STINKING RICH

The Four Myths of
the Good Billionaire

Carl Rhodes

Foreword by Joel Bakan

BRISTOL
UNIVERSITY
PRESS

First published in Great Britain in 2025 by

Bristol University Press
University of Bristol
1–9 Old Park Hill
Bristol
BS2 8BB
UK
t: +44 (0)117 374 6645
e: bup-info@bristol.ac.uk

Details of international sales and distribution partners are available at
bristoluniversitypress.co.uk

British Library Cataloguing in Publication Data
A catalogue record for this book is available from the British Library

ISBN 978-1-5292-3910-2 hardcover
ISBN 978-1-5292-3912-6 ePub
ISBN 978-1-5292-3913-3 ePdf

Cover design: Nicky Borowiec

Bristol University Press uses environmentally responsible
print partners.

Printed and bound in Great Britain by CPI Group (UK) Ltd,
Croydon, CR0 4YY

FSC
www.fsc.org
MIX
Paper | Supporting
responsible forestry
FSC® C013604

Contents

About the Author

Carl Rhodes is Professor of Organization Studies and Dean of the University of Technology Sydney's Business School. Carl studies the ethical and democratic dimensions of business, the economy and work. He is author of the bestselling *Woke Capitalism* (Bristol University Press, 2021) and frequently writes for the press in publications such as *The Guardian*, *The Times*, *Fast Company*, *Business Insider* and *The Conversation*.

Acknowledgements

First and foremost, I acknowledge that this book was written on the lands of the Gadigal People, in a place that bears the colonial name 'Sydney'. The Gadigal People have cared for their community, land and waters for thousands of generations, based on their deep knowledge of their country. In making this acknowledgement, I pay my respects to the Ancestors and Elders of the Gadigal People and acknowledge their ongoing status as the First Peoples of this land.

The invasion of Australia in 1788 brought with it what the British called 'civilization' but for Indigenous Australians it meant an era, still ongoing, of occupation and colonization. Murder, disease, displacement and disenfranchisement followed. So did inequality. This is not history, it is now. Today, Indigenous Australians experience poorer rates of life expectancy and employment than other Australians, as well as having a lower standard of healthcare, and greater rates of poverty, homelessness and incarceration. This is the reality of inequality in the country where I live and work. Inequality is not the result of an effective meritocracy bolstering the chosen few to great heights of wealth while those less worthy struggle; it is the result of the determined, systemic and self-interested social, political and economic system that elevates some people while preventing others from flourishing. It does not have to be this way.

I acknowledge the great support and encouragement I received from all the staff at Bristol University Press. Special thanks go to Paul Stevens, an extraordinarily committed publisher, who worked arduously to ensure this book would be the best it could be. Early drafts and proposals received insightful and constructive feedback from Dr Théo Bourgeron and Dr Tom Calvard from The University of Edinburgh, Dr Simon Pek from the University of Victoria, Professor Philip Roscoe from the University of St Andrews and Professor Andrew Sayer from Lancaster University. Each deserves thanks for their contribution to shaping the ideas and arguments contained in the book. Thanks too to Professor Joel Bakan for being, in his words, a 'fellow traveller', and for generously agreeing to write the Foreword to the book.

In the process of writing the book, I had a number of opportunities to present the developing ideas in both talk and writing. Some early thoughts that led me to the idea of the book were published in 2021 in an article in *The Conversation* titled, 'The AFR's 2021 Rich List shows we're not all in this together'.[1] The discussion of trickle-down economics in Chapter 2 had its first incarnation in an article in *Common Dreams* called, 'Is woke capitalism the new trickle-down economics?'[2] That chapter also draws on my 2022 article, 'Billionaire activism reveals the failure of Australian democracy', which was published in *Independent Australia*.[3] What became the opening passages of Chapter 4 was based on an article I was commissioned to publish in *The Guardian* in 2022 entitled, 'Patagonia's radical business move is great – but governments, not billionaires, should be saving the planet'.[4]

In April 2023, I was invited to talk to Philip Clark and his listeners on his Australia Broadcasting Company (ABC) radio talkback programme *Nightlife* on the topic of, 'Is it ethical to be a billionaire?'[5] Professor Sharon Friel and Dr Nicholas Frank from the Australian National University's Planetary Health Equity Hothouse invited me to speak as part of their seminar series in July 2023, providing an important forum for me to present my then work in progress in public.[6] I am grateful for each of these opportunities and how they helped me in the process of the larger project of writing the book.

I especially thank Professor Alison Pullen of Macquarie University for the ongoing dialogue that never fails to sharpen my thinking.

Carl Rhodes

Foreword

People with capricious power – dictators, despots, monarchs, oligarchs, feudal lords, colonial masters, theocrats, even slaveholders – typically insist on two things: first, that they care about the people they subjugate; and, second, that, because of (among other things) their closeness to God, racial superiority, family ties, military might, financial acumen or genius, they deserve the power they have. Unjust power is thus moralized and mythologized throughout history. And, also throughout history, the resulting moralizations and mythologies are routinely debunked by people who struggle against injustice and the power that sustains it. Which is what this book does and why it is so important.

Today, billionaires and major corporations routinely moralize and mythologize their power as benevolent and deserved. They claim they care about, and want to help solve, the multiple crises afflicting humanity and the planet, and thus slyly obscure their own roles in creating and perpetuating those crises, and also the anti-democratic animus behind their putatively good intentions. Emblematic of the latter is Richard Edelman's (arguably the world's most influential business guru) remark in an interview that, because of 'big changes in its reliability ... as a potential good actor', business could now 'fill a void left by government'.[1] I followed by asking him whether he thought that might be a problem for democracy – to have non-democratic businesses filling voids left by democratic governments. Edelman's answer was frank, though chilling. 'I'm not much of a believer in political citizenship,' he said. 'I actually believe much more in the power of the market-place.'[2]

Edelman's underlying belief – that, because corporations have become 'good actors', they can, and should, govern society more and be governed by it less – is widely shared among today's capitalist elites and is helping legitimate neoliberalism and its favoured policies of deregulation, privatization and tax cuts. Putting a smiling face on corporations, the 'good' corporation idea – which, as I have demonstrated in previous work is pure myth[3] – putatively justifies freeing them from democratic controls and granting them greater control of public domains. In that way, the myth helps 'inoculate capitalism against the threat of democracy', as Quinn Slobodian describes neoliberalism's central aim.[4] Which is why, as I argue elsewhere, 'good' corporations are bad for democracy.

Carl Rhodes makes similar arguments in his previous book, *Woke Capitalism: How Corporate Morality is Sabotaging Democracy*. Now, with *Stinking Rich*, he turns his critical gaze on the billionaire class. Echoing the notion that, as Justice Brandeis of the United States Supreme Court reportedly said, 'we can have democracy ... or we can have great wealth concentrated in the hands of a few, but we can't have both',[5] Rhodes demonstrates and debunks the moralizations and myths that putatively rationalize the wealth and power of billionaires. Drawing out four myths about the 'good' billionaire – the *heroic* billionaire, the *generous* billionaire, the *meritorious* billionaire and the *vigilante* billionaire – he shows how these cultural tropes repress and obscure the indefensible and widening inequality billionaires personify, and how that inequality deepens injustice and corrodes democracy.

This book would be an important contribution at any time, but it is especially so now. We are in a moment of acute crisis for democracy. The rapid rise of right-wing illiberalism poses a dramatic and disturbing threat to democracy. Less dramatic, and steadily unfolding, is the threat to democracy of neoliberalism's corrosive inequality. The latter tends to get overlooked these days, overshadowed by the intensity of the former. *Stinking Rich* is a welcome and important corrective to that. Through his trenchant critique of billionaires and the myths that sustain them, Rhodes highlights neoliberalism's anti-democratic force – a crucial move in its own right, but particularly so because of neoliberalism's synergistic links to right-wing illiberalism.[6]

Neoliberalism yields social insecurity, despair and hopelessness for many, while creating untold wealth for a few. It thereby creates fertile ground for the rise of illiberalism and its demagogues and xenophobes. History shows all too clearly that the animating tropes of illiberalism – fear, grievance, hate and distrust – find resonance among people disenfranchised and excluded by severely tilted political economic systems.[7] As Rhodes reveals, billionaires help sustain the particular tilted system that is neoliberalism, using their immense wealth and power to push for policies that help them gain, keep and expand their obscenely unequal wealth. Thus, while most billionaires do not actively advocate or intend to promote right-wing illiberalism – though some of them notoriously do – they do in fact champion neoliberal policies that foster conditions conducive to right-wing illiberalism and corrosive of democracy.

The solution is to have more democracy, not less of it – to foster equal and effective political citizenship by creating the necessary foundations for social citizenship: equality and inclusion. Billionaires flagrantly contradict that aim in terms of who they are, what they do with their wealth and power and what they symbolize. Deconstructing the myths and moralizations that sustain them and their power is essential to bring about the change we need. Which is precisely why this elegant, rigorous and convincing book is so necessary.

Joel Bakan
May 2024

Preface

On 22 June 2023, a headline in *The New York Times* read, 'Elon Musk proposes "cage match" with Mark Zuckerberg'.[1] That's right, two of the billionaire wunderkinder of the tech world were ready to go toe-to-toe in brutal unarmed combat. It all started when Musk, responding to a competitive threat on Twitter from Zuckerberg's Meta, tweeted, 'I'm up for a cage match if he is.' Zuckerberg answered on Instagram with: 'Send Me Location'. At issue was Meta's strategy to release a Twitter-like product called 'Threads'. It was dubbed the 'Twitter Killer'.[2]

The proposed fight attracted worldwide attention. After all, how sensational would it be for two household-name billionaires to translate their business rivalry into an old-school fist fight? Rumour spread that the Italian Ministry of Culture had offered up Rome's Colosseum as a venue for the fight. The billionaires would be battling it out like Roman gladiators![3] The smackdown never happened, but hand-to-hand combat was an apt metaphor for the behaviour of billionaires who would fight, even to the death, like real-life superheroes vying for attention, power and manly domination.

Musk and Zuckerberg are members of a new class of elite global billionaires viewed by many as heroes who hold genuine superpowers. These are people who have scaled the heights of success that others can only dream of, staring in awe at their wealth and accomplishments. Billionaires often portray themselves this way, too. When Musk took over Twitter in 2022, he did not describe it as a business deal designed to further extend his outrageous fortune. His banter was about saving freedom and democracy, not making money. Musk, who described himself as a 'free speech absolutist', argued that Twitter should be the 'de facto public town square'.[4] A letter Musk sent to the chairman of Twitter in the lead-up to his buying the social media company read: 'I invested in Twitter as I believe in its potential to be the platform for free speech around the globe, and I believe free speech is a societal imperative for a functioning democracy ... Twitter has extraordinary potential. I will unlock it.'[5]

Mark Zuckerberg has made similar overtures. Back in 2017, he wrote a 5,700-word statement describing to the world what he saw as his company's mission. Spoiler alert: it was not about the traditional purpose of business to make fair profits, produce goods and services people need, pay tax to support society or create meaningful and fairly paid jobs. It was not even about profiteering through ruthless market domination. No, for Zuckerberg, the whole deal came down to using Facebook to 'develop the social infrastructure to give people the power to build a global community that works for all of us'.[6] Civic engagement, the sharing of ideas, strong institutions and a commitment to a common humanity: these are the things that Facebook is really all about, proffered Zuckerberg.

There we have it, the two men who built business empires that propelled them into the cadre of the world's richest people are not really in it for money! They are really democracy-loving freedom fighters. The true goal of the wannabe cage fighters, they would have people believe, is to use their power and position to change the world. Under their influence, the world can become a better place for everyone. The ambition is startling in its enormity ... and in its hubris. Such high-minded talk fails to account for the vast global system of economic inequality, sitting at the top of which are people like Musk and Zuckerberg. Today's world is one where the outrageous fortunes of billionaires are growing by the day. Oxfam reports that between 2020 and 2023,[7] the richest 1 per cent of the world's population sequestered almost two thirds of the wealth created in the world. That is US$42 trillion. In that same period, for every dollar of wealth added to a person in the bottom 90 per cent, each billionaire acquired US$1.7 million. The reality of a billionaire-driven world economy is not one of democratic emancipation and shared community. For too many, it is about hunger, poverty, homelessness and lack of opportunity. To makes things even more unequal, despite only about a quarter of the world's population living in the Global North, as of 2024 these nations were home to three quarters of the world's billionaire wealth.[8]

Much has been said about the inequities in wealth and power that the growing horde of billionaires represent.[9] This book joins and complements those discussions by seeking to understand how these inequalities are maintained through a cultural moralization of the ultra-rich. The problem the world is facing is much more significant than the billionaires themselves. Billionaires are a symptom of a global culture that accepts the gross inequality at which they are at the apex, and the attendant injustice that comes with it. If billionaires are seen as morally acceptable, 'forces for good' even, then calls to change an economically unjust system that created them get muted.

Those who might defend inequality as a natural outcome of a merit-based free economy, and there are many of them, have been prone to dismiss talk of economic justice as a manifestation of a 'politics of envy'. This has been going on for some time. Back in 1974, a year before she became the leader of Britain's Conservative Party and five years before being elected prime minister, Margaret Thatcher stated that she rejected 'vehemently *the politics of envy*, the incitement of people to regard all success as if it were something discreditable, gained only by taking selfish advantage of others'.[10] In 1983, two years after he became president of the United States, Ronald Reagan, speaking to the National Conference of the National Federation of Independent Business, said:

> if we're to rebuild our beloved land, then those who practice *the politics of envy*, who pit one group against another, must rise above their rancor and join us in a new dialog – to encourage, honor, and reward every citizen who strives to excel and make America great again.[11]

At the dawn of the neoliberal era, Thatcher and Reagan told the world that if economic progress was the goal, then inequality was necessary. The liberated rich would lead the world, and everyone would benefit in the long run, so the story went. As national economies the world over embraced economic deregulation, corporate tax cuts and the virtual end of trade protectionism, a newly globalized world economy emerged, intoxicated by the promise of economic freedom. The experiment failed. This failure was announced in 2016 by, somewhat surprisingly, the International Monetary Fund (IMF). It is surprising because, back in the day, the IMF was one of the main driving forces that translated neoliberal ideologies into political policies and global realities. In 2016, however, the research department at the IMF published an article called, 'Neoliberalism: oversold?'[12] Acknowledging that neoliberal policies had spread worldwide since the 1980s, the research failed to find any connection between neoliberalism and economic growth. Even though abject poverty had reduced since that time, the report demonstrated conclusively that neoliberalism had led to widening economic inequality. The report heralded the 'death of neoliberalism from within', the final end to a flawed global ideology.[13]

Ideology is much stronger than facts, and reducing calls for equality as a politics of envy remains part of regressive conservative politics to this day that defies that failure of neoliberalism. When the British government released its business and wealth-friendly national budget in 2022, it was widely criticized for only benefiting rich people. Not so, Chief Secretary to the Treasury Chris Philp retorted: 'We're not going to be driven in this by the politics of envy, we want everyone in society to succeed, rich or poor.'[14] The conservative prime minister of Australia, Scott Morrison, who was in office between 2018 and 2022, was known to regularly play the 'politics of envy' card to defend his corporate-friendly approach to government. In 2022, in the depth of the COVID-19 pandemic, many of Australia's largest corporations were under attack for taking government handouts to support the payment of wages to their employees, while simultaneously handing out lavish bonuses to their executives. Morrison waved off the scandal. 'I'm not into the politics of envy,' he said. The same empty refrain is being sung the world over.

Dismissing one's political opponents by accusing them of a politics of envy comes hand in hand with a moralization of unequal wealth. This is a topsy-turvy world where demands for justice are dismissed as selfishly motivated, bred out of unchecked absorption by the deadly sin of envy. The flip side of the politics of envy is the idea that the wealthy should be revered rather than begrudged. By this account, being rich means being a hard-working 'winner' whom others should respect and admire, exponentially for billionaires. Billionaires are role models for many people, presented as benevolent and effective – good, even.

Debates about the politics of envy reflect how conservative political ideals have led to a moralization of individual wealth, falsely defending it as the engine house of economic development that can benefit everyone. Together with such a political conviction comes the view that economic inequality is both economically necessary and the fair outcome of a meritocratic society. Fortunately, public awareness and political activism against billionaire excess and calls to action to address it are growing. 'Reduced inequality' is even one of the United Nations' Sustainable Development Goals.[15] Economist Thomas Piketty, whose extensive and renowned studies on inequality put him in a position to understand the true devastation it can cause, remains inspiringly optimistic. 'History teaches us that elites fight to maintain extreme inequality, but in the end, there is a long-run movement toward more equality, at least since the end of the 18th century, and it will continue,'[16] he argues. Such hopefulness, combined with a faith in the possibility of progress, can animate a political will to change things for the benefit of the vast majority of the world's citizens. No seemingly entrenched and immovable state of injustice is fixed as if history would ever stand still.

What is decried as the politics of envy is, in fact, a plea for economic justice. The obscene inequality of wealth and power that billionaires represent has certainly not gone unnoticed. The criticisms articulated in this book mirror calls for change that have been issued loud and clear across the world. The call was seen in activist movements such as Occupy Wall Street back in 2011. It is around today everywhere from the 'tax the rich' movement,[17] to the so-called 'eat the rich' genre of movies that explore themes of capitalism and inequality.[18] New demands for inequality can be found in the resurgent socialism of Bernie Sanders in the United States and Jeremy Corbyn in the United Kingdom. What is clear is that in recent years there has been a growing discontent with the wealth and power controlled by the world's richest people. Joining this call, this book examines how a certain moralization of billionaires secures their elite status and fosters a moral acceptably of inequality.

This book attests to the need for a new political imagination that can reinvigorate the democratic promise of shared prosperity at a global level. On the one hand, as the world tumbles into climate disaster, economic inequality and political populism, the ultra-wealthy need to be held to account for their power by society. More radically, a new political vision is needed for a future where the wealth created by human activity is shared by the many rather than hoarded by the few.

Acclaimed author Ursula Le Guin stated, when being awarded the National Book Foundation Medal for Distinguished Contribution to American Letters in 2014, that: 'We live in capitalism. Its power seems inescapable. So did the divine right of kings. Any human power can be resisted and changed by human beings.'[19] As a footnote to Le Guin's insight, it can be added that under contemporary capitalism, there is a profound risk returning to something akin to the divine right of kings, only now those kings are billionaires. All the more reason to resist. All the more reason to demand justice. All the more reason for change.

Carl Rhodes

1

The Righteous Rich

The date 3 May 2022 marked the release of Bill Gates' book *How to Prevent the Next Pandemic*.[1] In the book, Gates presents himself as a long-obsessed student of infectious diseases. He lays out his blueprint for how a future outbreak akin to what was seen with COVID-19 can be avoided. Gates puts forward 'a plan for eliminating the pandemic as a threat to humanity and reducing the chance that anyone has to ever live through another COVID'.[2] His strategy is political. He proposed the creation of a 'Global Epidemic Response and Mobilization' team as part of the World Health Organization (WHO). The team of 3,000 scientists, data engineers, diplomats and business experts would cost US$1 billion each year, for which they would monitor possible outbreaks and advise on rapid responses to prevent global escalation.

This was not the first time Gates had used his position of wealth and power to publicly proffer his views on how to solve the world's biggest problems. His previous book, published just a year earlier, was 2021's *How to Avoid a Climate Disaster*.[3] In that volume, he had similarly lofty ambitions as he did with his COVID book. A *New York Times* number-one bestseller, the book saw Gates put his mind to planning how the world can reduce its carbon emissions to net zero. Once again, Gates is positioned as the entrepreneur who can come up with bold and innovative answers that have evaded political and scientific experts worldwide. Gates offers a market-based solution, taking what he learned from a career of world-dominating business innovation and applying it to the climate crisis.

Gates' forays into solving the world's most urgent crises are illustrative of the place that billionaires play in today's society. Once upon a time, billionaires might have been imagined in the form of the Mr Monopoly character who adorns the centre of the long-popular board game Monopoly. Mr Monopoly, alternatively known as Rich Uncle Pennybags, is a stereotyped old-school industrialist, replete with a bloated belly, top hat and well-coiffured moustache. He is often seen running away, holding his hat and clutching a bag of loot. Pennybags is, quite literally, a monopolist whose goal is to create a real estate business empire by reducing all his competitors to bankruptcy. Winning, for Mr Monopoly, means owning everything and raking in exorbitant rents that leave his tenants impoverished.

Gates is no Pennybags, he is a particular example of a new breed of billionaires who are determined to use their wealth and power as a 'force for good'. Gates has been publicly hailed as a 'hero of progress'.[4] Using the fortune he made as the founder of Microsoft, and the architect of its domination of the software industry, in 2000 he and his former wife founded the Bill and Melinda Gates Foundation. This is the largest private charitable foundation in the world, backed by a staggering US$50 billion in endowment funds, more than 70 per cent of which was donated by the Gateses themselves.[5] The Foundation describes itself as 'a nonprofit fighting poverty, disease, and inequity around the world'.[6] No more Monopoly-style rentier capitalism; today's story, as represented by Gates, is one of the billionaires coming to rescue the world from the most wicked and entrenched problems governments and international political agencies have failed to deal with. The narrative is nothing if not epic, with Gates actively taking on the mantle of the hero who will lead us all to the promised land. He is a 'good' billionaire.

But wait, Gates and Pennybags are not entirely different characters. As head of Microsoft, Gates was a ruthlessly ambitious businessman. The fortune that enabled his Foundation to be built on such a gigantic nest egg was earned precisely through monopolistic business practices. If anything, Microsoft's whole business model relied actively, if not aggressively, on preventing competition. Microsoft's self-described approach to its competitors was to 'take away their oxygen supply', 'crush them' and 'knife the baby'.[7] Matt Stoller, Director of Research at the American Economic Liberties Project, opined that when it came to competition 'Microsoft brings a cannon to a knife fight'.[8]

Consistent with Gates' reputation as a dominating and ruthless monopolist, in the 1990s, the United States government sued Microsoft for uncompetitive behaviour in what became widely regarded as the biggest antitrust legal battle in history. The Federal Trade Commission's case against Microsoft, which was brought to the US Department of Justice in 1998, was based on the accusation that they had attempted to create a monopoly in the market for personal computers. The argument put to the US District Court for the District of Columbia was that by bundling its other products in with the Windows operating system used by personal computers, Microsoft had limited other software companies from selling their products, which amounted to unfair competition.[9]

Microsoft lost the case. The presiding Judge Thomas Penfield Jackson said at the time: 'Microsoft has demonstrated that it will use its prodigious market power and immense profits to harm any firm that insists on pursuing initiatives that could intensify competition against one of Microsoft's core products.'[10]

Uncontrite, Microsoft appealed, eventually leading to the ruling being overturned. Microsoft fought the law, and Microsoft won. John Naughton, Professor of the Public Understanding of Technology at the Open University in the United Kingdom, studied the case. He concluded that Gates' behaviour at the depositions was 'obnoxious and aggressive'. That was not the worst of it. Gates' demeanour was befitting of 'a mogul who is incredulous that the government would dare to obstruct his route to world domination'.[11] It would appear that Gates felt that the rules that govern other citizens should not apply to him. With such an air of personal exceptionalism, Gates behaved as if he should be above the law, guided not by society's shared and reasonable expectations but by the calling of his greatness.

Gates' behaviour as a business manager has led him to be described as 'an angry office bully',[12] a 'nightmare boss',[13] and a 'tyrannical technocrat'.[14] Paul Allen, who co-founded Microsoft with Gates, characterized him as a 'ruthless schemer who demeaned his employees and conspired to rip [him] off'.[15] Allen pulled no punches about his opinion of Gates, saying that Gates not only failed to give him his due credit in founding Microsoft but also that Gates withheld the financial share in the company that Allen deserved. Gates took 64 per cent of the company they founded in equal partnership, effectively costing Allen billions of dollars.[16]

Gates' confrontational and controlling management style has been called out specifically as bullying. Maria Klawe, a former member of Microsoft's board of directors, reports that Gates derailed attempts to implement diversity management in his company in expletive-ridden rants. 'Are you trying to effing destroy the company?', he was reported to repeatedly say when the board recommended that the Microsoft executive team should be more diverse.[17] 'A person like Bill Gates thinks the usual rules of behavior don't apply to him,' Klawe concluded.[18]

Gates even admitted to a reporter an astoundingly controlling management technique he used at Microsoft in its early years: 'I knew everybody's license plates so I could look out in the parking lot and see when did [*sic*] people come in [and] when were they leaving.'[19] The idea was that he wanted to know who was at work for the longest, this being a sign of the kind of workaholic commitment that he not only expected of himself, but also of his employees. If an employee wanted to get ahead at Microsoft, a good start would be to ensure that Gates saw their car in the parking lot at the weekend. More generally, Gates has been accused of berating employees in public, mocking his competitors and taking enjoyment out of purposefully creating conflict at work.[20] Employees have even reported actively avoiding going to meetings with Gates for fear of being yelled at.[21] Joel Spolsky, a former program manager at Microsoft, recalled how he would bring a member of his team to meetings with Gates for the sole purpose of keeping count of how many times Gates uttered the 'F-word'. 'The lower the f★★★-count, the better,' Spolsky surmised.[22] All this suggests a hostile and controlling management style built on an almost unquenchable and aggressive desire to succeed at any cost, with scant concern for the well-being of others.

There is an apparent contradiction between Bill Gates, the callous tyrant and aggressive monopolist, on the one hand, and Bill Gates, the generous benefactor and philanthropist, on the other. But perhaps there is not any real contradiction, and what unites the economic and political behaviour of billionaires like Gates is an underlying morality through which, on account of their wealth and success, they not only know what is best for others but also have the right to rule the world. The expression of this 'born to rule' mentality is different when it comes to corporate management and philanthropic giving, but the underlying moral position is the same. The rule is that 'might is right'.

For billionaires, the material benefit of wealth is not the goal – after all, they have more money than even the most profligate of hedonists could reasonably spend many lifetimes over. When it comes to billionaires' excursions into social and political activities, extreme wealth is the means to acquire and wield power to reshape the world to their own liking and do it all in the name of generosity and morality. The problem is that this is not a democratic image of shared responsibility and rule by the general will of the people, but a plutocratic image of (at best) benevolent responsibility and rule by the rich. When Gates' climate book made it to number one on *The New York Times* Best Sellers list,[23] the bonus cash he earned in royalties was surely meaningless compared to a pitch to control the global agenda addressing one of the world's most pressing, wicked problems.

Gates has taken a decidedly and explicitly stated undemocratic stance when he considers the role of business in the world. Speaking to the most elite business and political leaders at the World Economic Forum (WEF) Conference at Davos in 2008, he laid out his position unequivocally. 'Businessmen and businesses are best placed to save the world,' he stated.[24] In making this pronouncement, Gates evinced an unbounded belief that corporate capitalism is not just a means through which to create wealth, trade goods and services and organize an economy, but that its powers can also be applied unproblematically to economic, social, political and environmental problems that exist outside of the traditional purpose of business activity.

Back in 1966, the psychologist Abraham Maslow created what came to be called 'the law of the instrument'. In the opening pages of his book *The Psychology of Science: A Renaissance*, he wrote: 'if the only tool you have is a hammer, it is tempting to treat everything as if it were a nail'.[25] In the case of billionaires such as Gates, all the world's most wicked problems are the nails and business management is the hammer, in his case a very large, well-funded hammer. According to Gates, this new application of corporate managerialism to 'save the world' should be led by the very same people who own and manage businesses – people like him. Following this logic, it seems that how businesses are managed is a one-size-fits-all solution to whatever ails the world, even though it is industrial and commercial activity that have created these ailments, from economic inequality to climate change.

The billionaire 'solution' to social, environmental and political problems sees the power and influence of business increasingly encroach on the public sphere, taking over what was once the preserve of the government and public institutions. Effectively there is a transfer of political power from public into private hands. A purely utilitarian perspective would assert that this does not matter so long as the problems are solved. Such a view is politically convenient, if not naïve. The political implication is that billionaires, as private citizens, are using the wealth they accumulated at the expense of others to create equally obscene inequalities in power. The billionaire solution is markedly undemocratic if not megalomaniacal. What is presented as private benevolence is revealed as a ploy to use wealth to buy political power.

Conventionally, generosity is understood as a form of ethical behaviour where a person gives away their money or possessions to others for their benefit. Generosity is aligned with hospitality, unselfishness and kindness as one forgoes for oneself that which would help others. It is morally good. In Gates' case, his massive spending on what would have traditionally been regarded as public goods has not put him in the poorhouse – quite the opposite. As of 2024, *Forbes Magazine* listed Gates as the seventh wealthiest person in the world, with a personal fortune of US$128 billion.[26] It was just US$37 billion in 2018.[27] The fact that Gates benefited financially from the pandemic while others suffered has had no effect on his self-appointment as a benevolent saviour of a world in crisis. In 2022, as he planned to hand over a further US$20 billion to his own Foundation, he took to Twitter with the comment:

> I have an obligation to return my resources to society in ways that have the greatest impact for reducing suffering and improving lives. And I hope others in positions of great wealth and privilege will step up in this moment too.[28]

Gates' 'obligation' is not based on the shared rules and customs governing society, but on his own very personal moral convictions and preferences. Gates' charitable endeavours are not publicly accountable. He can do as he wishes without having to report to or be evaluated by anybody – he is the boss and he behaves as if he is a law unto himself. Worse still, the vast amounts of money at stake means that Gates and his Foundation wield massive power and influence over the sovereign states that receive his patronage. 'There ain't no such thing as a free lunch,' so the saying goes, and it certainly applies here. From the early 2010s, for example, Gates was the WHO's second biggest donor. The biggest was the US and third place went to the UK. Health policy analysts Natalie Huet and Carmen Paun explain how Gates' 'generosity' has bestowed on him the ability to sway the world's health agenda towards the causes aligned with his personal preferences. They write:

> Gates' priorities have become the WHO's. Rather than focusing on strengthening health care in poor countries – that would help ... to contain future outbreaks like the Ebola epidemic – the agency spends a disproportionate amount of its resources on projects with the measurable outcomes Gates prefers ... Some health advocates fear that because the Gates Foundation's money comes from investments in big business, it could serve as a Trojan horse for corporate interests to undermine WHO's role in setting standards and shaping health policies. Others simply fear the UN body relies too much on Gates' money, and that the entrepreneur could one day change his mind and move it elsewhere.[29]

Gates' massive political power is without a trace of public accountability or democratic control. In the words of international development expert Mark Curtis:

> This situation is clearly a threat to global democratic decision-making. The fact that a private funder occupies these influential positions is an indictment of the world's public aid system and of governments which should be holding the [Bill and Melinda Gates Foundation] to account. Moreover, the effect is that public policy-making is being skewed towards promoting private, corporate interests.[30]

Democracy is a form of government authorized exclusively by the will of the people, with that will being enshrined in institutions such as political parties, the judiciary and the legislature, all underpinned by the rule of law. When billionaires like Gates take on public works, none of the democratic controls that limit individual power or provide checks and balances on decision making apply. Billionaires can make personal and idiosyncratic decisions about what problems need to be solved and how to go about trying to solve them, just because they are rich. Robert Reich, Professor of Public Policy and former labour secretary of US President Bill Clinton, goes so far as to ask whether foundations such as Gates' are 'repugnant to the whole idea of democracy'.[31]

Reich compares philanthropic foundations to both businesses and public institutions. If a business is not able to be profitable because people do not want to buy its good and services at the price that they are offered, then it goes broke. Businesses are accountable to consumer demand, and if they fail to meet this accountability, they will eventually fold. Public institutions in democratic nations have a different kind of accountability. In this case, elected officials are responsible to a nation's citizens. If an official makes decisions most citizens do not approve of, they can be voted out of office and replaced. Foundations, Reich argues, are different because they are accountable to no one – not to the consumers, not to investors and not to citizens. There is no office to kick Gates out of if any majority of citizens do not like what he is doing. Gates is a benefactor who can spend his money however he pleases.

As a billionaire, Bill Gates can decide what he wants to do with his vast fortune in a manner that is unencumbered by the necessity of democratic deliberation and public accountability. Wealth knows no democracy. Although extreme, Gates is not unique. Today there are more billionaires globally than ever before, and their ranks are growing fast. From Elon Musk and Jeff Bezos to Mark Zuckerberg and Bill Gates, the vast wealth billionaires have accumulated represents the scourge of inequality spreading worldwide. If that wasn't serious enough, it is only half of the problem. What is different about today's billionaires is that the titanic power they wield is not just an affront to the hope of economic equality and shared prosperity; it is a threat to democracy, progress and justice. Gates is merely an illustrative example of a much bigger and much more disturbing phenomenon.

It is especially dangerous when billionaires use their wealth in pursuit of power and a desire to be answerable to no one but their own sense of moral righteousness and self-proclaimed expertise. But what exactly is the nature of the morality that would grant such extreme power to billionaires? What is so 'good' about billionaires? At play is what can be called the 'political morality' of today's growing class of billionaires. The term 'political morality' refers simply to the moral rationale used to justify exercising political power and authority. Understanding political morality in relation to billionaires is an important consideration in the twenty-first century. A defining characteristic of contemporary times is not just widening inequality represented by the ever-increasing number of billionaires the world is producing. Coupled with this, billionaires are using their massive wealth to encroach on political life. But is there a moral justification for billionaires using their wealth to exercise power in this way? And if so, does it hold up to critical scrutiny?

Historically, the moral justification of political power has come in many different forms. In ancient Greece, the philosopher Plato proposed a particular form of aristocracy as the best form of government. In *The Republic*,[32] written some two and a half thousand years ago, Plato imagined an ideal political society called 'Kallipolis' – the beautiful city. A central characteristic of government in Kallipolis is that it is ruled by the 'philosopher king'. For Plato, the philosopher is worthy of being ruler because he is devoted to truth and wisdom rather than appearance, honour or pleasure. The king has been bred to rule through education in all branches of philosophy for at least 15 years.

In contrast to Plato's belief that philosophical credentials and capability are the moral justification for holding power, in the monarchies of Europe, the right to rule was thought to be bequeathed by God. In what was known as the 'divine right of kings', the monarch's rule was justified because he or she was empowered to rule by God himself. As the one chosen by God, the king has no accountability to his subjects, instead ruling as the supreme sovereign, above and beyond the law. King James I of England described this doctrine in 1609:

> The state of monarchy is the supremest thing upon earth;
> for kings are not only God's lieutenants upon earth, and
> sit upon God's throne, but even by God himself are called
> gods ... Kings are justly called gods, for that they exercise
> a manner or resemblance of divine power upon earth:
> for if you will consider the attributes to God, you shall
> see how they agree in the person of a king.[33]

The political philosophy at play with the divine rights of kings is one where the monarch is effectively God, and so is beyond question and without higher authority. On that basis, a ruling monarch is a singular authority who rightfully holds power and demands obedience.[34]

Monarchy was still the most dominant form of political leadership in Europe well into the 1700s, but the Renaissance brought a resurgent interest in democracy as a form of government first imagined in ancient Greece. Through the democratic revolutions in France and the United States, as well as more peaceful transitions in other nations, democracy became an ideal that many nation-states both aspired to and implemented. At its most fundamental level, in a democracy, the justification for exercising political power comes from a single source – the common will of the people. Derived from the Greek words *demos* (people) and *kratia* (rule or power), democracy means, quite literally, the rule of the people. Democracies can be organized in many ways, but what ultimately unites them is the political ideal that any political leader can only claim authority on the basis that they are acting on behalf of citizens. Political theorist Wendy Brown describes how democracy is 'the only political form permitting us all to share in the powers by which we are governed', promising that 'power will be wielded on behalf of the many, rather than the few, that all might be regarded as ends, rather than means, and that all may have a political voice'.[35]

If the moral justification for the philosopher king's power is wisdom, the monarch's is God and the democrat's is the will of the people, then what validates the political power of today's new breed of billionaires? The brief discussion so far has already revealed contours of the answer to this question. Billionaires exercise power because they have the wealth and resources that allow them to do so, a variation on the tradition of plutocracy. Quite simply, the financial resources commanded by the wealthy allow them to get things done such that the fact of capital ownership itself bestows power on them. The moral position is that it is their money and that they earned it fairly, so they can do whatever they wish with it, including meddling in public affairs and the provision of public goods. This position is reflected in Bill Gates' involvement in climate and health. Gates has no special training or background in climate science or immunology to give him expertise, nor has he any power bequeathed as a representative of anyone else. His powerful influence stems only from his immense wealth and the social standing it has garnered for him.

Billionaire political morality also assumes that billionaires are justified in exercising political power on the grounds that what they have learned in the business world can be applied to solve political problems in ways that politicians and the public sector have failed. Being democratically elected or selected through a transparent and fair process – as is the case (at least ideally) with politicians and public servants, respectively – is irrelevant. Instead, with billionaires there is a cocktail of plutocracy and technocracy. This technocratic tradition is one where people hold power and authority on account of their technical and scientific know-how. With the billionaire this tradition is transmuted into a 'capitalist technocracy'. With capitalist technocracy, it is one's skills and knowledge as a successful (insofar as vast wealth is a measure of success) entrepreneur and business person that provide the expertise that justifies the use of power.

The most revered billionaires are the ones asserted to be 'self-made men', with the assumed meritoriousness of their success used to rationalize their political exploits. The greatness of the billionaire does not abate through their good deeds, and the exercise of political power must never diminish the power of the billionaire himself, and preferably expand it. This form of self-interest reflects the commercial origins of billionaire political morality, where there is always assumed to be a 'business case' for every act of putative generosity. The arbiter of the social value of any political venture is always the billionaire himself, with the meritoriousness of his (they are usually men) wealth giving him the final word. Remember, as far as assumed merit goes, Gates epitomizes the model of the self-made billionaire. He is the college dropout whose singular vision propelled him to greatness as the founder of Microsoft, spawning a revolution in pursuit of a vision to have 'a computer on every desk and in every home'.[36] When Gates was just 31 years of age, he became the then world's youngest ever self-made billionaire.[37]

The moral justification of billionaire politics arises from a particular type of pragmatic utilitarianism. The exercise of power enabled by wealth is justified because it leads to practical outcomes deemed to be positive to society. This is true, and no one can doubt that many have benefited from his largesse. Think, for example, of the millions of lives saved from the vaccination programmes his Foundation has supported.[38] The catch is that the judgement about what is positive is entirely at the behest of the billionaires themselves; after all, they are the ones bankrolling everything. Utilitarianism is especially important to billionaire political morality in that it also serves the purpose of disguising the fact billionaires are using their wealth to extend their power into the public sphere. This is a political morality that presents itself as being 'beyond ideology',[39] because it justifies itself on pragmatic outcomes unencumbered by explicit political discourse or debate. Billionaires are not doing politics, they are doing good! The catch is that they are the ones who get to define what constitutes the 'good' for the rest of us.

The combination of plutocracy, capitalist technocracy and utilitarianism that characterize billionaire political morality create a particular relationship between the billionaire and democracy. This is especially so as it concerns the rule of law and the ability of billionaires to rise above that rule through their political activity. The rule of law – the political precept that the same laws apply to all members of a community or society, regardless of the position a person holds – is a central dimension of liberal democracy. For all citizens to enjoy political equality the rule of law is essential. It is based on the fundamental principle that no exceptions to the accepted laws on a democratic nation are to be made based on wealth, class, family, race, gender or other possible axes of discrimination. A president, a professor or a plumber faces the same consequences if they break the law.

Democracy may have triumphed over feudal, aristocratic and monarchical forms of political organization in the West, but in the world today there is a return to a system where political power is derived from wealth. This is not the same as the old feudalism, which was based on land ownership. Business and financial assets are at the heart of the power of the new billionaire rulers. These people are stateless cosmopolitans who insist that the approach to business that made them wealthy can be applied to solve some of the world's most wicked problems, under their unelected leadership and moral conviction. The morality that comes with this is one where unfettered personal freedom, wily entrepreneurialism and sanctimonious individualism triumph over the will of the people and the promise of shared prosperity. The world and its problems become the billionaires' playthings when they exercise their personal moral convictions to call the shots on public and political matters. All of this is done without any public or democratic licence or accountability.

This book can be read as a trenchant critique of today's new breed of billionaires. That is, however, not really the purpose. The book seeks to explain how vast and widening economic injustice on a global scale is obscured by the moralization of the ultra-rich at a time when their political power is expanding globally. Four mythical archetypes of the 'good' billionaire justify the curse of widening inequality by presenting its most conspicuous beneficiaries as righteous and deserving. By undermining the one-sided falsehood of these archetypes, the intention is to advocate for revitalizing the democratic values of equality and shared prosperity. An important starting point in fulfilling this intention is to acknowledge that the immense social and political power billionaires possess cannot be explained by their wealth alone, even though that is, of course, a significant part of it. Coupled with the financial resources billionaires command is a set of interconnected myths that portray billionaires as a 'force for good'; myths that shield them, at least partially, from being held to account for the inequality they represent in such an excessive, if not vulgar form. In being portrayed as mythically righteous, resistance and change to an almost morbidly unequal global economy is held back. If equality is the political goal, the myths that perpetuate it need to be exposed, explored and undermined. That is the contribution this book hopes to make.

This book identifies and describes four mythical archetypes of the good billionaire, using them to delve into how inequality has been accepted through the moralization of the ultra-rich. Before getting to those myths, it is worth taking time out to consider what is meant by a 'mythical archetype'. The term 'archetype', as it is being used here, refers to an idealized model of the meanings and values attached to a particular type of person. Importantly, these models are widely understood and shared through cultures. According to the pioneering psychoanalyst Carl Jung, archetypes are part of our 'collective unconscious'[40] – a shared stock of knowledge ingrained in members of society without them even necessarily knowing it. These collective representations provide models through which people can understand and interpret the world in which they find themselves. Jung described an archetype as a 'collective personification [... and ...] the product of an aggregate of individuals'.[41] Archetypes also provide models, if they are of people, to which individuals might try to aspire. Jung's conviction was that archetypes were universal.

Jung locates archetypes as part of a collective unconscious that 'has contents and modes of behaviour that are more or less the same everywhere and in all individuals'.[42] Myths are the primary ways that archetypes are produced and reproduced. Archetypes are understood – as particular sets of character traits – because the archetype gets used repeatedly in the stories people hear and tell about other people. Jung proposed that there were a set of universal and primordial archetypes, such as the trickster, the wise old man, the hero, the magician and the lover. Even though Jung's idea that archetypes were universal and common to people of all cultures is now by and large discredited, the idea of the archetype is still important. Rather than being universal, archetypes are cultural; they develop as shared and dominant ways of understanding life that people are socialized into believing.[43] Archetypes are mythical in that they are used repeatedly in the stories people tell each other, whether those stories are about real-life events or are in works of fiction.

When archetypes become mythologized, they are embedded in a cultural meaning-making system. Mythical archetypes provide people with structures through which to understand the world, but they are not benign; they can also direct understanding in a way that favours particular interests. They translate reality through stories, and while those stories appear to be objective and descriptive, they shape the realities that people take for granted. This is very much the case for billionaires. Stories are told about them all the time – on the television, around the dinner table, on social media, in the movies and elsewhere. Even though many realize the billionaires are wrapped up in, and benefit from, a system of global inequality, the cultural stories people tell about them so frequently serve to moralize them – to make them out to be 'good' in one way or another. Uncovering and making these archetypes explicit is not primarily concerned with passing moral judgement on individuals. What is much more important is developing an understanding of how this moralization emphasizes some aspects of billionaire behaviour and character, while forestalling criticism about the economic destitution that lies on the flip side of the billionaire coin. These are archetypes that stand in the way of progressive change and in the way of realizing the promise of democracy.

The central chapters of this book describe four principal and interrelated mythical archetypes that serve to moralize billionaires and the inequalities they represent. The first myth is that of the heroic billionaire. This is a myth that casts billionaires as the heroic protagonists of the American dream gone global. Billionaires are the heroes with the right stuff to achieve greatness unavailable to mere mortals. Despite its appeal, this myth belies a cruel version of survival-of-the-fittest social Darwinism, where the rich are exalted and the poor are cast asunder as losers in life's game. The new American dream that billionaires are so often portrayed as exemplifying is not one of a new world emancipated from its feudal past and where everyone, irrespective of class, creed or colour can succeed. Instead, it is a dream where success is possible, but only for the select few who can approach the dizzy financial heights of being a billionaire. The dream turns into a nightmare as with the realization that the billionaire is the hero of a winner-take-all story that glorifies inequality by canonizing the ultra-rich.

Second comes the myth of the generous billionaire. In this case, the story goes that through their philanthropic efforts and personal good deeds, billionaires should be lauded for their generosity and benevolence. It is true that in what some call the 'new golden age of philanthropy',[44] billionaires are increasingly giving away large sums of money to good causes they support. Looking beyond the myth, there is a much more dangerous phenomenon where billionaires are using their wealth to engineer a transfer of political power from public into private hands, all at the expense of democracy. This is not to say that handouts from billionaires are not beneficial to their recipients. Clearly, they can be. Nevertheless, despite how much they give away, billionaires' wealth, collectively and often individually, keeps growing; so does the number of billionaires in the world.

The myth of the generous billionaire obscures the fact that the more they give away, the worse the economic inequality they are a part of is getting. Is it just possible that all this giving really serves to preserve the political and economic system that continues to benefit those at the top of a widening economic divide?

The myth of the meritorious billionaire comes third. Central to the moral defence of billionaire wealth is the claim that their riches are a meritorious reward for hard work and talent. It may be an ideal means to justify billionaire inequality, but the argument that extreme wealth is meritoriously earned suffers two different problems. The first problem is that the meritocratic credentials of billionaires are deeply questionable. It is true that many billionaires came from humble origins and deployed a unique set of talents on their way to the top of the economic pile. However, even when this is the case, a combination of luck, inheritance and family connections invariably underpin billionaire success more than merit. The second problem is that even if it is assumed that billionaires deserved their wealth on merit, meritocracy is an inherently unfair system that undermines democracy. A meritocratic society is one where economic inequalities are based on the employment of the talents and abilities that a person was born with and developed. But isn't being born with talent no more a matter of luck than being born into a land-owning aristocratic family? Even worse, should people with these talents for money-making be allowed to use their wealth to exercise power? Meritocracy, at least as a political ideal, ends up being an unfair winner-takes-all system that provides a false justification for inequality.

Fourth and finally, there is the myth of the vigilante billionaire. The classic vigilantes – think of the Lone Ranger, Batman or Dirty Harry – are heroized for taking the law into their own hands when public institutions fail to achieve justice. These are cultural figures whose personal values rule supreme as they single-handedly solve problems where others have failed. The vigilante is also an archetype associated with billionaires. Whether it be the climate crisis, global health or world poverty, billionaires are positioned as bypassing governments in trying to solve the world's biggest problems using their vast wealth, business acumen and entrepreneurial spirit to succeed where politicians have failed. Like vigilantes, they forsake bureaucratic interference to get things done, acting alone and with no public accountability. But this is real life, not the movies. The myth of the vigilante billionaire justifies social and political interventions by billionaires. In so doing, it also presages a new global plutocracy where the world is ruled by the rich on their terms.

The four myths of the good billionaire are presented independently, but each is not meant to represent any individual billionaire. In practice, the myths work together in different combinations and with different emphases, with a single person potentially being associated with all four through the stories that are told about them. Take Bill Gates. He is known by many as the hero who has made improving world health his life's work. He is also known as the generous benefactor of the Bill and Melinda Gates Foundation, as well as the college dropout who became one of the richest men in history based only on his own merit. Gates is also seen as a go-getting problem-solver, a virtual vigilante who will do whatever it takes to get things done on his own terms. The four archetypes, in this case all reflected in one person, provide a compelling justification for extreme wealth but scratching beneath the surface reveals them to be a subterfuge covering for a much more dangerous reality: the expansion of billionaire wealth and power sets democratic nations back to the feudalism and plutocracy that the democratic tradition overthrew long ago. Collectively, these myths need to be exposed such that billionaires do not stand in the way of shared prosperity. Exposing the myths might just reanimate the belief in popular sovereignty such that the only justification for the exercise of political power is the will of all the people, not the will of a wealthy minority.

Under the guise of being a force for good, billionaires are riding roughshod over the democratic social contract on a global scale justified by a self-styled freewheeling morality. Gone unchecked, this is a return to a form of feudalism and plutocracy that was the foe that the democratic tradition overthrew. The world's citizens do not have to be resigned to this domination by the wealthy. Demanding justice can only be done by invigorating the political will to assert democratic authority over the runaway train of political and economic inequality.

2

Money and Power

Who is the wealthiest person on earth? In the high-stakes race for the title of world's richest man (it has never been a woman), the frontrunner keeps changing. In fact, observing the leader board of lucre has become something of a spectator sport, enabled by the broad availability of data on the financial fortunes to the world's ultra-wealthy elite, most especially through the annual publication of the 'World's Billionaire List' by *Forbes Magazine*. In 2024, *Forbes* released its 38th annual list, and it was the longest one ever, with a record-breaking 2,781 billionaires, up by 141 on the previous year and holding a combined wealth of US$14.2 trillion. Fourteen of those listed were in the most coveted group, the club who had more than US$100 billion. These super elite were the 'lucky few', according to *Forbes*.[1] 'It's been a banner year for the mega-wealthy,' *Forbes* proudly declared.

In the sport of billionaire watching, 2021 was an especially thrilling race as international mega moguls competed for who could rise out of the wreckage of the COVID-19 pandemic with the biggest swag bag. *Forbes* has released its official list annually since 1987 and in 2012, it created the companion online 'Real-Time Billionaire List'. Here the race can be followed all year round on a website that charts the ups and down of each billionaire's net worth and the list is updated daily.[2] Finance and media company Bloomberg has also published a daily updated list since 2012. There can be found the rankings and details of the richest 500 people in the world. Like *Forbes*, Bloomberg reports their total net worth, how much their wealth has changed since the last update and how much richer or poorer they became over the past year.

Forbes and Bloomberg use different methodologies, and the net worth and ranking attached to individuals are not entirely consistent, although they are rarely widely different. Nevertheless, whichever system is used to garner knowledge about billionaire excess, the most excitement comes from watching the top ten, and they have a lot in common. First, to be in this leader pack, a person's wealth had to be valued as at least US$100 billion. When the counting stopped on 31 December 2021, *Forbes* reported that Elon Musk crossed the finishing line first with a mind-boggling wealth of US$277 billion. At number ten was investor Warren Buffett, who sneaked in with a relatively modest US$104 billion.[3] The rest were spread out in between.

The second thing the top ten had in common in 2021 was that they were all men. By the end of that year, the world's richest woman was Françoise Bettencourt Meyers, heir to the L'Oréal cosmetics fortune. She came in at number 11, with a wealth estimated at just US$93 billion,[4] a position she retained in 2023,[5] falling to 15 in early 2024.[6] Even though the number of women billionaires is on the rise, it is still the case that only about one in ten of the world's billionaires are female. As of 2024, there were still no women in the top ten.[7]

It is less strict, but third, being a super-billionaire seems to be more likely for White Americans. In the 2021 race, the only person with a top ten berth from outside the United States was Bernard Arnault, the French luxury goods magnate and head of LVMH Moët Hennessy Louis Vuitton. He vaulted up to the number three spot in 2021, with his net worth weighing in at US$176 billion.[8] The top ten were all White.[9]

Fourth, it helps a lot to be in the technology business. In 2022, 2023 and 2024, eight of the top ten were tech billionaires. The outliers were the previously mentioned investors Buffett and Arnault.[10] The technology boom has led to the flourishing number of billionaires in the world, with the number of tech billionaires tripling in the 12 years from 2008. The year 2008 was also that when Facebook's Mark Zuckerberg made his debut as a billionaire at the tender age of 23. By the 2020s, his personal wealth had increased by 7,500 per cent.[11] By 2024, there were a record-breaking 342 tech billionaires, the largest number in any industry, accounting for more than 12 per cent of the total billionaire population.[12]

In 2021, the race was on full bore, spectated by a media machine eager to capitalize on the voyeuristic (and profitable) sport of billionaire watching. At the beginning of the year, Bloomberg reported that Elon Musk took the lead after overtaking Amazon's Jeff Bezos. It was neck and neck, with Musk sneaking ahead by just US$1.5 billion. Bezos, who had been in the lead for three years, was relegated to the number two spot.

Musk had been doing something of a dash, as just a few months earlier he had raced past Bill Gates into number two.[13] By May, rank outsider French billionaire Arnault had leapfrogged to first place, pushing Musk back to the number three spot.[14] It was a brief sprint, with Bezos taking back the lead in June and Musk back to number two by August.[15] In a surprise ending, Musk regained the top spot again in September 2021, and he was still holding on to it at the end of 2023.[16] A humble winner? Far from it. His message was, 'I'm sending a giant statue of the digit "2" to Jeffrey B., along with a silver medal.'[17] Should one expect any less schoolyard masculinity from one of the richest and most powerful men in the world? Alas, no.

As amusing as the billionaire race might be as a spectator sport, all this talk of billions can be quite confusing. A billion is a number that is so huge, it is hard to imagine what it really means, let alone the hundreds of billions hoarded by the top ten. A few illustrations might help. Imagine starting counting right now. Counting one number per second and without stopping to eat or sleep, it would take 31 years, 251 days, 7 hours, 46 minutes and 40 seconds to reach a billion.[18] A billion dollars (that is about five days' work for Jeff Bezos) in US$100 bills would weigh about 10 tons. A billion dollars in US$1 bills laid end to end would wrap around the world four times over.[19]

Countries that are members of the Organisation for Economic Co-operation and Development (OECD) have average household net adjusted disposable income per capita as US$30,490.[20] Remember here that by international comparisons, members of the OECD are generally considered countries with relatively high incomes. That means the average person in the world's richest countries would have to work almost 33,000 years without ever spending a cent to get to their first billion. Clearly this is ludicrous but it illustrates just how extreme the very existence of a billionaire is.

Making it even more extreme is the fact that the number of billionaires in the world is on the rise. So is the immensity of wealth at their command. The year 2021 saw unprecedented growth, with the number of billionaires worldwide rising by 660 to 2,755.[21] It was steady after that, fluctuating to 2,668 in 2022, 2,640 in 2023 and 2,781 in 2024. Collectively, billionaires are worth more than US$14.2 trillion.[22] Between 2020 and 2024, the wealth of the five richest people in the world doubled. Meanwhile, 60 per cent of the world's population – that is 5 billion people – became poorer.[23]

Another way to think about what being a billionaire means is to consider how much richer billionaires are than others. In 2020, the team at the SMS marketing company SimpleTexting released an online calculator that does just that. It allows people to determine how their wealth and income compare to that of the richest tech CEOs.[24] Using the calculator shows that earning the average salary of US$59,428 in the US[25] would take Elon Musk 13 minutes. Dreaming of home ownership? The average house price in the UK was £288,000 in 2023.[26] Over at Facebook, Mark Zuckerberg would only have to work a bit more than half an hour to have that fully paid off. To be in the top 1 per cent of income earners in the US – that means being really rich – requires bringing home a whopping US$650,000 yearly.[27] That's less than an hour's work for Adobe's CEO, Shantanu Narayen.

The sheer magnitude of what a billion dollars represents is mind-boggling. Things get much worse and much more severe when thinking about what this means for inequality on a global scale. Each year the company Wealth-X, which describes itself as 'the global leader in wealth information and insight',[28] publishes its 'billionaire census' report. First released in 2013, the report provides a detailed analysis of, in their words, 'the status of the world's billionaires, who, despite being modest in number, hold immense wealth and wield a significant influence over the global economy'.[29]

Wealth-X is not concerned with inequality per se, they are a wealth intelligence business. That means they offer services to financial services, luxury brands and not-for-profits to provide insight and analysis into the goings-on of very rich people so that they can be targeted for business opportunities or philanthropic donations. The rich are not homogenous and can be segmented based on the extent of their enormous wealth. They are classified into three groups. First, there is the lowly 'very high net worth (VHNW) individuals, who have a net worth of between US$5 million and US$30 million. Next up the line are the 'ultra-high net worth (UHNW) individuals'. To be in this group requires being worth more than US$30 million. It is after that that things get serious. On top of the pile are the billionaires, who (obviously) have more than US$1 billion in assets. A subset of the last group are the new billionaires who recorded their first billion in the past year.

Wealth-X's 2021 billionaire census report told a tale of the growing excess of billionaire wealth at the very top. In a contracting and COVID-addled global economy, the number of global billionaires identified by Wealth-X's research was not only more than what *Forbes* estimated, but it ballooned by 13.4 per cent to 3,204. The 2023, report showed this levelling out at 3,194.[30] The impact on inequality was stark, as Wealth-X details:

> The uneven distribution of global wealth is evident at all levels of society and across all wealth tiers, but is increasingly stark when evaluating the world's super rich. In 2020, billionaires represented 1.1% of the global ultra high net worth (UHNW) population – those with $30m+ in net worth – yet held a staggering 28% share of cumulative UHNW wealth.[31]

Beyond Wealth-X's market segmentation, to be counted in the financial elite, the price of entry is US$10 billion. It is the small group of people in this class whose wealth is expanding at the most rapid rate, with tech billionaires being the most dominant. At the very apex of global wealth, things are ever more uneven, with the combined wealth of the 212 super-elite members of the US$10 billion-plus club in 2021 being just about as much as the German economy's annual market value.[32]

An especially fascinating 'fact' revealed in Wealth-X's report is the belief that 'the majority of wealthy individuals around the world have created their own fortunes'. What they mean by this is that rather than becoming billionaires by inheriting wealth, they 'made' this money through their own business and commercial ventures. Only 13.3 per cent of billionaires around the world inherited their wealth. Through a combination of inheritance and their own activity,

31.5 per cent made their money. It is reported that 55.2 per cent are self-made billionaires.[33]

The implication of this idea of the self-made billionaire is worth questioning. It implies that anybody can achieve extreme wealth and that inequality is akin to a fact of nature, resulting from some people exercising their naturally superior levels of entrepreneurship, innovation, business acumen and other personal qualities. Surely anyone who makes something themselves, rather than it being given to them, deserves to have it. This was a question that American member of Congress Alexandria Ocasio-Cortez addressed directly when she spoke with author and journalist Ta-Nehisi Coates on Martin Luther King Jr. Day on 20 January 2020.

Coates asked Ocasio-Cortez what she would say to billionaires who would claim that they deserve their riches because they ran and owned businesses that sold 'widgets' that yielded all that money. Ocasio-Cortez responded with clarity and conviction:

> Well you didn't make those widgets, did you? Because you employed thousands of people and paid them less than a living wage to make those widgets for you. You didn't make those widgets, you sat on a couch while thousands of people were paid modern-day slave wages. And in some cases, … real modern-day slavery, depending on where you are in terms of food production. You made that money off the backs of undocumented people, … black and brown people being paid under a living wage, … single mothers and all these people who are literally dying because they can't afford to live. And so, no one ever makes a billion dollars. You take a billion dollars.[34]

Ocasio-Cortez gets to the heart of the two fundamentally different perspectives on the source of economic value within capitalist economies. The first perspective is that economic value is created through the entrepreneurial spirit and dedication of those people who form, own and manage commercial enterprises. This entrepreneurial ideal is central to billionaire morality. From this perspective, ownership of the financial and material resources required to do business, coupled with the ability to leverage that productively, gives one the right to claim the profits of that business as one's own. By deploying capital productively, the return on that capital rightfully belongs to the capitalist. The other perspective, and the one that Ocasio-Cortez articulated, is that people's labour creates economic value as they transform the world's natural resources for productive human use. Labour, not entrepreneurship or capital ownership, is what 'adds value' in the production of goods and services. By this account, any excessive or unreasonable profits returned to a business owner constitutes the appropriation of value that rightfully belongs to the workers who produced it.

In contemporary Western societies, the first of these beliefs has become the most dominant. Under the guise of what some call 'neoliberalism', a dominant belief has been instilled that free enterprise market capitalism is something of a natural system to which there is no alternative. Going back in history to the 1980s, this was justified by what was called 'trickle-down economics'. The term 'trickle-down economics' had been in use since at least the 1930s but it only became a part of conventional political and economic rhetoric in the 1970s and 1980s, especially through the supply-side economics promoted by Ronald Reagan during his US presidency from 1981 to 1989. The idea that was peddled was that if the big end of town – big corporations and wealthy individuals – were taxed less and freed from the encumbrance of government regulations, then they would create more wealth and grow the economy. Through a natural process, some of this wealth would trickle down through the rest of the economy so everyone would benefit.

Trickle-down economics was a supreme con that operated through a false morality professing that market capitalism would benefit everyone. This has not stopped the same trickle-down logic from being wheeled out today to distract from the realities of what is nothing less than planned and government-sponsored inequality. Trickle-down economics is still very much de rigueur to justify the very existence of billionaires. Surely the enterprises they create will create growth in employment in ways that taxation and government spending cannot. This political conviction was shown in stark relief in 2016, when the European Union handed down a ruling to fine the Apple Corporation €13.5 billion for evading taxes in Ireland. Apple chief and billionaire Tim Cook was appalled at such an idea. It will have 'a profound and harmful effect on investment and job creation in Europe', he claimed. Cook did not refer to the term 'trickle-down economics' but it was the same idea – if Apple had to pay more tax, then benefits of its commercial activity would not find their way down to everyday people.

The Irish government entirely agreed. Irish Finance Minister Michael Noonan described the political position as one where '[i]t is important that we send a strong message that Ireland remains an attractive and stable location of choice for long-term substantive investment'. This rubs salt into the trickle-down wounds. Trickle-down might have been a corporate-friendly policy put in place by Reagan in the 1980s, but what makes it different 40 years later is that big corporations, not the government, are calling the shots. In effect, Apple was able to hold Ireland to ransom. If they did not do what they were told, then the investment would be taken elsewhere to a place where the government was more compliant.[35]

As well as being widely advocated by US President Reagan in the 1980s, trickle-down economics was still an active part of US President Donald Trump's tax policy during his administration in 2017–21. On 22 December 2017, Trump signed the Tax Cuts and Jobs Act into law. The act involved significant cuts in tax rates on corporate profits and investment earnings, in some cases down from 39 to 21 per cent. The income tax rate for the poorest people remained unchanged, but for a single person earning more than US$500,001 the marginal tax rate was slashed from 39.6 to 37 per cent.[36] Trump described the plan as 'the rocket fuel our economy needs to soar higher than ever before'.[37] He was wrong. The plan was 'a windfall for big corporations and wealthy Americans', but it failed in any way to stimulate economic growth or investment.[38] The basic result was that it was corporations and not workers who benefited most. It led corporations to create record-breaking share buy-backs of US$1 trillion.[39] If there was any trickling, it was going up, not down.

Nothing new to see here. Researchers David Hope and Julian Limberg conclude from their study of tax reforms over 50 years in 18 different countries that tax cuts for the rich result in 'no significant effects on economic growth or unemployment'.[40] Despite its failure, the trickle-down approach offered a means to use tax policy rather than direct government spending to manage economic growth. The promise was that if taxes were cut for those who have cash and capital, then they will deploy the extra income in a manner that stimulates the economy without the need for government intervention. The problem is that while such a theory provides a neat moral justification for a policy that in effect just makes rich people richer, it does not work. Tax lawyer Madeleine Burnette-McGrath explains:

> trickle-down economics is an unreliable and unstable economic system, which ultimately keeps money in the hands of the top corporate earners. Corporations are not altruistic and selfless in nature. If corporations and shareholders have excess post-tax cash amounts, they are unlikely to spend it on other people. Rather, they will spend it on themselves and on products and services they want and invest in.[41]

So why is trickle-down economics still in vogue today? There are several possible reasons. It could be a lack of political imagination by present governments. Surely, relying on established ideology is much easier than taking the political risk of trying something new. Even worse, corporations and their cashed-up CEOs may have become so powerful that governments are afraid to take them on. This speaks directly to how billionaire wealth has yielded so much power that they can call the shots over the elected representatives of the people.

Professor of Political Science and former US Labour Secretary Robert Reich shows that trickle-down economics is no accident; it is a policy that is hard-fought for by those who benefit from it the most – the rich. In his words: '[trickle-down economics] satisfies politically powerful moneyed interests who want to rake in even more. Armies of lobbyists in Washington, London and Brussels continuously demand tax cuts and "regulatory relief" for their wealthy patrons.'[42] Reich also shows that these same 'moneyed interests' provide financial support to institutions and think-tanks, such as the Heritage Foundation, Cato Institute and Club for Growth, all of which continue to this day to promote the trickle-down rip-off publicly.

Trickle-down economics is an example of what economist John Quiggin calls 'zombie economics':[43] a failed economic ideology whose corpse seems to keep coming back to life to scare us. These undead ideas refuse to go away, even when all evidence suggests they should be in the graveyard of poorly conceived or even dangerous notions. Mired in the creed of right-wing apologists and advocates of unfettered globalization, trickle-down economics has always been a scam. The trickle-down con trick provides the perfect means to do away with the progressive taxation and income redistribution policies that taxed the rich to benefit those less well-off. If anything, it is incredible that anyone was fooled by such a bald-faced and counterintuitive lie.

Accepting trickle-down economics means believing that if rich people contribute less to society through taxation and governments create policies that enable them to garner more wealth for themselves, then the real benefits will accrue to people who are not rich. This is an astounding piece of anti-logic. It is the right-wing equivalent of arguing that down is up and up is down. The reality is that up is more up than it was before and that trickle-down economics has been proved to be nothing more than a political fraud. That is not to say that nothing has changed about trickle-down since the 1980s. Back then, the argument was purely economic – stop taxing the rich and the natural mechanics of the economy will ensure that everyone benefits. In that scheme, billionaires and corporations were conceived of as quite passive. The invisible hand of the market was supposed to do its magic without the active will of the rich and powerful.

Today the belief in trickle-down economics remains but it has become moralized. Now many billionaires position themselves as being actively and deliberately focused on producing 'social goods'. This approach is exemplified in the person of Larry Fink. Each January, Fink, billionaire boss of asset management firm BlackRock, sends a letter to the CEOs of the corporations in which his company invests. In these letters, he takes it upon himself to outline his views on the most important issues affecting the business world. A well-known advocate of 'corporate purpose', Fink's letters have focused on the responsibility of corporations to address environmental sustainability, promoting workforce diversity and managing the impact of business on society. His mantra has been that people have lost trust in governments that have failed to solve social and political problems, and it is time for businesses to step up and do it for them.

In his letter released on 17 January 2022,[44] Fink slightly changed tack. He still went on about stakeholder capitalism and how corporations should pursue the interests of the customers, employees, suppliers and communities rather than just shareholders. In 2022, he added a direct statement that his approach to business was not 'woke' and 'is not about politics'. Fink protested against being accused of being a pin-striped political ideologue, claiming he was just figuring out the best way to do capitalism. What could be less woke than that? 'We focus on sustainability not because we're environmentalists, but because we are capitalists and fiduciaries to our clients,' he opined. In his 2023 letter, Fink distanced himself from wokeness even more, focusing his attention on the more traditional business interests of value creation and trust in financial systems.[45]

Fink's anti-woke position came at a time when conservatives had been attacking corporations for meddling in social and political issues. US Senator Marco Rubio commented that '[i]nstead of the patriotic leaders that capitalism needs, today America's corporate elite kowtow to the woke, Marxist mobs that dominate the internet and Hollywood'.[46] The same sentiment is heard around the world. The global hoo-ha about whether corporations were embracing left-wing politics was a perfect distraction. The idea that corporate bosses were becoming Marxists is entirely ignorant of corporate behaviours and of even the most rudimentary tenets of Marxism. That Rubio would suggest it was nothing more than a rabble-rousing attempt to gain political clout. That Fink would respond was simply taking an each-way bet on his capitalist credibility.

What this really brought up was how stakeholder capitalism was a moral extension of trickle-down economics. Despite apparent differences, they both serve the same purpose of making a fundamentally unfair economic system appear like it will benefit everyone. All that has to be done is make sure that rich corporations call the shots. Worrying about whether Fink and his CEO buddies are woke is just like being tricked by a magician misdirecting attention to hide the sleight of hand. Getting all worked up about corporate wokeness might just obscure the sham that trickle-down economics has led to massive deterioration when it comes to basic matters of economic justice.

On precisely the same day that Fink sent his CEO missive, Oxfam released their report *Inequality Kills*. As much as this was a coincidence, it belied a bitter irony. There was no evidence in that report to support the extravagant promises of either trickle-down economics or stakeholder capitalism – quite the contrary. Oxfam described how COVID-19 was a boom time for billionaires, with the top ten doubling their wealth. Meanwhile, 99 per cent of the world's population became financially worse off. The reality of economic inequality is the polar opposite of capitalism's false promises. Inequality means simply that people with economic means forcibly take a much more significant share of the world's wealth for themselves, leaving the rest to struggle, suffer or die. This language is not figurative: Oxfam reported that inequality was, at the time, a contributing factor to the death of 21,300 people each day. By contrast, 2021 saw the biggest growth in billionaire wealth on record. In the foreword to the Oxfam report, Jayati Ghosh, Professor of Economics at the University of Massachusetts at Amherst, summed it up like this:

> Unequal access to incomes and opportunities does more than create unjust, unhealthy, and unhappy societies: it actually kills people … And while they died, the richest people in the world got richer than ever and some of the largest companies made unprecedented profits. The hundreds of millions of people who have suffered disproportionately during this pandemic were already likely to be more disadvantaged: more likely to live in low- and middle-income countries, to be women or girls, to belong to socially discriminated-against groups, to be informal workers. … Now it appears that inequality is not just killing those with less political voice; it is also killing the planet. This makes the strategy of privileging profits over people not just unjust but monumentally stupid. Economies will not 'grow,' and markets will not deliver 'prosperity' to anyone, no matter how powerful, on a dead planet.[47]

Inequality – meaning that some 'stakeholders' claim the lion's share of the world's wealth at everyone else's expense – is the political issue of the twenty-first century. Stakeholder capitalism might be a feel-good corporate-friendly ideological companion to trickle-down economics. However, so long as some stakeholders are (extremely) more equal than others, it is a flimsy veneer trying to hide an economic system that produces ever-increasing levels of inequality.

Flying in the face of the promises of shareholder capitalism is a much broader and more important debate over the question of billionaire legitimacy. This question was spurred into public debate on 24 September 2019, when US Senator Bernie Sanders sent out the four-word tweet, 'Billionaires should not exist.' The tweet accompanied Sanders' unveiling of his proposed wealth tax.

Sanders proposed that any individual whose wealth exceeded US$16 million should be taxed up to 8 per cent of their wealth each year. It would start at 2 per cent for those who just scraped past the bottom threshold, with the full 8 per cent hit reserved for those with more than US$10 billion in their coffers. The modelling showed that while only 180,000 American households would be affected, the deal would raise a staggering US$4.35 trillion over ten years. 'We are going to take on the billionaire class, substantially reduce wealth inequality in America, and stop our democracy from turning into a corrupt oligarchy,' said Sanders.[48] Those calculations were done before the surge in billionaire wealth that happened during COVID, and during the pandemic Sanders developed a new proposal: the Make Billionaires Pay Act. Sanders noted that the richest 0.001 per cent of people in the US – that is the 467 billionaires – had accumulated US$731 billion in wealth during the peak pandemic period from 18 March to 5 August 2021. Sanders' proposal was to tax this unearned windfall at 60 per cent. He laid bare the vast inequalities exacerbated by COVID:

> At a time of enormous economic pain and suffering, we have a fundamental choice to make. We can continue to allow the very rich to get much richer while everyone else gets poorer and poorer. Or we can tax the winnings a handful of billionaires made during the pandemic to improve the health and well-being of tens of millions of Americans. In my view, it is time for the Senate to act on behalf of the working class who are hurting like they have never hurt before, not the billionaire class who are doing phenomenally well and have never had it so good.[49]

For Sanders, the very existence of billionaires is a 'moral and economic outrage'.[50] In 2023, he upped the ante even further by proposing that there should be a 100 per cent tax rate on earnings of more than US$1 billion.[51] He is far from alone in his views on tax policy, with slogans and hashtags like #MakeBillionairesPay and #TaxTheRich rallying cries demanding economic justice in an era of obscene inequality.

Billionaires may have clearly taken more than a fair share of the world's wealth but they did not do it on their own. The emergence of the new billionaires is a symptom of an unbalanced economic system that resulted directly from economic policy reform. The billionaires were just in the right place and the right time to milk that system for all it was worth. It was the rapid expansion of neoliberal economic dogma in the West from the 1980s that established a system that enabled the new billionaires to surge into existence. As British Member of Parliament Lloyd Russell-Moyle explains,[52] the creation of individual empires of wealth has resulted from government policy and regulatory reform.

As governments sought for their countries to compete in an increasingly globalized economy they reduced taxes on the wealthy, strengthened property rights in favour of the rich and eroded workers' rights. The value of state fiscal intervention designed directly to achieve fairer wealth distribution was set aside in the name of global capitalism. Individual enterprise is what was needed and that could only be unleashed by breaking the shackles of pesky regulations. The entrepreneurial spirit was unleashed, to be sure, but the gross inequality that billionaires represent cannot be dismissed as an unintended consequence. Russell-Moyle points to the 4 million children living in poverty in the UK. Are they just collateral damage in the competitive war for economic growth? Do the injustices of inequality really need to be accepted so as not to dampen aspiring entrepreneurs? The answer to these questions is, emphatically, no.

The extreme wealth of the rapidly expanded billionaire class is a vital sign of the urgent need for political resistance to gross economic inequality. The excessiveness of the wealth held by those at the very top echelon of the economic hierarchy is almost unfathomable in its proportions. The obscenity of the extreme wealth of billionaires is palpable and inexcusable, and the economic inequality is matched by an inequality in power that is equally dangerous and offensive. Billionaires are increasingly using their wealth not just to influence politics but to become major global political players, often rising above state leaders and government officials in their ability to influence the world. Inequality in wealth is accompanied by a sense of entitlement, with individual billionaires able to act as if unburdened from the responsibilities of the social contract that demands responsibilities for the effects of one's actions on other citizens. When, on 14 November 2021, Bernie Sanders tweeted, 'We must demand that the extremely wealthy pay their fair share. Period,' it caught Elon Musk's attention. Musk replied to Sanders the next day: 'I keep forgetting that you're still alive.'[53] It would appear that Musk's power leads him to believe that he is above being answerable for who he is or what he does. There is no political argument or justification, just a hurtful childish jibe, taunting a career politician who has spent a lifetime fighting for equality.

A telling story of billionaire entitlement came on 20 July 2021, when Jeff Bezos of Amazon personally took the first ride on his Blue Origin New Shepard rocket as it launched into outer space. It was all part of a billionaire space race that saw him and Virgin's Richard Branson competing to be the first entrepreneur to develop commercial space travel. When Bezos landed after his 11-minute space sojourn, he thanked the Amazon employees and customers who 'paid for all this'.[54] Apparently, it was a joke.[55] Surely, this was not so funny for the Amazon workers deprived of toilet breaks and under the constant surveillance of algorithm management.[56] Not so funny either, as US Senator Elizabeth Warren tweeted, for 'hardworking Americans who actually paid taxes to keep this country running while he and Amazon paid nothing'.[57] The space ride exemplified the way that billionaires can simply do as they wish at the expense of ordinary taxpayers and workers.

It was 60 years ago that an American first left the earth's atmosphere.[58] That's old news. What was new about Bezos' joyride is not scientific, it is commercial. Blue Origin is the aerospace company Bezos owns that launched him into space on the New Shepard spacecraft. The video on their website explains the company's mission, with Bezos connecting his 'passion' for space travel to his childhood experience of watching Neil Armstrong land on the moon. Bezos proclaims that going to space is about the future of civilization. He extols the civic virtue of 'a bunch of very entrepreneurial start-up companies doing amazing things in space'.[59]

The space race of the 1960s was rightfully criticized for its profligacy. Putting a man on the moon should not have been more important than addressing hunger and poverty on earth. Despite his claims about civilization, Bezos has received similar criticism.[60] Oxfam's Deepak Xavier pulled no punches: 'We've now reached stratospheric inequality. Billionaires burning into space, away from a world of pandemic, climate change and starvation.'[61] Watching Bezos launch himself into space is a startling sign of the state of political power in today's billionaire age. Bezos' power is bought with immense personal wealth at the expense of citizens and at the expense of equality. And then he has the gall to claim he is doing it all for the future of humanity.[62] Bezos only paid a true tax rate of 0.98 per cent as his wealth grew by US$99 billion from the mid-2010s.[63] That he decides to spend some of his tax savings on public projects of his own choosing is as downright feudal as it is self-aggrandizing. Bezos' high-flying shenanigans laugh in the face of any glimmer of hope that democratic popular sovereignty matters more than the whims of the wealthy. Such is the danger of the new billionaires and the inequality they personify.

Coming back to the question posed at the beginning of this chapter as to just how rich are billionaires, the basic answer is that they are by far much richer than anyone deserves to be. As a corollary to that, they are also far too powerful. A telling example of the moral complexities of how billionaire wealth is used to exercise political power came in February 2022 when Mike Cannon-Brookes, the billionaire co-founder and co-CEO of software company Atlassian, made a bold excursion into corporate climate activism. Working with the Canadian asset management firm Brookfield, he made a dramatic takeover bid for AGL Energy, the 185-year-old public company that operates Australia's biggest electricity generation business. The offer was A$9 billion.[64]

Central to the deal was a plan for radical decarbonization. AGL's self-penned climate statement asserted the company's commitment to a transition from fossil fuel to renewable energy:

> We know what the long-term future of energy will look like.
>
> Electricity from renewable sources, backed by flexible energy storage technologies will power our homes,

businesses and vehicles. Energy will be both affordable and smart, and greenhouse gas emissions will be much lower, helping us to tackle climate change.

At AGL, we accept the climate science behind this vision. By 2050, we believe that Australia has the opportunity to be carbon neutral and an energy superpower. We will play our part in achieving this and target reaching net zero emissions by 2050.[65]

Cannon-Brookes was not impressed by AGL's carefully worded commitment to carbon neutrality by 2050. Central to the business strategy behind the takeover bid was a commitment to accelerate the company's decarbonization. Specifically, Cannon-Brookes planned to bring the energy giant's carbon-dioxide emission to net zero 12 years ahead of schedule to 2038 and replace its coal-power stations by 2030.[66] *The Australian Financial Review* painted the deal as epitomizing the intersection of climate politics, billionaire political activism and the meteoric rise of private capital.[67]

Given, historically, the Australian government's woeful ineptitude in addressing climate change, Cannon-Brookes' bid was a breath of fresh air to many. 'On a global scale this is a massive decarbonisation effort,' he said, spruiking the deal. This came at a time when people around the world were discrediting the Australian government for its wilful failure to take meaningful action on climate change. Just six months before the AGL takeover bid, Australia had presented as somewhat of an international embarrassment at the UN Climate Change Conference held in Glasgow in November 2021. Then Prime Minister Scott Morrison had just been outed in the press for putting pressure on the UK to drop climate change targets from a bilateral trade deal.[68] Extinction Rebellion environment activists set fire to the Australian flag at a demonstration as the conference began. Why? 'To symbolise Australia's Climate Pariah status on the first day of COP26, and our major parties' chronic addiction to life-destroying fossil fuels.' The symbol was of a nation set left to burn by unscrupulous politicians.[69] Climate justice lawyer Kavita Naidu said at the time:

Australia is the pariah here right now. It has not enhanced its ambitions since 2015. Most countries are really stepping up to making sure that by 2030, so in the next decade, we see some real reductions in emissions. Australia is not giving that at all, we're playing with numbers ... Australia is just not stepping up and nobody is buying Australia's bullshit anymore.[70]

Cannon-Brookes certainly was not 'buying Australia's bullshit' and was ready to put his money where his mouth was to do something about it. Despite the Cannon-Brookes bid being rejected at an emergency meeting of AGL's board of directors, this story says a lot about the relationship between liberal democracy and billionaire politicking and the extent to which the past 40 years have seen a massive shift in political power toward the super-rich. It also shows that today's billionaires are willing and able to take on some of the most significant political challenges facing the planet, even when governments shy away from the challenge. Notably, around the same time Cannon-Brookes was trying to decarbonize AGL, the Australian government was spending A$31 million of taxpayers' money on an advertising campaign to drum up public support for its widely disputed climate plan. For the politicians, using public money to fund marketing designed to convince voters that its unproven plan for Australia to reach zero emissions by 2050 seemed more important than addressing the actual climate crisis. The plan the campaign was communicating contained no new policies.[71]

For a democratic country like Australia, the sad situation was that the nation's capacity to address the most urgent global problems came down to the voluntary actions of a billionaire business owner. Cannon-Brookes was nothing if not consistent. His billionaire activist position against climate change has been steadfast for many years. In 2018, Prime Minister Scott Morrison renewed his support for coal power, dubbing it 'fair dinkum energy' – 'fair dinkum' being Australian slang for 'genuine'. Cannon-Brookes retorted, 'Argh! Bullshit mate ... you've made me mad and inspired me. We need a movement.'[72]

Despite Cannon-Brookes gesturing as a political activist, his motives were also commercial. The billions that were put up to buy AGL were not a charitable donation; they represented a calculated business investment and like all investments, they demanded a return. For a business to put public interests above its financial interests would be commercially irresponsible. Cannon-Brookes certainly was not doing that. He said at the time: 'decarbonisation is a huge technology transformation required around the world and creates a lot of investible opportunities to both create a profit for the investment and to decarbonise at the same time'.[73] In the wake of the government's climate failure and as the elected politicians kicked the problem of the climate crisis into the long grass, a private business partnership tried to step up to use its significant financial might to try to fix the problem, so long as they could make money along the way.

Cannon-Brookes' attempt to take over AGL is part of a more significant trend. Under the guise of billionaire activism, societies are increasingly coming to rely on the ultra-wealthy to take political action on matters concerning the public good; at least what they decide counts as the public good. Billionaires have even been touted as the 'superheroes' that the world needs![74] The rub is that so long as there is no conflict between billionaires' espoused political convictions and the hard business realities of what it takes to become that rich, then everyone might be okay. At best, this exemplifies commercially viable single-issue politics that attaches itself to a particular cause without concern for the broader political or ideological movement of that cause. For Cannon-Brookes, decarbonization is clearly a cause he genuinely supports personally and politically. Contributing to the public good through paying tax is much less of a priority for his company Atlassian, however. Perhaps paying tax is not on the list of what billionaires think is 'good'. It is fine for Cannon-Brookes to contest the government's approach to climate change, but his company is not putting the needed funds into the public coffers that would enable them to invest in renewable energy. This contradiction should not be ignored.

Back in 2020, Atlassian was widely criticized for paying absolutely no tax on a revenue base of more than A\$1 billion per year and a market capitalization of A\$54 billion.[75] The following year they paid a very modest A\$11 million.[76] It is all legal, with the minimum tax resulting from offsets they claim from research and development expenditure all wrapped up in complex multinational corporate governance arrangements. As *Australian Financial Review* columnist Joe Aston described it, Cannon-Brookes and his business partner Scott Farquhar set up the arrangement back in 2014. It involves 'a highly complex London-based structure that enables the arbitrage of global tax codes and ensures their tech darling will pay very little tax for a very long time'. More colloquially, Aston described Cannon-Brookes as 'an epic freeloader'.[77] Cannon-Brookes himself has also profited handsomely. As of 2024, his personal net worth was US$13.3 billion.[78]

The even bigger political question that Cannon-Brookes' story raises is whether a sovereign nation should rely on the commercial and political interests of globally mobile billionaires to address its most severe problems? It is also worth asking how desirable such reliance is when the corporations these same people are wrapped up in can avoid paying their way in society the way pretty much everyone else has to. If the political future of democratic states lies in the hands of the wealthy, even when people agree with them, the world is on a dangerous path back to feudalism if it means that a relatively lawless minorly rules over everyone else. Cannon-Brookes' attempt to find a way for Australia to contribute to the global effort to address climate change is, in many ways, commendable. The fact that this responsibility has fallen into the hands of a private individual is not, nor is the way so many billionaires eagerly take responsibility for dealing with the world's most severe problems into their own hands. It is even worse if they do so because they believe that the official authorities have failed in their public duties.

The success of billionaire politics is the failure of democracy. The case of Cannon-Brookes and AGL might not raise an eyebrow among those who agree with his stance on climate change and the need for urgent action. In the wake of the Australian government's failure to take drastic action on what is inarguably one of the world's most pressing problems, the fact that someone with the power to do is trying to make a difference can appear like good news. Perhaps so, but this indicates a much bigger systemic problem that commonly goes unnoticed or is ignored. This problem concerns what happens to democratic politics and the democratic way of life when rich people get to call the political shots, whether people agree with them or not.

American billionaire brothers David and Charles Koch spent a fortune promoting reductions in corporate tax and the removal of government regulations on business, with remarkable success.[79] David Koch personally paid out billions of dollars supporting institutions dedicated to climate change denial. Anti-abortion, anti-union and anti-LGBTQIA+ groups have also benefited from the Koch brothers' largesse.[80] Their ability to do this, just like Cannon-Brookes' climate activism, resulted purely from their wealth and their willingness to use it to try to enforce their own political convictions on others. In the case of the Koch brothers, this is part of a new plutocracy where billionaires have purposefully funded activities designed to control political systems, steering them in directions that benefit the rich.[81] 'Stealth politics' is at play where billionaires surreptitiously rig the economic game in their own favour while remaining entirely unaccountable for the political power that they pay for.[82]

Think about the 63 billionaires who provided financial backing to Donald Trump's re-election campaign in 2020. These were the same people who benefited handsomely from the tax cuts and deregulation policies Trump pushed through as the US president. *Quid pro quo?* It was called the 'Trump Victory Fund' and received millions of dollars from the likes of oil pipeline tycoon Kelcy Warren, real estate developer Steve Wynn and casino boss Phil Ruffin.[83] Trump's 2024 campaign followed suit. Fair-weather-friend billionaires disavowed Trump after the January 6 insurrection and his presidential defeat in 2021. Back then, Trump was no use to them anymore. In early 2024, when it began to look like he might return to the White House, billionaires started flocking back in support, fearful of President Joe Biden's promise to raise taxes on America's richest citizens.[84] Billionaire hedge fund manager John Paulson even hosted a fund-raising dinner to support Trump's campaign. The cheapest ticket was US$250,000 per person and went up to US$814,600 to sit at Trump's table.[85]

Union-busting is another favourite political cause among the world's billionaires. In the US, the billionaire-funded Freedom Foundation defines itself as a 'battle tank that's battering the entrenched power of left-wing government union bosses who represent a permanent lobby for bigger government, higher taxes, and radical social agendas'.[86] Critics such as Bob Schoonover, president of the Service Employees International Union Local 721, says the real agenda is to 'silence the working class'.[87] People with billions of dollars can do such things.

Cannon-Brookes might want to use his money to fight climate change, but that is not the case for many of his fellow billionaires. If anything, history shows that billionaires have been especially active in trying to convince people that climate change is a hoax, especially if those billionaires have large stakes in the oil and gas industries. Take, for example, the hedge fund billionaire Robert Mercer's Mercer Family Foundation. Not only did the Foundation hand over US$15 million to help bankroll Donald Trump's 2016 campaign, the very next year, they forked out almost US$5 million to climate change denying think-tanks and not-for-profit organizations.[88] One of these organizations is the CO2 Coalition, whose stated purpose is to educate:

> thought leaders, policy makers, and the public about the important contribution made by carbon dioxide to our lives and the economy. The Coalition seeks to engage in an informed and dispassionate discussion of ... the limitations of climate models, and the consequences of mandated reductions in CO2 emissions.[89]

Other donors like to keep their identities secret, channelling their funding of the so-called 'climate change counter-movement' through anonymized contributions to foundations such as the Donors Trust and the Donors Capital Fund that in turn fund a variety of entities that argue against climate science and spread misinformation about climate change.[90] Billionaires connected with 'big oil' have been identified as behind much of the funding.[91] The Donors Trust, which investigative reporter Andy Kroll described as 'the dark-money ATM of the conservative movement', is a vehicle that enables the very rich to shell out millions of dollars for right-wing causes anonymously. Climate change denial is only one of the areas of focus. Other political activities supported by the Donors Trust have been attacks on trade unions, criticism of public education and campaigning against economic regulation.[92]

Irrespective of whether anyone agrees or disagrees with billionaires' choices about how to wield their power in the political sphere, it is always the case that they can do this purely because they are rich. In the absence of democratic controls over this billionaire politicking, the citizens of the nations in which billionaires operate have no power to change things. People are left at the mercy of the whims and fancies of the rich, much as was the case in the feudal societies that democracy replaced. In a genuinely democratic society, if people disagree with an elected leader, they have the power to vote him or her out through the electoral process, effectively stripping the leader of their authority. If one's authority is drawn from personal wealth rather than the popular vote, it cannot be easily stripped.

In contrast with democratically elected leaders, billionaires are more like dictators whose power cannot be held to account in the same way as heads of state, other elected officials and public servants. They are not subject to the social rules and norms that other members of society must live by. Good luck if a billionaire turns out to be a benevolent dictator flexing his or her muscles around their political interests. Not so good if the dictator is fickle, greedy or malicious.

The reality of the existence of billionaires is the reality of gross inequality in money and power. In the liberal-democratic world, the risk of their existence is the final displacement of popular sovereignty by the rule of billionaire warlords. The political question that the existence of billionaires begs is: should the basis of political rule be on the power that comes with wealth? The absolute cornerstone of democracy is that the single and only source of legitimate rule comes from 'the people', who are the ultimate authority that all must answer to. The status of people in democratic society is that of being citizens who have rights and responsibilities to others, and who submit to the rule of law to maintain social cohesion and political stability. The whole point of government by elected representatives, for all its failings, is an attempt at operationalizing the founding principle of popular sovereignty. In a democracy, those with governing power are only granted that power on the grounds that they represent the people. When billionaires exercise their substantial power on their own terms and as if they were answerable to no one, they are defying the founding principle of democracy.

The wealth billionaires possess is a damning condition where vast inequality is the scourge of a world that laughs in the face of the people it has made hungry and destitute. The political power that billionaires command and exercise is a rebuke to the very promise of a society, as Abraham Lincoln said in Gettysburg in 1863, whose rule was 'of the people, by the people, for the people'. Nothing could be further from the trajectory of the new breed of billionaires.

Criticizing billionaire politicking as undemocratic does not mean that, taken individually, political acts of billionaires are 'bad' in and of themselves. Indeed, many would agree that billionaires can and do use their power as a 'force for good'. Such thinking sidesteps the bigger political systemic problem. This is not a problem of casting moral judgement on the acts of individual billionaires, Cannon-Brookes being a worthy example. The real problem is the development of a political system where decisions that affect all members of a society (or even of the whole world) are made at the discretion of the wealthy rather than democratically. One might agree with some billionaires' choices and disagree with others. The problem is that they are the ones who are doing the choosing based on whatever criteria or conviction they personally advocate.

The expansion of billionaire wealth and power does not just represent a retreat from democracy, it also heralds a new feudalism. Professor of Political Science Jodi Dean lays it out with clarity and insight:

> Global financial institutions and digital technology platforms use debt to redistribute wealth from the world's poorest to the richest. Nation-states promote and protect specific private corporations. Political power is exercised with and as economic power, not only taxes but fines, liens, asset seizures, licenses, patents, jurisdictions, and borders. At the same time, economic power shields those who wield it from the reach of state law.[93]

Under the neo-feudal regimes, the fate of everyday people is at the whim and mercy of the rich and powerful as they stride around the world, making decisions that affect so many others. The collective political might of billionaires represents a wanton disregard for the social promise of democracy. Like medieval Europe's feudal lords, billionaires live on private estates high on the hill away from the common people, figuratively and often literally. On show is how billionaire-driven neo-feudalism is a system where the extremely wealthy are becoming the world's rulers as members of a newly emerged global aristocracy that places democracy and its promise of equality at stake.

3

The Myth of
the Heroic Billionaire

There is a reality TV show that first aired in the United States in 2019 on the Discovery Channel called *The Undercover Billionaire*. The star of the first series is Glenn Stearns, founder of the mortgage lending company Stearns Lending. In building Stearns' myth, the Discovery Channel portray him as the epitome of the American dream.[1] Stearns was not born with a silver spoon in his mouth. Quite the contrary, he endured a difficult childhood with both his parents being alcoholics and him suffering from dyslexia. Not an early success in life, Stearns failed the 4th grade. He became a father when he was just 14 years old and finished in the bottom 10 per cent of his high school graduating class. Everything suggested that Stearns had no chance of becoming one of life's 'winners'.

Then the plot twists. Under the guidance of mentors, Stearns reportedly was able to take charge of his life and pull himself up by his own bootstraps to get on the road to success. He was not going to let his humble and challenging beginnings define him. Stearns completed a university degree, the first in his family to do so. Meanwhile he worked as a waiter to earn a living until he could get his big break. That break came in 1989 when, at the age of 25, Stearns founded his own mortgage company and set out on the corporate road to riches. By 2010, the company was lending around a billion dollars a month. Since then, it has booked loans of more than US$150 billion. On the back of such successful growth, a few years later, in 2015, Stearns sold 70 per cent his company to investment management firm the Blackstone Group, after which its assets quickly grew to more than US$2 billion.[2]

Stearns' success did not go unnoticed in the public eye. In 2003, when he married Mindy Burbano, the wedding was featured on *The Oprah Winfrey Show*. It was called a 'real-life Cinderella story'. The couple were widely regarded as the epitome of the rags to riches, American success story. The American dream just kept building. In 2011, Stearns was the youngest person ever to be granted membership to the Horatio Alger Association of Distinguished Americans. This association prides itself on being 'dedicated to the simple but powerful belief that hard work, honesty, and determination can conquer all obstacles'.[3] According to Stearns' own website, this award 'is given to individuals in recognition of overcoming challenging beginnings in life and then climbing to the top of their fields with outstanding endeavours in giving back to others'.[4] At the time *The Undercover Billionaire* was first broadcast, Stearns' personal net worth was reported at US$500 million. It may have been a convenient exaggeration to call him a billionaire, but that's still very rich.

The premise of Stearns' *Undercover Billionaire* is summed up in the Discovery Channel's press release about the show:

> self-made businessman Glenn Stearns bet big that the American dream was still alive and well. Viewers watched as Glenn was stripped of his name, wealth and contacts and dropped into a city he's never been to see if he could build a million-dollar company in 90 days with only $100 in his pocket.[5]

The show is a homage to a certain vision of billionaires as heroic figures. By taking away all the money, fame and trappings of the billionaire, what is left is just the human being slung back to the bottom rung of life's ladder. So, what happened to Stearns in the show? Would his epic character shine through, allowing him once again to rise on account of his personal acumen and hard work? Or would the setbacks derail him, showing that his previous success was nothing more than blind luck? The Disney Channel did not disappoint and the promise of the American dream was kept alive. This is a classic rags-to-riches story, with Stearns cast as the hero.

Despite initial obstructions, including a health scare, throughout the show Stearns never loses his determination or self-confidence. His new business was aptly called Underdog BBQ, a food and beer joint in Erie, Pennsylvania. Building a loyal team of so-called 'underdogs', Stearns' business finally gets off the ground. The series comes to a finale with the store opening. After 90 days, the business is valued at US$750,000. Not quite a billion, but enough to retain faith in the American dream.

The success of *The Undercover Billionaire* demonstrates the still genuine appeal of the American dream – the belief that anybody, irrespective of their background, can achieve success in the US. The term 'American dream' was coined by James Truslow Adams in his bestselling book *The Epic of America*,[6] published in 1931. The book is a history of what Adams refers to as the 'outlook, character and opinion' of the ordinary American.[7] The dream that America promised was one of freedom and independence, unavailable in the old European world where immigrants to the US were coming from. So far so good, but the American dream that Adams portrays has some crucial differences to its billionaire variant that is perpetuated in *The Undercover Billionaire*.

In Adams' original version, the American dream is not so much about the individual success of the likes of Glenn Stearns. Adams praises the possibility of 'a richer and fuller life for all' that rails against the 'marked injustice' of the unequal distribution of wealth.[8] Adams' American dream is one that combines opportunity and justice in a new world. It is a promise of an America where the structural inequalities of European feudalism are replaced with the shared democratic hope of freedom, equality and social solidarity. This American dream houses a collectivist vision of a nation where all people can succeed and flourish, rather than an elite few rising to the top while others languish at the bottom. What Adams believed in was 'an American dream of a better, richer, and happier life for all our citizens of every rank'.[9] This is not a dream of heroic individualism where only the few can succeed. Instead, it is a democratic dream of a nation where all people can do well, thriving without the shackles of the class disadvantage or racial discrimination that they might have encountered in the 'old country'.

Adams would be no fan of today's billionaires, nor would he see these moguls as in anyway exemplifying the American dream. There was more than a hint of sarcasm when Adams explicitly proclaimed his distrust in 'the wise paternalism of politicians or the infinite wisdom of business leaders'[10] and, it can be assumed, billionaires too. Adams' values were deeply egalitarian, opposed to the kind of brutal economic elitism that today's billionaires represent. Indeed, Adams bemoaned the inequality of his day as being unequivocal evidence of the American economic system having not yet lived up to the promise of the American dream. This is:

> A system that steadily increases the gulf between the ordinary man [sic] and the super-rich, that permits the resources of society to be gathered into personal fortunes that afford their owner millions of income a year, with only the chance that here or there a few may be moved to confer some of their surplus upon the public in ways chosen wholly by themselves, is assuredly an unjust system. It is perhaps as inimical as anything could be to the American dream.[11]

What Adams said back in 1931 still holds true to this day, if not in a greatly magnified way. Adams' dream of shared prosperity in the context of an egalitarian society is a decidedly different American dream to the more contemporary version depicted in *The Undercover Billionaire*. In the show, the American dream is imagined in the form of a man who has nothing by way of wealth or resources putting his own unique and rare skills and abilities to work to accumulate a personal fortune. This is a dream where only the heroic minority succeed and the rest are left behind. For Adams, in contrast, the dream was of a society that offers every citizen the resources to prosper while not tolerating any person who would seek an unfair share of the nation's riches for themselves.

Leon Cooperman is an example of a billionaire who embodies the vast minoritarian individualization of the new American dream. Cooperman is former CEO and Chairman of Goldman Sachs Asset Management, during which time the Institutional Investor All-America Research Team ranked him as the number-one portfolio strategist for nine years running.[12] Cooperman was born in the US to first-generation Polish parents. The family lived in a one-bedroom apartment in New York's South Bronx.[13] In 2024, he was worth more than US$2.8 billion and lays claim to being the hero of the American dream. *Forbes Magazine* describes Cooperman as a 'Wall Street legend' who was the public school-educated son of a plumber.[14]

Cooperman himself has stated his view that '[m]y life is the story of the American dream'. His is the heroic billionaire version of the American dream, not the one that involves equal opportunity of means and fair distribution of ends. For Cooperman, the American dream is one where 'the 99 percent can still join the 1 percent. It's possible with enough luck and commitment.'[15] His version of the American dream is not one that imagines success for all. Instead, it means that while anyone *can* be successful, only the vast minority ever will be. This American dream is fundamentally dependent on the assumption of inequality. Sure, any person may be able to get a bigger share of the pie but it will always be at the expense of others whose lot in life is to scrape up the crumbs that fall from the edge of the pie tin.

Literary critic Lydia Kiesling recounts how Americans have long been obsessed with the rags-to-riches hero, at least since Horatio Alger's popular mid-nineteenth-century novels about boys from poor backgrounds whose hard work and determination led them into the middle classes. Kiesling explains, as an embellishment to the fairy tale of Cinderella, the rags-to-riches stories that Alger popularized reflected a hopeful optimism about class mobility and equal opportunity. From studying their memoirs and autobiographies, Kiesling concludes that today's billionaires have developed a marked tendency to tell the stories of their own lives as if they were characters in one of Alger's novels. They have become adept at re-narrating their lives so that they are the heroes of the story. In an era where social mobility is harder and harder to achieve, the American dream emerges as a culturally convenient moral justification of obscene wealth, couched in the familiar cold comfort of a worn-out story of individual success. In a perverse retelling of the myth of the American dream, a vision of shared prosperity is falsely used as a justification for sickening levels of inequality.

Billionaires claiming to be the heroic protagonists of the story of the American dream camouflage the underlying logic of billionaire morality. This is not new. In 1776, Adam Smith published a collection of five books that comprised *An Inquiry into the Nature and Causes of the Wealth of Nations*,[16] widely considered to be the foundation of modern economics. Often seen as a treatise on the value of free market economics, Smith's position is not one that unreflectively advocates the supposed virtues of laissez-faire capitalism. Smith was a critic of 'mercantilism', the colonial economic doctrine of the time that held that a nation would become wealthy if it maximized what it exported and minimized what it imported. In other words, by restricting international trade, national wealth would increase. Smith's criticism of mercantilism is that it increases inequalities. Conversely, the eponymous 'wealth of nations' could only grow if inequality was reduced. Political scientist Dennis Rasmussen surmises:

> [It is] indisputable that the alleviation of poverty was one of Smith's central concerns ... Smith states, explicitly and repeatedly, that the true measure of a nation's wealth is not the size of its king's treasury or the holdings of an affluent few but rather the wages of 'the laboring poor.'[17]

The danger of inequality, as Smith would have it, is that it distorts society to a position where the poor begin to see the rich as heroes. This admiration of the wealthy is misplaced, he suggested, and can only lead to unhappiness. Moreover, given that Smith doubted the moral character of the rich on account of their arrogance and avarice, any admiration of them was a distortion of morality. In an economy characterized by inequality, the society that ensues is one where the rich few enjoy the spoils of the world, where the rest strive futilely to be like them. It is easy to see how Smith's observations and insights from 250 years ago are deeply pertinent today.[18]

Smith was severely critical of the vastly accumulated wealth that allowed the rich to enjoy the bounty of trade without sharing it. The 'masters of mankind', that is the feudal lords of his time, adhered to what Smith called 'the vile maxim'. He wrote:

> All for ourselves and nothing for other people, seems, in every age of the world, to have been the vile maxim of the masters of mankind. As soon, therefore, as they could find a method of consuming the whole value of their rents themselves, they had no disposition to share them with any other persons.[19]

The rich spent their money on frivolous and unnecessary luxuries, while regular people struggled to survive. Despite the promises of free trade, little seems to have changed today as far as the 'vile maxim' is concerned, it is just that today's lords are the new billionaires. To rub salt into the wounds, today's masters continue to moralize inequality, arguing that their vast and obscenely unequal wealth is fair because they 'earned' it.

Even Donald Trump, perhaps the very personification of how the American dream has become a warped homage to selfishness and inequality, insisted that his financial success was entirely his own doing. In 2016, when he was running for the US presidency against Hillary Clinton, he was at pains to state that he started off his business empire when 'my father gave me a small loan of a million dollars' on which he had to repay with interest. The bolder claim was that he used that 'small loan' to kickstart a business empire and a personal net worth of more than US$10 billion. In truth, the loan was US$60.7 million.[20] As of 2024, *Forbes Magazine* assessed Trump's net worth as US$6.4 billion.[21]

Trump has long been adamant in presenting himself as if he was the heroic protagonist in a Horatio Ager novel and one who those who are not of the moneyed class should hold in envy and admiration. Political analyst Chris Cillizza explains the politics behind Trump's downplaying of his father's role in helping the young Donald get into business was to convince voters not just that he was like them, but that they, too, could aspire to the level of greatness he saw in himself.[22] Trump was exploiting the American dream by distancing himself from his own privileged background. The reality was that Trump was born into wealth and his success would not have been achieved without the support of daddy's money.

For Trump, the American dream was not about everyone having a chance at success but rather about classifying people as 'winners' and 'losers'. His self-told story was that he was born with the same chances as everyone else, but only because of his personal genius, business acumen, drive and talent was he able to become among the richest people in the world. All of this was in dispute – his intelligence has been questioned, his upbringing was privileged and his wealth is allegedly exaggerated. Never mind, this is the new American dream where only the chosen few can rise above the morass of losers that the successful leave in their wake. Despite the

'Make America Great Again' rhetoric that Trump used to galvanize American voters to back him, his self-revelation as an everyman who made it to the top reinforced the sham elitism of the new American dream.

The original American dream was a political project railing against the seeming immutable inequalities of class-based European feudalism. With bitter irony today, the dream has been transformed into a system of inequality that has revitalized the same form of feudal domination it once sought to abolish in the name of democracy. If anything, Trump exploited the very inequality that he benefited from to try to convince the American public that under his rule, a long-dead American dream could rise for the ashes like a phoenix. He was explicit. When in 2015, Trump announced that he would be running for the US presidency, he ended his address by stating: 'sadly, the American dream is dead … But if I get elected president, I will bring it back bigger and better and stronger than ever before, and we will make America great again.'[23] The rest is history.

Back in 1960, arguably the heyday of American dreaming, Martin Luther King Jr. addressed the Annual Freedom Mass Meeting of the North Carolina State Conference of Branches of the National Association for the Advancement of Colored People (NAACP). The topic of his address was, 'The Negro and the American Dream'. This dream was quite different from that of Donald Trump's crazy cocktail of individual success and competitiveness. The date was 25 September and the place was Charlotte, North Carolina. King's dream was not of riches, it was of social equality. In Charlotte, he famously said that the unfulfilled dream of America, as enshrined in the Declaration of Independence, was 'the dream of a land where men of all races, colors and creeds will live together as brothers'.

The real America was nothing like the dream. King described it as schizophrenic in that it was torn between two 'selves':

> A self in which she has proudly professed democracy and a self in which she has sadly practiced the antithesis of democracy. Slavery and segregation have been strange paradoxes in a nation founded on the principle that all men are created equal. Now more than ever before America is challenged to bring her noble dream into reality.[24]

This was the same dream that King declared again three years later on 28 August 1963 at the March on Washington, where he most famously and powerfully said:

> Even though we face the difficulties of today and tomorrow, I still have a dream. It is a dream deeply rooted in the American dream.
>
> I have a dream that one day this nation will rise up and live out the true meaning of its creed: 'We hold these truths to be self-evident, that all men are created equal.'
>
> I have a dream that one day on the red hills of Georgia, the sons of former slaves and the sons of former slave owners will be able to sit down together at the table of brotherhood.
>
> I have a dream that one day even the state of Mississippi, a state sweltering with the heat of injustice, sweltering with the heat of oppression, will be transformed into an oasis of freedom and justice.
>
> I have a dream that my four little children will one day live in a nation where they will not be judged by the color of their skin but by the content of their character.
>
> I have a dream today![25]

Native Americans considered 'savages' by the conservative advocates of the American dream were similarly excluded from the American dream. The promise of the American dream was always blind to structural aspects of American culture that bestowed privilege on certain people by virtue of race and class and literally enslaved and oppressed others to create wealth for the few.[26] To this day, the US is plagued by racial inequality, with Black and Hispanic people earning less than other groups. Data from 2019 shows that the wealth of the median White family was US$184,000. Black households had just US$23,000. For Hispanic households it was US$38,000. This differential has been largely unchanged for the past 50 years. Parallel structures of disadvantage exist internationally. During the COVID-19 pandemic, for example, inequality continued to widen across the world, with women, members of ethnic minority groups and people in developing countries being especially disadvantaged. It was not just about money; it was about the right to life. Oxfam reports that people who lived in Bangladesh were five times more likely to die from the virus than a White person in Britain. In Brazil, Black people were 50 per cent more likely to die from COVID than White Brazilians.[27]

That billionaires are the poster children of the new American dream is less about the real possibilities for the advancement of ordinary citizens, instead ironically serving as justification of obscene inequality by heroizing the rich. To believe the contemporary version of the American dream, where anybody can be rich if they just apply themselves, implies that those who are not rich deserve not to be. This dream reflects a merciless moral system. People who are not financially successful simply do not have the right stuff. Following this cultural logic, being poor does not come about from structural inequalities, minority discrimination, class position, educational opportunities or family wealth, it is simply because the poor are losers. This is an American dream where the cream rises to the top. Billionaires are deserving of their wealth because they made it in the world while others did not. They are heroes. In this culture of extreme individualism, a person's life outcomes – be they success or failure – are entirely the responsibility of that person. People experiencing poverty just do not dream hard enough, it would seem.

The new American dream is not one of shared prosperity, but a dream in which a minority of individuals can acquire the lion's share of the world's wealth at the expense of others. This new American dream is not restricted to the US; it is, perhaps more accurately, the global neoliberal dream. One might even define neoliberalism as the globalization of the American dream. As the Berlin Wall fell on 9 November 1989, capitalism was declared triumphant as both a desirable and inevitable global economic system. This momentous event did not just symbolize the end of communism in Europe but also the liberation of capitalism around the world. Philosopher Francis Fukuyama famously declared the 'end of history' that arose from 'an unabashed victory of economic and politic liberalism' over state communism.[28] In this same era, British Prime Minister Margaret Thatcher wanted everyone to be a capitalist. If the class conflict between workers and capitalists is what fuels the desire for a socialist alternative, Thatcher responded by attempting to eradicate the apparent contradiction by offering capital ownership to everyone.

Speaking to the Conservative Party Conference in the seaside town of Blackpool on 11 October 1985, Thatcher preached:

> Come with us then towards the next decade. Let us together set our sights on a Britain: – where three out of four families own their home; – where owning shares is as common as having a car; – where families have a degree of independence their forefathers could only dream about. A Britain – where there is a resurgence of enterprise, with more people self-employed, more businesses and therefore more jobs.[29]

With this dream of all citizens being property owners vested in the stock market, Thatcher updated the American dream and yanked it free from the US. When everybody is an owner of capital, there will, in this vision, be no need for trade unions, state enterprises, wage control or government housing. Thatcher promised a new utopia, a new dream, where everyone had the opportunity not just to succeed in life but to do so as a heroic capitalist.

So where did Thatcher get these ideas? It all links back to an Austrian economist called Friedrich Hayek whom Thatcher met in 1975 just after she became the leader of the British Conservative Party. Like Thatcher, Hayek was a virulent critic of socialism and staunch advocate of free market capitalism. Hayek's influence on Thatcher was long-lived. In 2003, some ten years after Hayek died, Thatcher was awarded the Preis der Friedrich-August-von-Hayek-Stiftung that was set up in honour of Hayek. In her acceptance speech, Thatcher said, 'Hayek is, therefore, the prophet not of doom and disaster, but of peace and plenty. His is a voice of wisdom for our time, and for all time. We should listen to him.'[30]

Thatcher took heed of Hayek's doctrine for her whole career as party leader and then prime minister. A defining moment that demonstrated her commitment to Hayek's theories came in 1975, when she visited the Conservative Research Department, a section of the party seen at the time as a breeding ground for the right-wing political elite.[31] On this occasion, Thatcher was being advised that the party should adopt a middle-of-the-road approach to politics, somewhere between the extremities of both left and right. Thatcher was having none of it. In response, she grabbed her copy of Hayek's

1960 book *The Constitution of Liberty*,[32] which it appears she just happened to have with her, and whacked it down on the table. 'This is what we believe,' she proclaimed.[33] No middle ground for Thatcher.

Hayek provided Thatcher with a fully formed justification for the market liberalism that she was so enamoured of. After all, he had won the Nobel Prize for Economics in 1974. Who could argue with that? Thatcher promised a vision for a Britain, if not a world, that would be better for all. Speaking to the Conservative Women's Conference in 1980, she explained how the radical free enterprise system she supported would benefit everyone:

> A generous society encourages talent and reaps the reward for doing so. Academic excellence, for example, isn't just about elites. It's about raising teaching standards in a way that benefits every child. Business success isn't just a selfish aim. Profits spread beyond those who make them and bring jobs and prosperity.[34]

All well and good for selling policies about tax cuts for the rich, but it is quite different from what her guru Hayek wrote in that very book she slammed on the table at the Conservative Research Department.

Hayek's *The Constitution of Liberty*,[35] as the title portends, is a book about freedom. Across almost 500 sprawling pages, he attempts to do nothing less than resurrect the value of individual liberty and free society to prevent what he saw as the decline of Western civilization at the hands of an ever-encroaching socialism. Hayek defines 'liberty' as the absence of coercion. The idea is that a person is free if other people are not pushing them into doing things they do not want to do. The moral of the story is that, as much as possible, people should be able to do whatever they want without anyone trying to interfere with their choices. All this talk of freedom culminates in a consideration of economic liberty, with much of Hayek's attention being on the freedom of markets.

Hayek agrees with Thatcher that free markets are the vehicle of social and economic progress in the long run, yet he is less sanguine (or at least more frank) about what this means for shared economic prosperity here and now. When Thatcher supported what she called 'popular capitalism', she was suggesting that everyone was going to benefit. Speaking to the Zurich Economic Society in 1977, she said:

> We need a free economy not only for the renewed material prosperity it will bring, but because it is indispensable to individual freedom, human dignity and to a more just, more honest society.[36]

There is a clear emotional appeal. Free market economies with limited government interference would not only make everyone freer, they would make people richer, too. For Hayek, however, inequality is the price paid for freedom and he is so singularly gripped by the value of freedom that he thinks this is a price well worth paying.

Economic progress is the goal and if achieving that means that some people acquire the lion's share of the spoils of that growth then so be it, Hayek proffered. This is not just a matter of history, it is happening today and billionaires are a symptom of a global economic system determined to grow at any cost. The rise in inequalities that have been witnessed since the 2008–2009 Global Financial Crisis have been accompanied by economic growth. As billionaires filled their coffers with an ever-increasing share of the world's wealth, wages stagnated for workers in developed countries and for many, employment became increasingly precarious.[37] No problem, says Hayek: 'the large economic advance that we have come to expect seems in large measure to be the result of ... inequality and to be impossible without it'.[38] This is not about billionaires earning or deserving their wealth, inequality is a built-in feature of the economic system they operate in.

Thatcher's dream of popular capitalism never came true. Hayek's grim acceptance of inequality did. Some 30 years after Thatcher marketed her dream of every British citizen being a capitalist, just 19 per cent of adults owned shares and the percentage of traded shares owned by individuals dropped from 20 to 11 per cent. Rates of home ownership were unchanged.[39] As far as inequality is concerned, in 1980, the top 1 per cent of earners took a 3.44 per cent share of total income. It has risen steadily since. It was 5.74 per cent in 1990, 8.06 in 2000, after which it stabilized at around 8 per cent.[40]

Thatcher's dream of shared prosperity through business ownership may have failed but the cultural belief in 'popular capitalism' became increasingly entrenched on a global level. Throughout the 1980s, across the world corporate tax rates tumbled, as did taxation of the very rich. By 1989, what came to be known as the 'Washington Consensus' was firmly established as the dominant policy position of the IMF, leading to structural reforms to economies across the developing world, lest they not have access to IMF dollars. The 'consensus' was that the privatization of state enterprises, the liberalization of markets, corporate deregulation and the general withdrawal of government from economic affairs was the one and only way to secure global economic growth. At the heart of this new consensus was a blind ideological belief in market fundamentalism,[41] which was shackled to liberal democracy and exported around the world. The promises were big and the conviction was even bigger. It didn't work. The biggest growing world economy in the latter part of the twentieth century was China's and they certainly did not abide by Washington's rule book. Developing countries that were dependent on the IMF, in Latin America in particular, fared more poorly. Growth was sluggish and inequality got worse.[42]

Despite all evidence of its failure to be realized, the new American dream lived on. If the neoliberal model produced inequality, the best thing one could do was dream of being one of the people who gets a bigger share of the pie. The newly globalized American dream rose up to a point where it professed that anybody, fighting for themselves, could get ahead of the pack and attain personal riches by being a capitalist in a world that had been reformed specifically to allow that to happen. The hero of the neoliberal dream is the successful entrepreneur: a newly iconic figure valorized for his or her ability to succeed in the free market.[43] With the markets liberated, the only things standing in the way of the neoliberal hero's success was his or her own ambition, tenacity and hard work. This was not the world of shared prosperity but a world of winners and losers where the winners were morally deserving of their victory.

The globalized American dream promulgated the idea that anyone could make it if they just tried hard enough. It also cemented the truth that only the very few would. Rubbing salt into the wounds, billionaires parade around the world fuelling the dream with outlandishly heroic claims that they did it all themselves and that they deserve the astronomical volume of wealth that they have taken from the world. Finance journalist and author Helaine Olen calls out the way that in contemporary culture, the billionaire is a 'man (because it is almost always a man) who is better than us mere mortals, able to solve any business or political or philanthropic problem that comes his way'.[44] Part of the problem, Olen explains, is because when men become billionaires they enter a self-congratulatory 'feedback loop'. Billionaires are surrounded by sycophants praising them and never challenging any of their ideas or schemes. Shut off from criticism by an entourage of lickspittles, billionaires rise above the world of mortals, believing themselves to be self-made heroes whose acumen knows no bounds.

The American dream personified in the billionaire is a social Darwinist nightmare. Social Darwinism is a doctrine that holds that Charles Darwin's principles of evolution and the 'survival of the fittest' apply equally to human societies as they do the development of whole species. Just as particular species will adapt, survive and thrive because of their superior qualities, so will superior individuals and social groups. Over the years, social Darwinist ideas have been used to justify everything from market competition in the economy to educational achievement in schools. Put simply, a person wins because they are superior in their fitness to thrive – it is a matter of 'natural selection'.

The term 'social Darwinism' takes Darwin's theories of how species develop and applies them to the progress of people in society and is largely attributed to nineteenth-century English philosopher Herbert Spencer. In society, too, people are subject to a 'survival of the fittest', he argued, such that those who thrive in life do so because of their inherently superior ability to endure. It was Spencer who coined the phrase 'survival of the fittest' in his 1866 book *The Principles of Biology*.[45] He wrote:

> This survival of the fittest, which I have here sought to express in mechanical terms, is that which Mr. Darwin has called 'natural selection, or the preservation of favoured races in the struggle for life.' That there goes on a process of this kind throughout the organic world, Mr. Darwin's great work on the Origin of Species has shown to the satisfaction of nearly all naturalists. Indeed,

when once enunciated, the truth of his hypothesis is so obvious as scarcely to need proof. Though evidence may be required to show that natural selection accounts for everything ascribed to it, yet no evidence is required to show that natural selection has always been going on, is going on now, and must ever continue to go on.[46]

A central tenet of social Darwinism is that the process of natural selection is not just about the biological development of species, but about the progress of human society from generation to generation. Spencer was adamant that 'society advances when its fittest members are allowed to assert their fitness with the least hindrance, and where the least fitted are not artificially prevented from dying out'.[47]

In the burgeoning industrial capitalism of the nineteenth century, social Darwinism found a special footing in the world of industrial capitalism. One of Spencer's most ardent followers was nineteenth-century American steel magnate Andrew Carnegie. Carnegie was a forerunner of today's billionaires, one of his generation's wealthiest people. Alongside the likes of J.P. Morgan, Cornelius Vanderbilt and John D. Rockefeller, Carnegie was one of the robber barons of the Gilded Age, amassing great fortunes from creating and exploiting industrial monopolies. Carnegie also described himself as a 'disciple' of Spencer, declaring that 'before Spencer, all of me had been darkness, after him, all had become light – and right'.[48]

In Carnegie's hands, the brutal logic of the 'survival of the fittest' turned from biological and social evolution to human behaviour in the capitalist economy. For Carnegie, the law of competition in business is simply a version of Darwinism.[49] Carnegie favoured a winner-takes-all approach to commerce, where those who were the best would dominate over others based on their merit and acumen. Echoing Spencer's conviction that social Darwinism justified the supremacy of laissez-faire economics, Carnegie held that fierce industrial competition was essential to human progress. As a corollary, Carnegie also professed that extreme economic inequality was justified by the 'survival of the fittest' doctrine. Poverty might be unfortunate for those suffering from it but it was essential for the larger goal of human progress, Carnegie maintained. In his own words:

> while the law [of competition] may be sometimes hard
> for the individual, it is best for the race, because it insures
> the survival of the fittest in every department. We accept
> and welcome therefore, as conditions to which we must
> accommodate ourselves, great inequality of environment,
> the concentration of business, industrial and commercial,
> in the hands of a few, and the law of competition between
> these, as being not only beneficial, but essential for the
> future progress of the race.[50]

Carnegie evinced a Darwinist defence of the massive economic
inequality produced by early capitalism, inequalities that he
personally benefited from on a huge scale. He vainly claimed that
he was among those 'fittest' who are not only deserving of wealth
on account of their superiority among men, but also because him
being wealthy (as far as he was concerned) was of benefit to the
overall progress of humanity.

Although support for social Darwinism has ebbed and flowed
over the years, it is front and centre in billionaire political morality
today: the reason that billionaires are so deserving of their wealth is
because they have won life's game on account of their superiority
over their fellow humans. Even more, there is nothing that can or
should be done about this vast inequality because it is natural. The
American dream has become a nightmare and it has done so on
a global scale. Gone is the hope that everyone can succeed if just
given a chance and in its place is the conviction that inequality is
the natural outcome of some people being more 'fit' to prosper than
others. The problems of the Darwinist American dream are not
just a matter for people in the US. The dream, and its promise of
progress driven on merit and hard work, has spread around the world
through a process of cultural globalization.[51] In what, for example,
gets called the 'Indian dream', the 'Chinese dream' or the 'Brazilian
dream', the promise is the same: that success is open to everyone,
regardless of their origins. Everyone can be a hero. The globalized
American dream is blind to structural inequality and an impediment
to material success, selling the idea that the only thing that stands
in the way is oneself.[52] By implication, failure to achieve the dream
is the personal individual failure of those who Donald Trump calls
'losers' and a 'suckers'.[53]

58

The new American dream of individual success for the heroic few at the expense of widening inequality is central to the moral justification of billionaire wealth and power. By this account, the billionaire reaps the benefits of the laws of nature. According to the logic of billionaire morality, inequality in both wealth and power is natural, inevitable and desirable. The responsibility of the billionaire is merely to allow nature to take its course as the world's wealth is showered on him. The problem is that this morality is a thin distraction, desperately trying to obscure the fact that inequality is fundamentally unfair because it results from patterns of advantage and exploitation that favour the wealthy.

In the US, for example, between 2021 and 2025, Americans will inherit US$72.6 trillion. Around half of that will come from just 1.5 per cent of all households. It is getting worse. The amount that will have been inherited between 2011 and 2035 will be just US$34 trillion. To make matters even worse, much of this wealth transfer will be done using financial mechanisms that will protect the benefactors from inheritance tax. So much for hard-earned wealth![54] It is true that only a minority of billionaires are heirs to other people's fortunes. It is also true that a similar minority came from Horatio Alger-like humble beginnings. According to *Forbes Magazine*'s research into the 400 richest people,[55] only 20 per cent came from working-class or poor backgrounds, while 30 per cent has inherited wealth. The major group, comprising 60 per cent, came from middle, upper middle or wealthy families. University of California, Berkeley, Professor Public Policy Robert Reich points out that most wannabe billionaires not only have family support but also have a safety net of returning to relative material comfort should their entrepreneurial ventures fail. Reich writes:

> But portraying themselves as rugged individuals who overcame poverty or 'did it on their own' remains an effective propaganda tool for the ultra-wealthy. One that keeps workers from rising up collectively to demand fairer wages, and one that ultimately distracts from the role that billionaires play in fostering poverty in the first place.[56]

The original American dream may have reflected a democratic aspiration for a fairer society, but perversely the new billionaire version of the American dream is a scam designed to provide a cloak of moral legitimacy over a political and economic system rigged for vast inequality.

The new American dream embodied in the figure of the billionaire finds virtue in individual competitiveness and personal wealth accumulation, all garnered at the altar of free market capitalism. This is a game of winners and losers, where the financially victorious not only have the money and power but are morally justified in the exalted social positions they occupy on account of their wealth. These are the self-made 'men' who deserve everything they have. At least that is the fable they perpetuate and that works to shield them from criticism.

Musk, for example, has been frequently extolled for being a 'self-made' billionaire, especially by himself. If anything, Musk comes across as being self-consciously anxious about any suggestion that his extreme wealth is nothing but the result of his own genius and hard work. On 21 September 2022, Robert Reich released a four-and-a-half-minute video on Twitter. It was titled, 'Self-Made Billionaires are a Myth'.[57] In the video, Reich questioned the idea that anyone can become a billionaire with enough hard work and commitment. This myth, Reich notes, was especially duplicitous in the era of wage stagnation and expanding wealth inequality in which Musk acquired his fortune.

The reality of the situation, Reich re-emphasizes, is that billionaires commonly come from upper-middle-class and wealthy backgrounds. Their life stories are less about 'rags to riches' and more about 'riches to more riches', he argues. Along with Caitlyn Jenner, Bezos and Gates, Musk was singled out by Reich as a billionaire from a privileged background. Reich explains that Musk's family owned a South African emerald mine. Reich's point was that when people from wealthy families use that wealth as a springboard to engage in entrepreneurial activity, they are not really taking any personal risks. The rich can do so simply because they are rich. In other words, becoming a billionaire requires a birthright that is open only to the few, even though they often go to great lengths to deny this. Reich says: 'If your safety net to joining the billionaire class is remaining upper class – that is not pulling yourself up by your bootstraps. Nor is failing to pay your fair share of taxes along the way.'[58]

On the very same day the video was released, Musk reacted to Reich on Twitter. Musk sounded angry! 'You [sic] both an idiot and a liar,'[59] he tweeted impetuously. This response resounded with the fact that Musk has gone to great lengths to insist that he is a self-made man and deny that he grew up in privilege. Much of the hoo-ha revolves around the idea that his father owned the emerald mine that Reich referred to. Whether the mine existed or not is shrouded in mystery. What is not at all mysterious is Musk's doggedness in asserting that it did not. On 29 December 2019, he took to Twitter again:

> He [Musk's father] didn't own an emerald mine & I worked my way through college, ending up ~$100k in student debt. I couldn't even afford a 2nd PC at Zip2, so programmed at night & website only worked during day. Where is this bs coming from?[60] ... This is a pretty awful lie. I left South Africa by myself when I was 17 with just a backpack & suitcase of books. Worked on my Mom's cousin's farm in Saskatchewan & a lumber mill in Vancouver. Went to Queens Univ with scholarship & debt, then same to UPenn/Wharton & Stanford.[61]

The relative privilege of his upbringing is clearly a sore point for Musk and obsessively denying it is all part of his need to assert his own heroic self-made status. Whether or not the mine existed is less relevant than the central part of billionaire morality that discussions of it reveal – the idea that the power one has gained through money is entirely one's own and the result of nothing less than entrepreneurial genius, business acumen and an extreme work ethic.

'Self-made man' is a term coined by US lawyer and politician Henry Clay back in 1832. Clay was full of admiration for the 'enterprising self-made men, who have whatever wealth they possess by patient and diligent labor'.[62] The idea of the self-made man – as it emerged in nineteenth-century America – was embedded in a deeply colonial narrative. Never mind that these rugged individuals garnered their wealth in an economic system characterized by the appropriation of land that was not their own as they dispossessed or murdered native peoples to acquire it. Never mind, too, that American prosperity was built on the forced enslavement of Africans uprooted from their homeland to labour for the good of White America. Self-made? Hah! It was never the case; so-called self-made wealth was made through theft and exploitation. This heroic myth serves to glorify selfishness by making individual success the measure of a 'man'. American Studies scholar Heike Paul puts it as follows, '[a]s part dream, part fantasy, and part prophecy, the foundational myth of the self-made man seems to be powerful enough to defy the overwhelming evidence of its own baselessness'.[63]

The myth of the heroic self-made man relies on the assumption of 'competitive equality' with all born equal and with fair chance to compete for a place at the top. The person who makes it to such lofty heights of success does so because they are a winner of their own making. Together with this mythical assumption of equality of opportunity comes a moral defence of the outrageous inequality of outcomes that characterize the real world. There is no need to dig deep to find the falsehood of the myth. To begin with, the very history of the self-made man precluded, if not contributed to preventing, the possibility that a woman might be successful on her own terms. Equality of opportunity is similarly a bald-faced lie as intersections of class and race define much of the opportunity open to people around the world. Despite all evidence to the contrary, the myth lives on, proclaiming that, again following Paul:

> hard work, moral integrity, and discipline lead to material success and that experiences of crisis and failure – rather than being indicative of larger social, political, and economic problems – constitute chances for self-improvement.[64]

The idea of the heroic self-made man beholds a harsh morality. The underlying belief is that whether a person is successful or unsuccessful, rich or poor, they get their just deserts at the end of the day. Good luck, social privilege, social class, gender and racial prejudice are irrelevant in the myth of the self-made man. In this fairy tale, success is all down to hard work and good character.[65] If the self-made men have only themselves to thank for their material success, what does that say about those who have not succeeded materially? The implication is that they are lazy, morally lax and without discipline. Moreover, because of that, they deserve any destitution that falls upon them. The dark side of the myth of the heroic self-made man is the assertion that if a person is poor, it is because they are unmotivated or incompetent.

Whether the likes of Musk lived off an emerald mining fortune or not hides that bigger lie about the self-made billionaire. Clearly there are some billionaires who literally started out with nothing. Spanish billionaire Amancio Ortega, best known for his fashion company Zara and worth US$106.8 billion in 2024, is the son of a railway worker.[66] Aldi's founder, billionaire Karl Hans Albrecht, was the son of a baker and a small grocery-store-owner in Germany. When he died in 2014, he left behind US$25 billion.[67] Pharmaceutical magnate Zhong Huijuan started her career as a chemistry teacher in the Chinese city of Lianyungang. Her 2024 net worth was US$8.6 billion.[68] Even if a billionaire rose from a humble background, it is still worth asking if they really 'earned' their billions through their own work. The word 'earn' has a moral character to it. It implies that the financial rewards that one receives in return for one's labour are justified. Earning implies an exchange of work and effort for money or other things of value and is rooted in an ethic of reciprocity – the equality of give and take. If a person earns less than they rightly deserve, they are being exploited. If a person earns more, then they are unfairly taking part of someone else's fair share. When a person earns something, they are entitled to it and considered worthy of what they receive in return for the effort they have put in. Justice is central to earning because it implies a fair deal between what one does and what one gets for it. How does someone earn a billion dollars? It is certainly not through wage labour. Imagine getting paid US$100 per hour (that's about 14 times the minimum wage in the US), working 40 hours per week for 48 weeks per year and saving half of the income. Doing that hard work, it would take 8,680 years to 'earn' the first billion. Clearly for the vast majority of the world's population, earning a billion is radically inconceivable.

Wage earners make money by exchanging their work and time for money in the labour market. Billionaires do not 'earn' their money that way. For billionaires, 'earning' is about winning the jackpot in the high-stakes game of shareholder capitalism. In Musk's case, the bulk of his riches came from his part-ownership of the electric car manufacturer Tesla, which he bought with funds from selling his shares in the online payment company PayPal. When electric cars started to become more popular from the late 2010s, Tesla was an industry leader and its market value skyrocketed by a whopping 1,100 per cent in five years.[69] Musk's insanely high net worth was a result of the appreciating value of his company on the stock market, rather than directly as a payment or return from work he has done. The question is, does a billionaire like Musk deserve the billions of dollars that he owns, in the same way that factory workers deserve the hourly rate that they get paid?

The new American dream proffers that billions can be legitimately earned and deserved, even by people from the humblest of backgrounds, the ranks of which Musk claims to be a member. Musk's billions were acquired at a time when financialized capitalism had already come to rule the economic roost on a global level. He exploited, but did not create, the system of capitalism that made him ultra-rich. This new form of capitalism, as it took hold through the rapidly globalizing economy from the 1980s onwards, shifted business attention away from the established tradition of pursuing long-term fundamental growth through investment and profitability. In its place, the purpose of business was recast as being to maximize shareholder value. Shareholder primacy became the new mantra of corporate governance.

Business organizations can have many different economic goals, whether they be profitability, growth, market share or creation of long-term value, but in the heady days of a fast-maturing neoliberalism, it was the shareholder who became king. The world was changing in the 1980s as a resurgent political belief in the capability of free markets to usher in a new era of globalized capitalism took hold in the corridors of political power in the West. Economic liberalization was going to solve the problems of the economic stagnation and runaway inflation that had plagued the 1970s. As Western economies faced new global competition from the East, especially Japan, Western corporations sought to reinvent themselves. Governments both initiated and supported the changes. Tariff walls fell, public corporations were privatized and corporate taxes were slashed. Business had been liberated. Capitalism was cool.

The new-found zeal for unbridled global capitalism came with a new master – the shareholder. The headline of economist and Nobel Prize winner Milton Friedman's 1970 article in *The New York Times* that 'The Social Responsibility of Business Is to Increase Its

Profits',[70] had, by the 1980s, become an unquestioned (if not morally convenient) mantra for businesses and politicians. They followed the free market Pied Piper dutifully, if not enthusiastically, as they leapt on the gravy train of shareholder primacy. Well, it was gravy for them at least. Another Nobel Prize-winning economist, Joseph Stiglitz, offers a telling explanation of why Friedman's shareholder advocacy was met with such enthusiasm in the corporate world:

> The free-market ideologue and Nobel laureate economist Milton Friedman was influential not only in spreading the doctrine of shareholder primacy, but also in getting it written into US legislation ... Friedman's thinking not only handed greedy CEOs a perfect excuse for doing what they wanted to do all along, but also led to corporate-governance laws that embedded shareholder capitalism in America's legal framework and that of many other countries.[71]

Musk personifies this approach. His actual salary as CEO of Tesla was just US$56,000 per annum – that is less than the minimum wage for school teachers in the US.[72] Even with that being so low, he refused to ever cash his pay cheque, instead getting rich based on the value of his substantial stock holdings.[73]

A telling example of the ways that billionaires are still entwined with shareholder primacy came in early 2023 when, following their pandemic boom, the world's biggest technology companies started to get worried about lower than anticipated revenues and the possibility of a recession in the US. The tech companies did not dilly-dally in formulating a response. It came swiftly in the form of massive employee layoffs. Alphabet, the parent company of Google, let go of 12,000 workers, equivalent to a staggering 6 per cent of the company's workforce. What was the result? The share market rewarded Alphabet handsomely with a 6 per cent increase in their share price. The workers' loss was the owners' gain and they gained a lot. Google was founded by Larry Page and Sergey Brin. The share price hike saw Page's fortune rise by US$4.9 billion. Brin chalked up an additional US$4.5 billion. That's how shareholder primacy works, quite literally the shareholder is number one and they are rewarded at the expense of the employees.

To become wealthy on the returns of financial capital and share ownership is to be a *rentier* and it is central to the new American dream. Being a rentier means that earnings do not arise because of what a person does but because of what they own. More and more people are getting rich this way. It has become so extreme that the whole system has come to be referred to as 'rentier capitalism'. Political economist Brett Christophers defines rentier capitalism as 'an economic system not just dominated by rents and rentiers, but, in a much more profound sense, substantially scaffolded by and organized around the assets that generate those rents and sustain those rentiers'.[74] Essentially, under rentier capitalism, those with economic and political power, such as Musk, can appropriate excessive value from the economy. To make matters worse, a company like Musk's Tesla actively avoids paying corporate tax,[75] and has enjoyed many billions of dollars of government subsidies over the years.[76] It all sounds much more like taking than making.

At best, billionaire morality is a self-perpetuating myth where the ultra-rich have convinced themselves and others that they deserve their vast fortunes because they made them themselves. At worst, this morality is a manipulative con trick designed to ensure that those from whom that wealth was taken do not demand a fairer distribution of the world's prosperity. Casting billionaires as heroes justifies inequality, placing the billionaires on a pedestal high above the rest of us. These are the masters of the universe, so aloft that they are immune to the daily struggles of everyday people that they have risen above through their own efforts and smarts. Operating under the illusion that they earned their wealth fair and square, billionaires are exonerated from any responsibility for the unequal system that they benefit from so handsomely. The myth of the heroic billionaire not only excuses the takers for the inequality they represent but also makes them out as heroes. It is a morality based on a self-righteous and self-aggrandizing lie that extreme wealth is earned and that by virtue of that, and despite all evidence to the contrary, the world is fair.

4

The Myth of
the Generous Billionaire

The twenty-first century has been called the 'new Gilded Age'.[1]
From the advent of 1980s globalization through to the wake of
the Global Financial Crisis of 2008–2009, a new form of big
philanthropy has developed as the world's richest people hand over
more and more of their fortunes to support charitable foundations,
public causes and political advocacy. Just as the robber barons of
the late nineteenth century ushered in the first Gilded Age, today's
billionaires are stepping up to fund what they deem to be the public
good.[2] In the first Gilded Age, the likes of Andrew Carnegie, John
D. Rockefeller and Meyer Guggenheim took it upon themselves
to direct their wealth to create universities, museums, hospitals
and libraries. The goal was to bring culture and education to the
labouring American masses.

American industrialization created dynasties of extreme wealth
that survive to this day. This was the same industrialization that
generated an era of economic inequality. Economist Henry George
wrote in 1879 that the technological changes that transformed the
American economy created a situation where:

> Some get an infinitely better and easier living, but others
> find it hard to get a living at all. The 'tramp' comes with
> the locomotive, and almshouses and prisons are as surely
> the marks of 'material progress' as are costly dwellings,
> rich warehouses, and magnificent churches ... unpleasant
> as it may be to admit it ... the enormous increase in

productive power which has marked the present century and is still going on with accelerating ratio, has no tendency to extirpate poverty or to lighten the burdens of those compelled to toil. It simply widens the gulf … and makes the struggle for existence more intense.[3]

Philanthropy did nothing to abate the poverty and inequality of the Gilded Age. If anything, it justified that inequality by portraying the rich as kind and generous benefactors who would bring education and culture to the impoverished classes.

Today's billionaires are on to a similar adventure, a second Gilded Age.[4] This time the inequality has not been produced by industrialization but by neoliberalism. Globalization, the expansion of free trade, the financialization of the world economy and the growth of information technology industries have all led to the twin outcomes of significant economic growth and growing economic inequality. And just like it was in the first Gilded Age, inequality is coupled with philanthropy. What is different is that today's Gilded Age is global and goes beyond investing in cultural pursuits. The neoliberal robber barons are funding everything from public health, social services, medical research, education, to abating the climate crisis and beyond.[5] Benevolent feudalism is back with a new political flavour.[6]

What is the magnitude of the philanthropic efforts of the modern-day robber barons? Each year *The Chronicle of Philanthropy* lists the 50 biggest donors to charity in the United States. In 2023, the top 50 gave more than US$11.9 billion. The biggest donor was media tycoon Michael Bloomberg, who gave US$3 billion. Nike co-founder Phil Knight and his wife Penny Knight came in second, with donations of US$1.2 billion. Michael and Susan Dell were third, with just under US$1 billion.[7] The list goes on, with billionaire after billionaire giving substantial sums to fund causes related to science, the environment, health and human rights, gender and racial inequality, youth work, education and poverty alleviation.[8] It all appears like unbounded generosity.

Americans might be the biggest philanthropists but large-scale philanthropy is a global phenomenon. *Forbes Magazine* keeps a record of Asia's 'heroes of philanthropy'.[9] Gautam Adani is on that list. With massive business interests in ports, airports, cement, power and energy, Adani has many times vied to be India's richest person, as well as having held the mantle of Asia's richest. In 2022, his net worth reached a peak of US$124 billion, which at the time made him the fifth richest person in the world, just ahead of Buffett.[10] To celebrate his 60th birthday in 2022, he made a massive philanthropic pledge of 600 billion Indian rupees. That is about US$7.7 billion. Health education and skill development were his causes of choice.[11]

In Australia, Melanie Perkins and Cliff Obrecht, founders of software company Canva, handed over most of their shares to create the Canva Foundation. The official announcement was that: 'We have this wildly optimistic belief that there is enough money, goodwill, and good intentions in the world to solve most of the world's problems. We feel like it's not just a massive opportunity, but an important responsibility and we want to spend our lifetime working towards that.'[12] The pair committed to giving 80 per cent of their share of Canva to the new foundation to support charitable initiatives. Hong Kong's Jean and Melanie Salata, Thailand's Joon Wanavit, Malaysia's Brahmal Vasudevan and South Korea's Michael Kim are all members of the world's ultra-rich class who are conspicuous in their giving.[13]

The generosity of today's billionaires seems extraordinary. On face value, it could be believed that they are taking their hard-earned lucre and selflessly putting it to the service of the greater good. Such is the myth of the generous billionaire. Things are not as simple as they seem. Understanding how billionaire generosity really works starts with an appreciation of the positive correlation between economic inequality and billionaire philanthropy. As was the case in the first Gilded Age, when inequality worsens, the ultra-wealthy give more and more wealth away but that does nothing to curb the vicious spread of inequality. Quite the contrary, it is commonly the case that those who give are the ones whose personal net worth continues to grow the fastest. To mark the tenth anniversary of Gates' and Buffett's Giving Pledge in 2020, Chuck Collins, Helen Flannery, Omar Ocampo and Kalena Thomhave of the Institute for Policy Studies, Washington, DC, released a report on the net worth of the people who initially signed up to the Pledge.[14] Remember that in its own words, 'The Giving Pledge is a promise by the world's wealthiest individuals and families to dedicate the majority of their wealth to charitable causes.'[15] A noble sentiment, no doubt.

The Pledge involves Gates, Buffett and more than 200 others from among the richest people around the world having committed to giving away most of their wealth to address problems facing society.[16] Gates' own foundation shelled out a staggering US$7.7 billion in grants and charitable contracts in 2023 out of an endowment of US$75.2 billion.[17]

The facts support the assertion that the generosity of billionaires does not, in general, lead to them being less rich. Quite the contrary. The Institute for Policy Studies' report[18] showed that the 62 billionaires who pledged in 2010 saw their collective net worth grow by 95 per cent in ten years – from US$376 billion to US$724 billion. Whatever they gave, they seemed to have acquired much more. At the extreme, nine of these billionaires saw their wealth more than triple in this period. Mark Zuckerberg topped the list, with an almost unimaginable 1,783 per cent increase. Other big winners were venture capitalist John Doerr, whose wealth grew by 416 per cent and Salesforce co-founder Marc Benioff, whose stash went up by 400 per cent.

These results led the researchers to question whether billionaire philanthropy meant that the rich were using the act of 'giving' to further sequester rather than surrender wealth. The researchers also questioned how philanthropy is not just about money, it is also about power. The report documents how charitable billionaires largely give their money to private foundations controlled by family members or to funds whose operations they control. While the money is technically given away, control over it remains in the hands of the billionaires. The report concludes that the organization of billionaire philanthropy:

> allows wealthy donors and their families to retain significant philanthropic and cultural power and, in some cases, personally from foundation assets through fees and salaries. It enables those donors to retain significant managerial control over millions of philanthropic dollars.[19]

Different billionaires give in different ways and care needs to be taken not to assume that they are cynically lining their own pockets under the guise of giving, even though that may be so in some cases. A telling example came in 2022 when Yvon Chouinard, the founder and owner of Patagonia Inc., announced that his family was transferring 98 per cent of the company's stock to a newly created not-for-profit organization dedicated to combatting climate change.[20] The media applauded Chouinard for 'giving away his company' for the planet.[21] It was billed as an unprecedented and extreme act of generosity. Chouinard was not on the back foot with his own views of the significance of his decisions and actions. He claimed he was doing nothing less than 'turning capitalism on its head'.[22] The widespread admiration of Chouinard was a telling sign of a world eagerly awaiting heroes who would solve the climate crises created by industrial capitalism and left to worsen by inept governments the world over.

Chouinard launched his first business, the climbing gear Chouinard Equipment, when he was just 19. It was 1957, and Chouinard was a climbing enthusiast who wanted the gear that would allow him to move to the next level. No one was making it, so he took the initiative to do it himself. He personally forged climbing spikes and ran the business out of a chicken coop in Burbank, California. All went well for the young Yves and by 1970, Chouinard Equipment was the largest climbing-equipment supplier in the United States. Around this time, Chouinard diversified his business into retailing clothing for climbers. The apparel was a huge success and in 1973 he spun that off into a dedicated clothing business he called Patagonia. The company was named after a mountain region in South America that is home to the notoriously difficult to climb Monte Fitz Roy. Chouinard himself conquered this mountain in 1968.[23] The new company revolutionized the outdoor clothing industry, appealing to fashion-conscious shoppers as much as to hardcore mountain climbers. Along the way, Chouinard became extremely wealthy.[24] Despite his financial success, he always claimed that he never really wanted to be a businessman, let alone a billionaire.[25]

As well as being a lucrative business enterprise, Patagonia was also well known as a radical pioneer in responsible business, an approach attributed mainly to the values of its founder. Patagonia is the company that provided its employees with training courses on civil disobedience. The company's policy was that it would help pay the bail of anyone who completed this course should they ever get arrested at a peaceful protest. Then there was the environmental internship programme where Patagonia's staff could take two months away from their jobs to work for environmental groups, all on full pay.[26] At a broader level, Chouinard founded the campaign '1% for the Planet', urging other companies to donate 1 per cent of their sales revenues to environmental restoration. He led by example and the campaign built a membership of more than 5,700 businesses.[27]

Chouinard's announcement concerning 'giving away' his company was the logical, if not extraordinary, conclusion to his 50-year commitment to a corporate purpose of being in business to save the planet.[28] On 14 September 2022, he publicly released a letter headed, 'Earth is now our only shareholder'.[29] In this letter, Chouinard spelled out the next chapter for Patagonia. The ownership of the company would be transferred from the Chouinard family to two entities. The first was a trust and the second was a non-profit organization. This bold move aimed to 'protect the company's values', fight the environmental crisis and defend nature.

Practically, Chouinard's plan meant that each year, about US$100 million of non-reinvested profits was expected to be given to a newly created non-profit organization called Holdfast Collective. Holdfast would have a 98 per cent share in Patagonia and would hold all of it in non-voting stock. The exact nature of Holdfast's work was not specified other than in the very general idea of its environmental purpose. Patagonia described this purpose as to 'fight the environmental crisis, protect nature and biodiversity, and support thriving communities'.[30] Holdfast was an organization recognized as tax exempt under the US Internal Revenue Code 501(c)(4). This means that, unlike public charities, it would be legally allowed to endorse political candidates, make political donations and fundraise for political organizations, among other political activities.[31] The remaining 2 per cent of the non-voting stock, but all the voting stock, was destined for the Patagonia Purpose Trust.[32] This is an organization Patagonia depicted as having been 'created solely to protect our company's values and mission' to save the planet. That means that the Trust has veto power over decisions like the composition of the board of directors, the organizational structure and the company's operations.

No longer being Patagonia's owner, what would Chouinard's role be in the future? The Q&A on the Patagonia website said, 'The Chouinard family will guide the Patagonia Purpose Trust', will 'continue to sit on Patagonia's board', and will 'guide the philanthropic work performed by the Holdfast Collective'.[33] It would appear that while Chouinard was giving away the ownership of his company, he was not giving up any control. If anything, these changes would immortalize his life's work by preserving the values and purpose he has long espoused and by providing a legal vehicle for political activity. In practical terms, it is unclear what exactly he was giving away. It promised to be pretty good for business, too, with Patagonia's competitive advantage wrapped up in its climate activism. Chouinard's announcement could surely only bolster that advantage.

This all begs the bigger question about the role of extremely wealthy business people in today's society. The ranks of the ultra-rich are growing fast, as discussed in earlier chapters, with swathes of new billionaires being added to the list each year. Coupled with that is a new zeal, among the rich, for seeing 'business as a force for good'. Chouinard was way ahead of his time when he was growing Patagonia from the 1970s. Does that mean what Chouinard did to the ownership structure of Patagonia was qualitatively different from the behaviour of other billionaires, who, like the robber barons of old, are queuing up to give away their fortunes to their favourite good causes? Philanthropy is the height of fashion for the well-heeled billionaire about town! What makes Chouinard relatively unique is that rather than making an abstract no-strings-attached promise to the likes of The Giving Pledge, he literally relinquished his assets. As of 2023, he lost his place on the *Forbes* list of billionaires.[34]

Chouinard's stated ambitions were explicitly political as much as they are environmental. 'Hopefully this will influence a new form of capitalism that doesn't end up with a few rich people and a bunch of poor people,' he told *The New York Times*.[35] It is easy to admire Chouinard for his generosity but it is harder to agree with his hopefulness for a new capitalism. Chouinard may have been a reluctant billionaire. He said he was 'pissed off' when he was first listed on the *Forbes* list of the richest people in the world in 2017. Good for him, but that does not undermine a global economy that continues to produce such vast inequity as governments watch on with learned helplessness.

That Chouinard and others contribute to addressing the climate crisis and dealing with other global problems through their individual action is undoubtedly good; after all, governments worldwide have failed for decades. The rub, however, is that this is all part of a well-developed global system, where private interests increasingly take over responsibility for dealing with public and social problems. As with Chouinard, the wealthy elite insist on calling the shots – in this sense, he is no different to many other billionaire philanthropists. Chouinard may have relinquished his assets but did not relinquish his power. If anything, he bolstered it. Rather than addressing the underlying political and economic system that creates inequality, billionaire generosity provides it with a moral justification. It serves as an excuse not to fundamentally change the political and economic system that produces the vile reality of inequality.

When Patagonia announced its bold changes, what exactly the Holdfast Collective would spend its US$100 million a year on was not disclosed. Nevertheless, the nature of the new ownership structure suggested it would in no way be open to public scrutiny. The same goes for the many other public causes sponsored by corporations and billionaires. Once upon a time, corporations would have been accused of hypocritical greenwashing, as if a thin veneer of paint could hide the unsavoury realities underneath. Greenwashing is still alive and well but today's corporate political activism is anything but superficial. It heralds a deep-seated shift in power relations on a global scale – a shift which sees the power of billionaires grow even further. At the same time, it does nothing to rebalance grossly unequal economic relations.

The neoliberalism of the 1980s saw a beginning in a shift in economic power from the public to the private sector through widespread reforms involving the privatization of publicly owned companies, corporate deregulation and the removal of international trade restrictions. The late neoliberalism of the 2020s is also seeing a power shift in the same direction. The difference is that this time it is not just economic power that is being transferred, it is political power. It is the relationship between billionaire philanthropy and this political power that is key to understanding the myth of the generous billionaire. Part and parcel of the changes that are afoot is that billionaire business owners are taking over as society's moral agents and political actors, using their apparent generosity to address what they see as society's greatest problems. It was great that Chouinard put his company to work for the future of the planet. What is not great is how, in the 'new capitalism' he professes, people's lives and futures are increasingly dependent on the power and generosity of the self-elected rich elite rather than being ruled by the common will of the people. Whether billionaires do good or bad, everyone else remains at their mercy. No matter how benevolent they might be, they are accountable only to themselves.

Chouinard provides one example of the connection between billionaire philanthropy and billionaire control but it does not exhaust its possibilities. The ways that generosity is yoked to power can come in many forms. Just one month after Chouinard's announcement, on the other side of the world from his home in Jackson, Wyoming, a different facet of billionaire generosity was being revealed. This case involved Gina Rinehart, Australia's richest citizen and the 55th richest person in the world. Her net worth in 2024 was US29.9 billion.[36] Rinehart is the executive chairman of the mining and agriculture business Hancock Prospecting. Hancock Prospecting is a privately owned company making its money mainly from iron ore, coal, beef and dairy. Rinehart personally owns 76.55 per cent of the company, with the remainder owned by her daughter Bianca Hope.[37] Rinehart took over the then financially troubled company after the death of her father, Lang Hancock, in 1992. Under her leadership, Hancock Prospecting became among the world's most successful mining companies.[38] Along the way, Rinehart became one of the world's richest and most powerful people. To get an idea of just how rich she is, as of 2021, Rinehart controlled 9.2 million hectares of land. That is 1.2 per cent of the landmass of the entire continent of Australia.[39]

Rinehart takes pride in her generosity. Dubbed 'the iron lady behind a long list of philanthropy', she has funded a range of causes and projects focusing on health and the well-being of young people. Sport is a particular passion. She has supported swimming since the 1990s, later extending to volleyball and rowing. Domestic violence and breast cancer are other causes that have benefited from Rinehart's largesse.[40] In 2023, to celebrate her 41 years at the helm of Hancock Prospecting, Rinehart gave away 41 prizes of A$100,000 each to her employees. The prizes were raffled randomly, with potentially life-changing amounts given to the lucky few who won.[41]

Adding to her long history of philanthropy in sport, in September 2022 Rinehart announced that she would provide A$15 million to support the cash-strapped Australian women's national netball team, the Australian Diamonds. The pandemic had not been good to netball, with Netball Australia, the sport's national governing body, charting losses of A$7.2 million in two years. They were in debt to the tune of A$4 million and had received notice from their auditors that their status as a 'going concern' was in doubt.[42] Against this backdrop, Netball Australia announced Rinehart's gift with a combination of relief, fanfare and deference. 'The Origin Australian Diamonds are excited to announce Hancock Prospecting has joined as high-performance program partner until the end of 2025,' ran the press release. The partnership would cover investment in coaches and athletes, as well as competitions and training camps. Hancock Prospecting's logo would be emblazoned on the Diamonds' uniforms. 'This is a major investment for our sport and is a huge contribution towards the ongoing success of the Diamonds ... We are incredibly grateful to this leading Australian private company, Hancock Prospecting, for its significant support and partnership,' said Netball Australia CEO Kelly Ryan.[43]

The celebrations did not last long. Not all the Diamonds' players shared Ryan's enthusiasm, especially Donnell Wallam. Wallam, a proud Noongar woman from Korijekup, Western Australia, was the third ever Indigenous Australian to play for the national netball team.[44] She took exception to the idea of wearing the Hancock logo on her uniform. The reason came down to statements made by Rinehart's father, founder Lang Hancock, when he was interviewed on television in 1984. In addressing the supposed 'Aboriginal' problem Hancock said of Indigenous Australians:

> Those that have been assimilated into, you know, earning good living or earning wages amongst the civilised areas, those that have been accepted into society and they have accepted society and can handle society, I'd leave them well alone. The ones that are no good to themselves and can't accept things, the half-castes – and this is where most of the trouble comes – I would dope the water up so that they were sterile and would breed themselves out in future and that would solve the problem.[45]

Hancock's was a cruel statement of violent racism by a powerful land-owning White man. It echoed the horrors of some of the darkest moments in Australian colonial history. The idea that Indigenous Australians would or should simply die out as a race of people following the European invasion in 1788 was a core belief in Australia's early White society. Nineteenth-century White Australians not only considered Indigenous Australians to be uncivilized and inferior but were also largely thought to be a 'doomed race' who would wither and die as part of the West's inevitable march of progress. Such was the arrogance of the new colonial Australians. The assumption was that as British rule became more and more established, Indigenous people would eventually become extinct because of the social Darwinist survival of a superior White race.[46] *The West Australian* newspaper described the dominant view in 1912 as:

> 'The survival of the fittest' is the primary law of evolution, and no more striking example of its inexorable truth need be looked other than is afforded by the decay and rapid extinction of the Australian aboriginal race which is going on under our very eyes, before the advance of the all-conquering white race.[47]

Hancock's praising of assimilation not only represented his social Darwinist pretensions but it was also deeply tied into the shameful Australian government policy that led to what came to be called the 'stolen generation'. The stolen generation refers to Indigenous children who were forcibly removed from their own families and brought up in White foster families or in state institutions. The policy targeted Indigenous children who were of mixed race, especially those able to 'pass' as White. It is estimated that one in three Indigenous Australian children were 'stolen' from their families between 1910 and 1970.[48] Untold pain resulted as families were torn asunder by a thick-headed racist government policy designed to 'breed out' blackness through forced assimilation. This policy also involved encouraging Indigenous women with fairer skin to live with White men. If Indigenous Australians would not die out in accordance with the natural laws of social Darwinism, they had to be bred out. Generations of Indigenous Australian children and their families suffered and continue to suffer today because of the kinds of ideas that Hancock espoused.

Hancock's outspoken support of the horrors of Australia's racist history were made even worse by his shocking suggestion of sterilizing Indigenous people to breed them out; the statement of a White eugenicist madman, clearly. It is hard to find fault with Donnell Wallam for refusing to wear a uniform that bore this man's name, and she considered seeking an exemption from having to do so. Non-Indigenous players supported Wallam in solidarity. Others expressed concerns over Hancock Prospecting's climate record. When the Diamonds played their next game, which was in New Zealand, they wore the old uniforms that did not have the Hancock logo on them.[49] Public controversy ensued. The Chair of Netball Australia, Marina Go, stepped down.[50] Many members of the public called for Rinehart to apologize for her father's statements some 40 years earlier. She did not do so. Meanwhile, conservative politicians entered the fray, name-calling the netball players as ungrateful for Rinehart's generosity.[51] In the end, under strong pressure, Wallam agreed to wear the logo. The very next day, Hancock Prospecting announced that it had changed its mind and withdrew the sponsorship.[52]

The public statement Hancock Prospecting released on 22 October 2022 read:[53] 'Hancock has advised Netball Australia (the governing body of netball in Australia) that it has withdrawn from its proposed partnership effective immediately.' A second media release the same day read:

> It is unnecessary for sports organisations to be used as a vehicle for social or political causes ... sport is at its best when it is focussed on training and good and fair competition, with dedicated athletes striving for excellence to achieve their sporting dreams to represent our country at their very best ... there are more targeted and genuine ways to progress social and political causes without virtue-signalling or for self-publicity.[54]

What can be given can be so easily taken away. Indigenous sportsman and activist Anthony Mundine summed it up: '[Rinehart] could have apologised for her father's comments, distanced herself from them and told us that she doesn't believe those things. Instead, she pulled her money out.'[55] The Rinehart netball saga reveals one central facet common to all billionaire philanthropy. When it comes to the various causes that receive financial backing, at the end of the day the decision of who gets the financial support and who does not is the decision of the donor. The billionaire is in charge, always, with the recipients held ransom to their supposed benevolence.

At the root of billionaire philanthropy is a more general belief that the wealthy rightfully deserve political and economic power. That was evident in 2016 when Rinehart advocated for the Australian government to take a leaf out of Donald Trump's playbook when it came to economic policy. Rinehart travelled to Washington, DC, to meet Trump's campaign team, including campaign manager Kellyanne Conway and the former mayor of New York, Rudy Giuliani. What did she learn from this trip? She opined:

> People close to the president-elect and his campaign advised that their countrymen told them they wanted, firstly, less government tape, secondly less taxation, and for the USA to grow and be economically strong again, and provide more sustainable jobs. And how exciting, this is exactly what the president-elect, and his team, are advising they want to deliver for America and its struggling economy … Trump's team members advised that the president-elect wants to cut federal government tape by 50 per cent in his first months of office, and that he wants to cut company tax to 15 per cent. What a kickstart to the American economy that will provide![56]

The economic liberalism Rinehart espouses prizes limiting public authority in the form of government so as to enhance the economic power and freedom of corporations and their wealthy owners. Doing so, she claims, will provide benefits to everyone, all rising on the heels of business success. It all adds up to limiting the power of the democratic state in place of enhancing the power accorded to private interests – those of the ultra-rich in particular.

Rinehart's support for Trump, and his brand of billionaire capitalism, did not end in 2016. Trump launched his 2024 presidential campaign at his Mar-a-Lago resort in September 2022. Rinehart was there in person to cheer him on. Her visit was not entirely surprising, given that Rinehart has been named as a member of an elite group called the 'Trumpettes' – an elite group of high-profile women who support Trump. In 2018, Rinehart was awarded the honour of being the 'Trumpette of the week', after being previously dubbed 'lead Trumpette in Australia'.[57] When the who's who of Australian Business were invited to dinner at the White House by Trump in 2019, Rinehart was on the guest list.[58] Trump and Rinehart have a lot in common, especially when it comes to championing corporate deregulation and tax cuts.[59]

The cases of Chouinard and Rinehart are strikingly different examples of the myth of the generous billionaire. The two cases do, however, share one key feature. For both, putative generosity is coupled with a desire for control. To make sense of this, it is worth stepping back for a moment and considering what is meant by the very idea of generosity. This is a matter addressed most famously by the French sociologist Marcel Mauss in his book titled *The Gift*, first published in 1924.[60] Mauss' research was focused largely on gift exchange among ancient peoples and civilizations from Polynesia to Melanesia to North-West America. His work sought to understand the function of gifts in these societies and to use that knowledge to shed light on modern society. Mauss found that while gifts are ostensibly given voluntarily and out of generosity, or even altruistically, their social function is quite different to that. He argued that gifts serve the same purpose as contracts. A gift is a form of economic transaction, albeit one that does not directly involve money. Instead, gifts are infused with a moral obligation: to accept a gift from another person is effectively to be in debt to them. Conversely, in giving a gift to someone, it is reasonable to expect them to have a reciprocal obligation. Gift giving and receiving assumes cooperation and reciprocity. In receiving a gift, one is always expected to show appreciation in one way or another.

Mauss explains that the giving of gifts comes with an expectation to reciprocate that is understood by both the giver and receiver. Gifts are thus a form of non-monetary economic exchange. In the societies Mauss studied, gift giving was not restricted to individuals. Gifts were exchanged between clans and tribes, often accompanying hostile relations. These gifts served to establish the nobility, power and wealth of the givers and to justify their sense of importance and superiority. In giving something to others, one gains a certain power over them by asserting one's status as having both the wealth and magnanimity to be able to give. Things had not changed with the advent of modernity. Mauss elaborates:

> A considerable part of our morality and our lives themselves are still permeated by this same atmosphere of the gift, where obligations and liberty intermingle … The unreciprocated gift still makes the person who has accepted it as inferior … Here we also see come to the surface … the 'basic imperialism' of human beings … We must give back more than we receive.[61]

What appears as generosity is actually economy, indeed the 'most ancient system of economy',[62] according to Mauss. The ancient system of the gift economy sheds light on how billionaire philanthropy works. The question that Mauss' thinking begs, as it relates to the myth of the generous billionaire, is about whether the philanthropic excess of billionaires is truly motivated by a spirit of civic-minded and altruistic generosity or whether there are more self-interested motives at play.

When considering the apparent generosity of the ultra-wealthy in funding charitable foundations and causes of their choosing, it is naïve to assume that this is simply a matter of selfless do-gooding altruism. The question is, what do billionaire philanthropists expect in return for their economic largesse? One possible answer comes in what Professor of Economics James Andreoni has called 'warm-glow giving'.[63] Andreoni accepts that when people give money to charity, their motivations are not necessarily altruistic. To use his terms, giving is 'impurely altruistic',[64] in that the giver themselves gets a benefit from the giving in the form of feeling good about themselves for being generous. In other words, they get a warm glow in return for their giving. In some cases, this warm glow might be in the form of assuaging potential feelings of guilt about being so much better off than others in the world, especially those in the direst economic conditions.

It is quite conceivable that billionaires feel good about themselves on account of their philanthropic efforts but there is more to their gift giving than a warm glow. This is where power comes into the equation. Expert on philanthropy and ethics Paul Vallely writes:

> Philanthropy is always an expression of power. Giving often depends on the personal whims of super-rich individuals. Sometimes these coincide with the

priorities of society, but at other times they contradict or undermine them. Increasingly, questions have begun to be raised about the impact these mega-donations are having upon the priorities of society.[65]

Vallely argues that the relationship between democracy and philanthropy is fraught. The problem is that individual giving bestows power on the giver. That is not to say that donations are not put to good use, some are and some are not, but rather that the billionaire giver gets to decide on what are ostensibly political choices. This was the case with the examples of both Chouinard and Rinehart. Philanthropy entails a transfer of power to the rich. The billionaire German shipping tycoon and philanthropist Peter Kramer, someone with deep inside knowledge, has argued, that:

> [Billionaire philanthropy] is all just a bad transfer of power from the state to billionaires. So it's not the state that determines what is good for the people, but rather the rich want to decide. That's a development that I find really bad. What legitimacy do these people have to decide where massive sums of money will flow? ... That runs counter to the democratically legitimate state. In the end the billionaires are indulging in hobbies that might be in the common good, but are very personal.[66]

Even non-governmental organizations like the Global Policy Forum and specialists in global governance have warned governments that taking money from billionaires should not be done without considering the risk and unintended consequences, especially the lack of accountability, reliability and monitoring.[67]

The myth of the generous billionaire masks the realities of how billionaire philanthropy entails an exchange where what is given with apparent generosity is actually exchanged for political and social power. There is more to it than that, however. Mauss explained that since ancient times, gift giving has been a means to build social cohesion between groups with different interests. The gift is a vehicle for solidarity and cooperation. With billionaire philanthropy, this cooperation is between the billionaires themselves and the rest of society (essentially, people less wealthy than them). There are plenty of genuine reasons for antagonism here, not least the vast economic inequality that the billionaires personify. These forms of inequality have spawned calls for socialist revolutions, as working people actively resist those who profit handsomely from their labour while they are paid barely enough to survive. Is it just possible, then, that another return the billionaire class gets from its collective giving is the prevention of class tensions that might arise from economic inequality? If this is the case, then billionaire 'generosity' ensures that the very system that enables wealth and inequality to grow is not disrupted.

Undermining the myth of the generous billionaire surfaces how billionaire giving is a ruse to secure the wealth, power and privilege of the billionaire class. Bezos' philanthropic activity is a good example. As the founder of Amazon, Bezos is one of the richest people in the world. In fact, he held the title of the number-one richest from 2018 to 2021, dropping to number three in 2024, with a net worth of US$194 billion.[68] In 2022, Bezos announced that he intended to hand over most of his immense fortune to charity during his lifetime. He did not say exactly how he would do this or who he would give it to, but it was a public commitment, nonetheless.[69] The causes Bezos has committed to are combatting climate change and unifying society across political and social fault lines. As far as climate is concerned, he has already committed US$10 billion to his own Bezos Earth Fund.[70]

Journalist Whizy Kim specializes in reporting on the power and influence of the wealthy. In her analysis of Bezos' massive philanthropic commitment, Kim sees through the idea that it is a simple act of selfless generosity that the myth of the generous billionaire perpetuates.[71] Kim draws special attention to the utter lack of transparency of Bezos' commitment. He has not even signed the Giving Pledge, instead just making a public statement of his good intentions. What is noticeable, however, is that Bezos' announcement came at a time when his company Amazon has received special public scrutiny. In the early 2020s, Amazon was accused of price gouging during COVID, was subject to protests over working conditions and was widely considered to be crowding out smaller businesses in its continued quest for growth and market share. Reports of increased carbon emissions and accusations of tax avoidance have also plagued Amazon. A few months after Bezos announced his wealth giveaway, Amazon laid off almost 18,000 workers.

Kim observes the myth that:

> Philanthropists have long leaned on their ability to do a
> lot of good for society as a justification for deeply unequal
> wealth distribution. If, in the end, their riches were
> benefiting the public – wasn't that wealth well-earned?[72]

The heart of the myth of the generous billionaire is that these acts
of apparent kindness serve to preserve and extend the inequality
of wealth and power that billionaires benefit from, and they do
it both individually and systemically. This is not altruism but a
form of exchange where the charitable gifts are traded for social
acceptability not just of individual billionaires, but also of the warped
political system that brought them into existence in the first place.
Philanthropy is not designed to change the system but to preserve
it. This process has been called 'moral laundering'.[73] If this is a deal,
then the billionaires are getting the better end of it.

The idea that billionaire philanthropy is less an act of giving and
more an act of power is confirmed by management scholars Mairi
Maclean, Charles Harvey, Ruomei Yang and Frank Mueller.[74] They
explain that this power is enacted by protecting the wealthy from
criticisms over the means through which they made their money.
Further, it extends billionaire power from the economic realm into
the social and political sphere. Maclean and colleagues reinforce that:

> Elite philanthropy ... is not simply a benign force for
> good, born of altruism, but is heavily implicated in
> what we call the new age of inequalities, certainly as
> consequence and potentially as cause. Philanthropy
> at scale pays dividends to donors as much as it brings
> sustenance to beneficiaries [... it ...] functions to lock in
> and perpetuate inequalities rather than remedying them.[75]

Elite philanthropy is not something to be lauded, and the idea
that it is the best way to solve the world's problems is a myth
that is both false and dangerous. If anything, the existence of
this philanthropy is a sign of the extent to which the world's
interconnecting political and economic systems have failed most
people. The outcome is continued vast inequalities, holding the

world's populations at the mercy of a non-accountable minority of extremely wealthy people.

Billionaires giving away their money to fund projects for the public good come in stark contrast to their behaviour, in many cases, when it comes to paying tax. For most citizens, the tax system provides the mechanism through which a portion of their earnings are directed towards initiatives deemed to be of general benefit to society. Whether it be roads, hospitals, schools, defence or welfare, tax revenues are spent by governments in a way, in democratic countries, that is designed to be collectively good and publicly accountable. When billionaires make sizeable gifts to charity, they are not channelling their money through such a socially controlled process, but rather through one that is largely privately controlled by them. The billionaires decide how much is spent and they decide what it is spent on. The added sweetener is that, in most countries, charitable donations are tax deductible,[76] serving to further impoverish the public purse.

Do billionaires pay their fair share of tax? This is precisely the question that Oxfam researchers asked in 2022,[77] with specific references to billionaires in the US. Their results were even more startling than one might imagine. Oxfam found that American billionaires, in general, paid a lower rate of income tax than most working families. The effective income tax rate of the top 400 billionaire families was a paltry 8.2 per cent. The nationwide average was 13 per cent. When it came to the 25 richest, it got even more extreme. Their true tax rate was just 3.4 per cent. No wonder they have plenty of money to direct to the charitable causes of their own choosing.

ProPublica investigative journalists Jesse Eisinger, Jeff Ernsthausen and Paul Kiel searched through and analysed the US Internal Revenue Service records to reveal even more shocking facts about billionaire tax contributions (or lack thereof).[78] In 2007, and again in 2011, Bezos paid no federal income taxes at all – zero dollars. Ditto for Musk in 2018. The analysts at ProPublica then calculated what they call the true tax rate of the 25 richest Americans for the period 2014 to 2018. By 'true tax rate' they mean the total tax paid divided by the total amount of wealth growth. By this reckoning, Buffett paid 0.10 per cent, Bezos 0.98 per cent, Bloomberg 1.30 per cent and Musk 3.27 per cent.

This is all legal. So how do they get away with it? A common strategy is for billionaires to ensure that they receive relatively low pay packets. Instead of using official earnings to finance their luxury lifestyles, they borrow money against their significant shareholdings and other investments. The result is that they have a load of cash to splash but none of it is taxable. Tax lawyers are employed to make sure that all of this is done in a way that is both within the rules and effective in avoiding any substantial tax paying. Ed McCaffery, Professor of Law, Economics and Political Science at the University of Southern California has dubbed the strategy 'buy/borrow/die'. It goes like this:

> STEP 1 – BUY: Purchase appreciating assets that do not generate income, such as stocks, real estate or even valuable art works and fine wine.
>
> STEP 2 – BORROW: Borrow money against the asset's appreciation and then live off that money while officially earning little or no actual taxable income.
>
> STEP 3 – DIE: Never pay back the money that has been borrowed, simply let the debt accumulate until you die. At that point, your heir can sell your assets to pay off the debt you lived off.[79]

In the US, where more billionaires reside than anywhere else, extreme tax avoidance is not only legal in its tax system but is also seen by some as virtuous. In 2016, presidential nominee Hillary Clinton criticized Donald Trump for not paying taxes. Trump did not disagree but instead of apologizing, he responded, 'that makes me smart'. He added that he was personally a better overseer of the money than the state.[80] These smarts all add up to a virtually tax-free life. This is why billionaires only pay a true tax rate of 3.4 per cent in the US.[81] McCaffery sums up as follows:

> The tax-law doctrines that allow those who already have financial wealth to live, luxuriously and tax-free, are simple. They follow the steps in what I have dubbed Tax Planning 101: Buy/Borrow/Die … We are letting capital off the hook, and ratcheting up taxes on labor,

at precisely a time when deep-seated and long-running economic forces suggest that this is precisely the wrong thing to do. It is time – past time – for change.[82]

Our times have been described as the 'golden age of élite tax avoidance'; a time where the brazen wealth hoarding of the ultra-rich and the refusal of many to pay their fair share into the public purse has resulted in political turmoil, social division and a reduction in many states' ability to fund education and health.[83] Along the way, the idea of fairness as a feature of liberal-democratic nations falls further into the abyss.

The problem is not limited to the US. In France, for example, researchers at the Paris School of Economics found that effective tax rates of the richest 0.1 per cent decreased as their incomes grew. In practice, this amounts to a regressive tax system.[84] One in seven UK-related billionaires are formally residents in tax haven countries so that they can avoid paying British tax, even though many of them own substantial assets in the UK. Monaco, the Channel Islands, the Isle of Man and the Bahamas are especially popular.[85] Internationally it is well known that the super-rich use tax havens to avoid and evade tax at the expense of everybody else.[86] Oxfam reports that:

> Worldwide, only four cents in every tax dollar now comes from taxes on wealth. Half of the world's billionaires live in countries with no inheritance tax for direct descendants. They will pass on a US$5 trillion tax-free treasure chest to their heirs, more than the GDP of Africa, which will drive a future generation of aristocratic elites. Rich people's income is mostly unearned, derived from returns on their assets, yet it is taxed on average at 18 percent, just over half as much as the average top tax rate on wages and salaries.[87]

The reduced contribution of the rich to public funds has all been aided and abetted by governments across the world who, over the past 40 years, have progressively cut tax rates for the wealthy while implementing higher taxes on goods and services. Such taxes hit the poorest people the hardest. On top of that, many billionaires and corporations fund lobbyists who actively ensure that their financial interests are reflected in tax policies.[88]

We are in a situation where billionaires are giving away billions of dollars while paying as little tax as possible – often nothing. This giving is not neutral, it is a specific form of exchange. Money is exchanged for power. Moreover, this is done by reformatting the nature of the relationship between the ultra-rich and everyone else. In a world of vast inequality, billionaire morality suggests that those who suffer hunger, illness, homelessness and poverty (for example) should not blame a system that produces inequality but should be grateful to the billionaire masters for whatever meagre alms they might receive. On another level, as the world plunges further into climate disaster resulting from the ravages of centuries of industrial capitalism, who might be expected to graciously address the catastrophe? The capitalists themselves!

The special form of philanthropy that sees billionaires as coming to the rescue of an ailing world has been called 'philanthrocapitalism' – a term first used by Matthew Bishop and Michael Green, authors of the 2008 book *Philanthrocapitalism: How the Rich Can Save the World*.[89] Bishop and Green are gushing in their admiration of billionaires for what they see as both their generosity and their efficacy. Philanthropy can be done better if it imitates capitalism, they argue. The trick, as they would have it, is for the new philanthropists to 'apply the secrets behind [their] money making success to their giving'.[90] Note well that these secrets are not the ones about ruthless monopoly competition and the exploitation of workers. They are the assumed secrets to thinking big and being hugely successful. Former US President Bill Clinton wrote the foreword, summing up the book's message as:

> In *Philanthrocapitalism*, Matthew Bishop and Michael Green show the remarkable extent to which private wealth can advance public good by applying entrepreneurial skills, speed and score-keeping to our most persistent challenges ... the twenty-first century has given people with wealth unprecedented opportunities, and commensurate responsibilities, to advance the public good.[91]

The new philanthropy achieves 'leverage' by being 'strategic', 'engaged', 'impact oriented' and 'knowledge based'. Some call themselves 'philanthropreneurs'.[92] The explicit underlying assumption is that the profit motive can drive public good and that pursuing that public good is best understood as a business strategy.

Matthew Bishop, Michael Green and even Bill Clinton might have faith in the redemptive possibilities of the philanthrocapitalism of the good billionaires but others have been far more sceptical. In this regard, sociologist Linsey McGoey has been especially insightful and erudite, arguing connivingly that 'the ascendancy of the philanthrocapitalist approach represents a subtle but profound displacement of belief in the need for democratic checks and balances on the use of public funds for private enrichment'.[93] Philanthrocapitalism conveniently ignores the long-held political distinction that recognizes the inherent contradictions between public good and private interests – a political concept known as the 'separation of powers'. This separation is based on the idea that the public good is a shared responsibility of 'the people' based on the common will of all citizens as represented by democratically elevated government and public institutions. No individual by virtue of personal wealth or power has the right to dictate the public good based on their own personal views, biases or preferences. Hence, public and private powers need to be separated to avert the possibility that public funds might be used for private gain and to prevent minority interests of the wealthy dictating public policy for the majority.

There is 'no such thing as a free gift', McGoey argues in her book of that title.[94] McGoey dares to ask who exactly benefits from the new age of billionaire philanthropy. She shows that massive philanthropic efforts from, for example, the Bill and Melinda Gates Foundation or the Chan-Zuckerberg Initiative, wield so much power that they can dictate the direction of global development. Moreover, as the world increasingly relies on billionaire benevolence to solve its problems, the inequalities in power and wealth that those billionaires exemplify in extremis are sewn into the fabric of global society. Is it really possible to believe that the paternalistic rich will look after the best interests of everybody as the system of inequality that bestowed such wealth on them continues to get worse?

The myth of billionaire generosity is the belief that the ultra-rich are selflessly giving away their wealth in an act of charitable altruism.

The reality is quite different. Philanthrocapitalism is an economic transaction. In exchange for giving away some wealth, what the wealthy get in return is a cocktail of plutocratic power and the assurance that there will be no real changes to the system that enables them to become so rich in the first place. So long as the myth of the generous billionaire is in place, there will be no real progress towards economic equality and shared prosperity.

5

The Myth of
the Meritorious Billionaire

In 2019, *Forbes Magazine* named Kylie Jenner as the youngest
billionaire of the year, as well as the youngest ever self-made
billionaire.[1] The title was previously held by Mark Zuckerberg, who
notched up his first billion when he was 23. Jenner was just 21 years
old at the time. She acquired her fortune through the company
Kylie Cosmetics, which she founded in 2015, not long after her
18th birthday. It all started with the 'Kylie Lip Kit', which consisted
of a matte liquid lipstick and matching lip liner. The product was
initially released on 30 November 2015. Not only was the product
out of stock within seconds but the interest was so extreme that the
website that was selling the lip kit literally crashed. 'Kylie Jenner's
Lip Kit Sells Out, Ruptures Internet', ran the headline in *Vanity Fair*
on the day. Jenner even had to send out an emergency tweet to calm
down her fans: 'Nobody be upset! There's so many people trying to
buy at once so there are some tech issues,' she wrote.[2]

By February 2016, production exceeded 500,000 units, and
Jenner's trajectory to billionaire status was established. Success
followed success as the business expanded its offerings to include a
broad range of cosmetic products. Blushers, bronzers, brow kits and
body wash could soon be found on the Kylie Cosmetics product
list, with product releases selling out time and time again. When a
holiday collection was put on the market ahead of Christmas 2016,
it sold out in 24 hours, yielding US$19 million in revenues. After
being in business for 18 months, sales had reached US$420 million.
By 2019, Kylie Cosmetics was valued at US$1 billion.[3] Kylie herself

owns three Hollywood mansions, a fleet of cars reported to be valued at US$6 million and a private jet. For spare change, she charges more than US$1.5 million for a post on her Instagram account.[4]

Forbes determined that Jenner's ascension to the billionaire class was meritocratic because of her fortune not having been gained purely through inheritance of money or business interests – that is their explicitly stated criteria. *Forbes* described Jenner as being in the 'self-made who got a head start from wealthy parents and moneyed background' category. Jenner,[5] born on 10 August 1997, is the second daughter of Olympic athlete Caitlyn Jenner and Kris Houghton. Their first child was older sister Kendall. Kris also has four other children from her previous marriage to celebrity lawyer Robert Kardashian: Kourtney, Kim, Khloé and Robert Jr.[6] When Kylie was ten years old, she shot to fame as part of the smash hit reality television show *Keeping Up with the Kardashians*. Produced by Kris Jenner, *Keeping Up with the Kardashians* turned her children into celebrity superstars, opening their somewhat chaotic family life up for the world to see. *Harper's Bazaar* magazine described them as 'the world's most famous family'.[7] Amid scandal and controversy, a global public was drawn to them, eager to lap up each outburst, argument and dysfunction.

The show's massive popularity made the Kardashian-Jenners one of the wealthiest families in the world. The show ran for 20 seasons and led to 14 spin-offs, as well as providing its stars with the public platform to create various business ventures. Social media was key, with the family boasting an eye-watering 1.2 billion followers on Instagram alone.[8] Between them, the Kardashian-Jenners launched 26 businesses since their climb to fame on reality television. Kylie's half-sister Kim Kardashian started up KKW Beauty and KKW Fragrance in 2017. Two years later, in 2019, she launched her 'shapewear and lounge brand' SKIMS. Kourtney has a health and wellness business, and Khloé opened a denim brand. Sister Kendall worked as a model from age 14 and became a brand ambassador for Estée Lauder.[9] She also owns the brand 818 Tequila. As for Kylie, she was modelling when she was 14, using US$250,000 of her earnings to set up the cosmetics business that propelled her to billionaire status.[10]

Given her celebrity upbringing, Kylie's status as a self-made billionaire was questioned publicly. Whether Jenner could have

THE MYTH OF THE MERITORIOUS BILLIONAIRE

become a billionaire had it not been for her being born White, wealthy, healthy and famous dominated the discussion. Many suggested that she could not have. That is not to say that Jenner did not work hard at her business, but it is to say that all that hard work would have amounted to much less, possibly nothing, if it was not for the privileged circumstances she was born into.[11] Jenner wasn't having any of it. When confronted, she doubled down on her self-made standing, saying '[t]here's really no other word to use other than self-made because that is the truth. That is the category that I fall under. … I did not get money from my parents past the age of 15. I used 100% of my own money to start the company, not a dime in my bank account is inherited, and I am very proud of that.' More surprising than Kylie becoming a billionaire was her insistence that her wealth was entirely meritoriously earned. Even more odd was how she backed this up with the damning insinuation that her parents had abandoned her financially at a tender age:

> The self-made thing is true … my parents told me I needed to make my own money, it's time to learn how to save and spend your own money, stuff like that … What I'm trying to say is I did have a platform, but none of my money is inherited.[12]

The idea that Jenner made a fortune alone as a teenager cut off from financial support by her parents makes for a particular version of the myth of the meritocratic billionaire but one that does not bear up to scrutiny. Critics have pointed out that Jenner's success largely stems from her fame in *Keeping Up with the Kardashians*. Given her background, she did not have to borrow money to start her business or face the challenges and hardships that befall other wannabe entrepreneurs. Jenner had a well-known name, celebrity status and ample money, as well as a mother who managed the financial side of her business for a 10 per cent cut. Kylie's mother, Kris Jenner, is commonly seen as the epitome of the 'momager' – a mother who manages her famous children. In the *Cambridge Dictionary*'s entry for the word 'momager', Kris is the example used to illustrate the term. The entry is:

momager

noun [C]   mainly US   informal   humorous

the mother of a famous person who is also their manager:

Momager Kris Jenner is the brains behind the Kardashian franchise[13]

Kris reportedly manages the careers of all of her children, including organizing campaigns, acquiring jobs and administering their businesses.[14]

Whether Jenner created the idea for Kylie Cosmetics has even been questioned. In 2017, make-up artist Vlada Haggerty alleged that Jenner had taken the look and style of her original work, including the golden fingertips and dripping lip gloss. Haggerty went on to claim that this was not the first time Jenner had passed Haggerty's work off as her own.[15] Haggerty threatened to sue Jenner for copyright infringement; the pictures used in the Kylie Cosmetics looked remarkably like ones Haggerty had posted just a month earlier. This was not the first time this had happened, with other Haggarty images having allegedly been appropriated by Jenner. The photographer who took the picture of Haggerty's make-up work, Julia Kuzmenko McKim, said:

> It breaks my heart to see how large brands take independent, unprotected artists' work and use them to multiply their wealth, In an ideal world, big brands would easily prevent such backlashes by hiring the artists who have already created something that they would love for their own campaigns.[16]

The matter was settled out of court, with neither party commenting on the nature of the settlement. What the whole episode showed, however, was that Jenner's claims of having independently earned her wealth were far from uncontested.

The questioning of whether Kylie Jenner's status as a meritorious billionaire was myth or reality was an immediate forerunner to the media and internet uproar about 'nepo babies' that arose a few years later. In 2023, Kylie came third in a list of the 'most-searched nepo babies'.[17] 'Nepo-' is short for 'nepotism', the idea being that the nepo babies became stars because of their family history – and the money, fame and contacts that come with that – rather than on the back of their own hard work and talent. The uproar about Kylie Jenner's claim to be a self-made billionaire all happened before the term 'nepo baby' had become part of the internet's lingua franca, and there had been many nepo babies before that. Consider, for example, Judy Garland's daughter Liza Minnelli, Henry Fonda's daughter Jane Fonda, Francis Ford Coppola's nephew Nicolas Cage or Jerry Stiller's son Ben Stiller.

So where did the new term 'nepo baby' come from? It started with a tweet. In February 2022, Canadian tech-support worker Meriem Derradji posted on Twitter: 'Wait, I just found out that the actress that plays Lexie is a nepotism baby omg [weeping emoji] her mom is Leslie Mann and her dad is a movie director lol.'[18] Derradji was referring to actress Maude Apatow, who played the lead role of Lexie in the HBO teen drama series *Euphoria* released in 2019. Unbeknown to Derradji at the time, she had coined a term that would dominate the media and the internet as the public debated whether merit played any significant role in celebrity wealth and fame. Throughout 2022, Hollywood stars were 'outed' for nepotistic family connections, including Dakota Johnson (daughter of actors Melanie Griffith and Don Johnson), Maya Hawke (daughter of actors Uma Thurman and Ethan Hawke), Willow and Jaden Smith (daughter and son of actors Jada Pinkett Smith and Will Smith), Zoë Kravitz (daughter of actress Lisa Bonet and singer-songwriter Lenny Kravitz), Brooklyn Beckham (son of singer Victoria Beckham and football player David Beckham) and so many more.[19] When *New York* magazine featured nepo babies as its cover story in December 2022, it ran with the headline: 'She has her mother's eyes. And agent. Extremely over-analysing Hollywood's nepo-baby boom.' 'We love them, hate them, disrespect them, and obsess over them,' the magazine claimed. The magazine even named 2022 as the 'year of the nepo baby'.[20]

Nepo baby is generally a derogatory term reflecting a social awareness that worldly success is not a function of merit. It is a cultural critique of the myth of meritocracy. The term was a reminder that the social networks, cultural capital and money that accrue to a person merely because of the family they were born into play a significant part in their success. When it comes to Kylie, many think it is her sister Kim Kardashian who is the world's biggest nepo baby on account of her US$1.8 billion net worth, but Kylie still vies for number one given that she was named as the youngest ever billionaire.[21] In reference to Kim, Kylie and others, the term nepo baby registered outrage over the unearned privilege that enabled a select few to climb to the top of their chosen fields because of who they were, not just what they did. At a time, in the 2020s, when billionaire-driven inequality was being rubbed into people's faces and when economic injustice was fuelling political populism around the world, the nepo baby symbolized how gross unfairness had become increasingly normalized. The glitzy world of the Hollywood nepo babies shone like a microcosm of a broader society that simply accepted that the promise of meritocracy and equal opportunity had become a pathetic joke.

That 2022 was the year for the nepo baby was not just about Hollywood, it registered a more general malaise with the apparent lack of justice in play when someone gets a head start in life by virtue of their parents and relatives. Once upon a time, birthright belonged to people from royal families who were destined to be king or queen simply by being born in the right manor. The idea of the nepo baby suggests that wealth, fame and celebrity are new sources of birthright in today's world, and people are increasingly aware that meritocracy is not what it appears to be. In countries that pride themselves on liberal-democratic politics, openly advocate for meritocracy and see equal opportunity as a virtue, the nepo babies reveal how the reality of those cultures is quite different from their rhetoric. Nepotism has been around since time immemorial, and when it comes to getting to the top today's Hollywood seems to operate more like feudal Europe than a contemporary democracy based on the virtues of freedom and equality.

Adrian Wooldridge, author of *The Aristocracy of Talent: How Meritocracy Made the Modern World*,[22] explains how, once upon a time, meritocracy was a radical idea that emerged as an alternative to the dominant view that people's lot in life should be determined by the family they were born into rather than by their own hard work and talent. Meritocracy promises a certain kind of equality that ensures that status within a social hierarchy is not fixed. In a meritocracy, the circumstances of one's birth do not, and should not, determine the material quality of one's life. Meritocracy is offered as a noble idea that testifies to democratic values of equality and justice. It is also the basis of equal opportunity and the justification for public education.

Wooldridge argues that nepotism is a direct affront to social justice and social progress that he sees as intrinsic to meritocracy:

> The pre-modern world was one of family connections and personal favors. Kings and Queens ruled as well as reigned. Families controlled the commercial world. Civil service jobs were handed down to relatives. Oxbridge colleges awarded fellowships automatically to descendants of college founders. The word 'nepotism' derives from Latin and was first used to describe the Catholic church's practice of allowing popes to appoint their nephews (who were often illegitimate children) to the College of Cardinals.[23]

Much of the discussion of nepo babies in 2022 focused on how nepotism, as it exists today, is a regression to the state of historical injustice that Wooldridge documents. It should be relegated to the past. There is a second, less-considered, reason for the backlash against nepo babies and it is not just about nepotism per se. As Kylie Jenner exemplified, people labelled as nepo babies can push back vehemently against their detractors, claiming that their success was just deserts for their talent and hard work. The denial of nepotism rubs salt into the wounds of nepotism itself. Take Lily-Rose Depp, the actress daughter of model Vanessa Paradis and actor Johnny Depp. She defended herself, claiming that while her parentage may have got her auditions, it was her talent alone that got her the job:

> The internet cares a lot more about who your family is than the people who are casting you in things. Maybe you get your foot in the door, but you still just have your foot in the door. There's a lot of work that comes after that.[24]

Actress Gwyneth Paltrow, the daughter of Emmy award winner Blythe Danner and producer and director Bruce Paltrow, pushed the argument further by insisting that it is more difficult for kids of famous parents to make it in Hollywood. Like Depp, she admitted that being a nepo baby provided access, adding, 'I really do feel that once your foot is in the door, which you unfairly got in, then you almost have to work twice as hard and be twice as good.'[25]

Imposter syndrome is a psychological state first identified by psychologists Pauline Rose Clance and Suzanne Imes in 1978. It refers to a feeling, especially prevalent among high-achieving women, that they somehow do not deserve their success; that they are phoneys who will be found out one day. Clance and Imes write:

> Despite outstanding academic and professional accomplishments, women who experience the imposter phenomenon persist in believing that they are really not bright and have fooled anyone who thinks otherwise. Numerous achievements, which one might expect to provide ample object evidence of superior intellectual functioning, do not appear to affect the impostor belief.[26]

Journalist and activist Sonali Kolhatkar[27] astutely notes that nepo babies suffer from the exact opposite of imposter syndrome – they believe that they fully serve their success and that it is entirely attributable to their hard work, excellence, merit and superiority, even though all objective evidence shows that this is an extreme overstatement, if not an entire falsehood. Kolhatkar calls this the 'insider syndrome' – a deeply held belief among the wealthy elite that 'they are deserving of unearned privilege'. What is exceptionally pernicious about the insider syndrome, Kolhatkar goes on to explain, is that it hides the realities of how the class system works to perpetuate inequality. The 2022 spread of the outing of nepo babies can be seen as an exercise in raising class consciousness, revealing how meritocracy is, in Kolhatkar's words, 'a myth built on smoke and mirrors, on lies and false confidence'.[28]

More salt in the wounds of an ailing meritocracy comes when nepo babies keep quiet about their family tree. 'A new generation is finding out that their favourite celebrities, talented as they may be, have benefited from a system that is not strictly meritocratic,' explained Anna Kambhampaty and Danya Issawi in an early and influential commentary published in *The New York Times*.[29] Kambhampaty and Issawi argued that public interest in nepo babies was a matter of disillusionment, especially as many of those outed had not made their family connections public in the past. These were the nepo babies who were operating under the public pretence that their stardom and wealth were entirely down to their merit, and their fans were only just finding out about it.

Not all nepo babies are billionaires like Kylie Jenner and Kim Kardashian, but those who are illustrate just how far a person can go when spring-boarded to success by celebrity birthright. Nepo babies being outed revealed to many the secret that while society pretends that a system of merit whereby only those deserving of success through talent and hard work should succeed applies to everyone, the reality is different. The myth of meritocracy was revealed as a one-sided story. Not only was the story untruthful but its deception was entirely for the benefit of those who falsely claimed their success was meritoriously deserved.

Meritocracy presents itself as a system of justice. The person most qualified and experienced for the job will get it, irrespective of their creed, colour or connections. The most talented and hard-working people will reap a greater share of life's material rewards. While regular people have to strive for opportunities to get ahead in life, nepo billionaires and other nepo babies start the race way ahead of the pack just because they were born to the right parents. The nepo baby scandal of 2022 triggered a massive sense of injustice generated by inequality, an injustice that flies in the face of the democratic rhetoric of liberty, equality and solidarity. The myth of meritocracy reveals the reality of systemically generated inequality, the beneficiaries of which are unwilling to recognize or admit to its own privilege.

The nepo babies laid bare not only how wealth and social status are self-perpetuating but also how their success is effectively a barrier to opportunity, social mobility and equality for everyone else. By claiming that their success was merit based, the nepo babies were trying to keep the nepotism a secret. The same can be said, by and large, of billionaires as well. Early-twentieth-century sociologist Georg Simmel's work provides great insight into how this secrecy works and why it directly affronts the pursuit of democratic equality. Simmel explains how secrecy is an essential part of establishing groups of elites. Exclusive groups, for example, billionaires and Hollywood celebrities, are actively formed through what Simmel calls an 'aristocracy-building motive'.[30] This motive leads people to want to be seen as 'special' in the sense of being better and of more value than others. To do so, people form special groups that exclude other people and consider themselves elite.

The aristocracy-building motive is in play from the schoolyard to the King's court to the corporate C-suite. Simmel's unique insight into the workings of elitism is that building the division between an elite group and everyone else requires 'secrecy and pretence of secrecy'.[31] Secrecy preserves a sense of aristocracy and exclusiveness because it prevents those who are excluded from knowing how elite groups operate or, more importantly, from being able to dismantle them. Simmel makes the crucial point that secrecy allows elites to 'oppose general, fundamentally sanctioned laws'.[32] In other words, the secrecy of ultra-wealthy elites enables them to become billionaires because no one knows how they really get away with it.

Applied to the nepo babies and billionaires, Simmel rings an alarm that by exaggerating their meritocratic attainment, the babies can keep the truth hidden. That truth is that meritocracy is a scam that preserves the ability of the wealthy to secure and enhance their wealth through non-meritocratic means. If they admitted that their material excess was gained by anything other than their own merit, they would be open to public scrutiny over their unfair nepotism – precisely what happened in 2022 – and this is to be avoided at all costs. The poorly kept secret is that the distribution of wealth across society is a rigged game. Central to the rigging is getting people not in the elite group to believe that the same principles of merit and reward apply to rich and poor alike. For Simmel, the in-group (in the present case, nepo babies and billionaires) develop a sense of 'group egoism' that provides them with the moral justification for their existence. It may well be the case that the wealthy elite truly believe their success is entirely attributable to an overflow of talent. Even worse, that belief bolsters their own egos. This effectively immunizes them against all evidence that their mere accident of birth gave them the opportunity for wealth and fame. No matter what criticism and antagonism they encounter publicly, the in-group must maintain its position as holders of the secret.

Wherever there is money, nepotism will be found. Although the 2022 year of the nepo baby focused on well-known celebrities, the same happens in all walks of life from politics to education and, of course, to billionaire business. When Zach Dell, son of Dell Computer founder Michael Dell, founded a tech company in 2013, it was no surprise that the investors were his dad's friends, including

Marc Benioff, CEO of the company Salesforce.[33] Zach, who was in high school then, had the connections to raise US$585,000 in capital.[34] Clearly, it was good to have friends in high places, for example, having a father with a net worth of US$50.3 billion, making him the 23rd richest person in the world.[35] Zach also had great advisors, including Tinder's co-founder Whitney Wolfe Herd. Herd would have been especially helpful, given that Zach's business was based on a dating app called Thread. It was pretty much like Tinder, only targeted specifically at university students who were looking for relationships.[36] Despite all of this, Zach clearly stated that his father was not an investor in his entrepreneurial venture, perhaps as an indicator of him not relying on daddy's money to fund his business.[37] According to Zach, he did it the hard way:

> Early on, it was tough to convince investors to roll the dice on an 18-year-old kid, but after a while, word started to spread that I was the real deal, and some of the top investors in the industry were willing to hop onboard.[38]

The app failed but Zach did not. He went on to found another start-up business before settling into a career in the finance industry, initially as a private equity analyst and then as a tech investor. Richard Reeves and Kimberly Howard of the independent research group, the Brookings Institution,[39] explain how, the wealthier a person's background, the thicker and higher is the 'glass floor' that prevents even the less bright offspring of the rich from any real downward mobility. The 'glass ceiling' means that people from gender, class, racial and other minority groups can see what it is like in the higher levels of society but are faced with an invisible barrier to reaching them. Conversely, the glass floor applies to the privileged few who can see that some people are worse off than them, but no matter how much they fail, an invisible floor prevents them from falling down the social and economic hierarchy. Meritocracy? It seems that nepo babies simply cannot fail.

For contemporary sociologist Brooke Harrington, Simmel's ideas on secrecy reveal much about how wealth is not just an economic matter but is a central part of today's culture and politics. Harrington explains that secrets are a 'practical means of protecting material assets and interests from scrutiny or seizure'; they give billionaires moral and practical resources to protect, justify and retain their wealth. Secrets are essential to the preservation of economic inequality, most especially in societies that claim to be meritocratic and democratic. The secret that the rules of meritocracy do not apply equally to all effectively shields the wealthy from accountability. It also shields them from demands for economic redistribution that would threaten their excessive wealth. From time to time, the secrets get out, such as with the year of the nepo baby.

Another telling example of a leak in the hold of billionaire secrecy came in the form of the Panama Papers Scandal in 2016. This scandal involved 11.5 million files being leaked from Mossack Fonseca, which at the time was the world's largest offshore financial services provider – its business was providing banking and other services to people outside of the countries where they lived or did business. The papers revealed the complex ways that people of extreme wealth were using clandestine offshore tax havens to minimize the tax they pay. From Panama to the Bahamas to the British Virgin Islands, companies were set up for the purpose of anonymously holding bank accounts and property controlled by intermediaries elsewhere in the world for the direct purpose of avoiding or evading tax. Nothing is necessarily illegal in these financial arrangements, even though it is possible to use them for money laundering.[40]

What was scandalous about the Panama Papers leak did not concern the legality of the arrangements. There were some instances of fraud and crime involved but, in many cases, what was revealed was entirely within the law. The real scandal was not about illegality. It was about how the world's wealthy elite hid their fortunes and their tax avoidance from public scrutiny. The Panama Papers revealed the secret. Politicians, celebrities and business people alike were taking complex steps to ensure that they did not have to play by the same rules as everyone else and that the secrets of their wealth were kept hidden (especially from the prying eyes of tax authorities). The revelation of how the ultra-wealthy operated under a different set of rules was made worse by the elaborate lengths they went to ensure that people outside of their privileged group did not know what they were doing. It was not just the way wealth is hidden that shocked people. Equally, if not more, pernicious were the unmeritorious ways it is earned and maintained and the fact that a different set of rules apply to the ultra-rich.

The nepo babies and the Panama Papers show, first, some of the ways billionaires and other wealthy elites do not earn their elite status by merit alone and, second, that a combination of access to social and economic networks enables them to both grow their own wealth and to build barriers to entry that prevent others from joining their club. Such is the myth of the meritocratic billionaire. These cases show how the reality of the antimeritocratic nature of this elitism is actively kept secret, keeping alive the lie that meritocracy reflects a shared set of rules and values that applies equally to all. This secret is all part of how inequalities of both opportunity and outcomes are maintained. Billionaires are justified through the myth of meritocracy and claiming that the wealth is all deserved meritoriously is central to the scam.

The myth of meritocracy that is deeply embedded in contemporary capitalism has become even stronger over the course of the twenty-first century. In 2001, UK Prime Minister Tony Blair was riding high. He was coming to the end of his first term as prime minister and commanding a significant lead in the opinion polls ahead of his re-election for a second term. The key themes that informed Blair's election campaign were meritocracy, choice and opportunity. Blair focused on education as a way of creating a level playing field where all citizens could compete fairly for the opportunity to succeed in a new Britain.[41] As he set out on his campaign for his New Labour Party, he proselytized:

> There is much talk in politics of the need for a big idea. New Labour's big idea is the development of human potential, the belief that there is talent and ability and caring in each individual that often lies unnurtured or discouraged ... Our ideology is the development of the human mind to its fullest natural extent, building national strength and prosperity by tapping the potential of all the people.[42]

Questioned on his political position, Blair argued that he operated outside of the distinction between left and right. 'We are what we believe in. We are meritocrats. We believe in empowering all our people,' he proclaimed.[43] Blair's belief intimated that everyone could compete for their share of the bounty of global wealth and those who deserve it most will benefit most. He offered a market version of meritocracy where the just rewards for a person's hard work would be fairly measured by what the market deemed that labour to be worth. When he was first elected prime minister, Blair even went as far as to say, 'The Britain of the elite is over ... The new Britain is a meritocracy where we break down the barriers of class, religion, race and culture.'[44] Britain's rigid class system, royal family and aristocratic history represented everything different to the meritocratic ideal. Against this backdrop, Blair's embrace of meritocracy signalled his desire for a radical break with history, one where a new global culture of opportunity and equality could herald a bold future where prosperity was available to anyone prepared to work for it.

Blair was a man of his time, championing what was to become the age of meritocracy for citizens, workers and wealthy elites alike. Business was a central protagonist. In 1997, Steven Hankin of the top-shelf consulting firm McKinsey and Co. coined the phrase 'the war for talent', signalling the intensification of competition between major corporations. This competition was not a fight over customers and revenues but over hiring the 'best' people from what was portrayed as a small pool of the most talented executives. Hankin and his colleagues researched the 'war', publishing their results in the McKinsey Quarterly.[45] Their call to arms was:

> Companies are about to be engaged in a war for senior executive talent that will remain a defining characteristic of their competitive landscape for decades to come. Yet most are ill prepared, and even the best are vulnerable. You can win the war for talent, but first you must elevate talent management to a burning corporate priority ... A war once conducted as a sequence of set piece recruiting battles is transforming itself into an endless series of skirmishes as companies and their best people, and in particular their future senior executives, under constant attack.[46]

The battle between corporations over the most meritorious executives was to be fought on a global scale, with warlike competition fast becoming the dominant metaphor for recognizing and exploiting people's merit. The 'talent mindset' which the McKinsey consultants insisted that successful companies need to adopt was symptomatic of the age of meritocracy that they were part of ushering in. This was a 'global meritocracy',[47] where the barriers to success were not geographical but simply down to the position of talent and the willingness to work hard. In this new global system, competition was the central organizing principle as individuals are pitted against each other in the world labour market-cum-corporate colosseum. The war for talent was not simply a business strategy. The global meritocracy that it reflected was deeply political and had a significant influence on the economic, educational, immigration and social policies of many governments around the world. Global meritocracy was abetted by a global war for talent, making skilled workers the new commodity traded by the world's corporations. The latter parts of the twentieth century saw governments of advanced economies worldwide investing in education to increase their stock of 'human capital'. Emerging economies such as China, India, Brazil, India and Russia similarly invested in the development of 'talent' as part of their engagement in the global economy.[48]

To this day, meritocracy remains a political catchcry across the world. In 2023, author and entrepreneur Vivek Ramaswamy was busy making a bid to become the Republican candidate in the 2024 presidential election. He laid out his case in an article published in the *Wall Street Journal* entitled 'Why I'm Running for President'.[49] The byline read: 'America has lost sight of the ideals that made it great – freedom and merit foremost among them'. Ramaswamy tells his own story as being the very embodiment of meritocratic success. His parents legally immigrated to the United States and their children worked hard, started businesses and were financially successful. 'We must embrace merit in who gets to succeed in America,' wrote Ramaswamy. This meant doing away with affirmative action for women and minorities entirely and making job appointments based on racial diversity illegal. It also means embracing free speech by removing all censorship of ideas, no matter how damaging or hateful. Ramaswamy reflected the ongoing appeal of the meritocratic ideal.

Despite Ramaswamy's enthusiastic American conservatism, the idea of merit is not limited to one side of the political spectrum or one side of the globe. In Greece, for example, Alexis Tsipras, head of the left-wing opposition party, Syriza, claimed that they 'will come to power to create, to build infrastructures of trust, meritocracy, accountability and transparency'.[50] On the opposite end of politics, when far-right politician Jair Bolsonaro was president of Brazil between 2019 and 2022, championing meritocracy was central to his political rhetoric and appeal.[51] Meanwhile, in Malaysia, Deputy Human Resources Minister Mustapha Sakmud has blamed the lack of meritocracy on his country's brain drain. He claimed that people prefer to take their talents overseas where they are valued. Meritocracy is deeply associated with being modern and progressive. In Sakmud's words: '[d]eveloped countries have better laws that protect their workers' rights from any discrimination, and also provide better salaries. They are based on meritocracy, unlike in our ecosystem, which is sometimes based on connections or who you know.'[52]

Meritocracy as a guiding political principle cemented the centrality of individual competition as a central value of twenty-first-century liberal-democratic culture on a global level. Meritocracy is fair only if it comes with the belief that it is fair that the best 'man' wins, not just in the sporting arena but in all walks of life. Professor Jo Littler explains in her book, *Against Meritocracy*,[53] that meritocracy's claims are worthy of deep scrutiny. Equal opportunity may promise class mobility, equal opportunity and a fair playing field in life but it does so by putting in place a culture dominated by competition and self-interest that pits people against each other as rivals in life's game. This was not just being instituted in the UK; as Littler explains, Blair's adoption of meritocracy was very much influenced by US President Bill Clinton, with the two of them representing the face of market-friendly yet socially liberal politics that were taking hold at the time. The focus was on ensuring that, at least notionally, all citizens could have equality of opportunity but could also expect an inequality of outcomes (depending on how meritoriously they took the opportunity). Personal competition in the world of meritocracy was akin to business competition in the free market. Blair and Clinton's promise was one where access to education would provide the possibility of social mobility to all and provide avenues out of inequality. In other words, everyone having access to education would herald a world where people 'earn what they learn'; the market would sort out the rest.

Accepting meritocracy as the moral bedrock of democratic and capitalist societies provides billionaires with a perfect escape route from accusations that they are undeserving of their wealth. By claiming to have achieved their obscene wealth meritoriously as self-made men, billionaires specifically exploit the idea of meritocracy to provide a moral justification for their excess. After all, the inequality of outcomes is entirely to be expected. Such is the double-edged sword of meritocracy. On one side, it promises a just distribution of the world's prosperity based on hard work, intelligence and acumen. On the other side, it has not only resulted in vast inequality but has also provided the benefactors of that inequality with a moral justification for their uneven share of the world's wealth.

The growth of the new class of billionaires is very much aligned with the global embrace of meritocracy since the late twentieth century. Didier Jacobs, Senior Economist with Oxfam, makes a convincing case about how the claim of meritocracy by billionaires is a scam.[54] Jacobs explains that those who defend extreme wealth and its attendant economic inequality almost always do so through an argument related to meritocracy – that is, inequality is morally justified if the ultra-wealthy earn their money fairly. In other words, it is all okay to be filthy rich if that wealth is deserved. In response, Jacobs asks whether extreme wealth can ever be meritocratic. His answer is no. Jacobs explains this using the 'ladder of demerit'. There are six rungs of the ladder. As each rung is climbed, the likelihood of wealth being meritocratic diminishes. The top two rungs are 'crime' (for example, drug trafficking and fraud) and 'cronyism' (for example, funding political campaigns and using friends or family to garner influence). These are definitely deemed not to be meritocratic. The following two rungs are 'inheritance' (where a billionaire's wealth was simply given to them as an heir) and 'monopoly' (where money is made by overcharging customers because of unfair market power). Arguably these are directly unmeritocratic. With monopoly, a billionaire technically 'earns' their money by taking risks, working hard and being talented. Nevertheless, Jacobs sees this as unmeritocratic because they abuse market power to receive a disproportionate compensation for their work. The bottom two rungs are 'globalization' (earning money through international trade) and 'technology' (earning money through the innovative use of new technology). These are arguably meritocratic sources of wealth.

Jacobs' main point is that even though some ways of becoming a billionaire appear more merit based than others, none are truly meritocratic. Globalization, for example, has helped almost all billionaires create or increase their wealth because it ensures the businesses they own or invest in have a broader customer base from which to grow profitably. This provides economies of scale, leading to higher market concentrations and higher profits. Billionaires may take advantage of this economic situation but they did not create it. Jacobs writes that globalization happens:

> Independently of the actions of extremely rich people, so they don't merit them. For example, although it takes effort, talent, and risk-taking to gain market share by exploiting economies of scale, extreme wealth continues to grow even when market share stabilizes, because the market itself continues growing regardless of billionaires' actions.[55]

Becoming rich off the back of technological innovation is also not the haven of the meritocratic billionaire. The issue is that although technology is transforming many industries, professions and occupations, and while making money from it can be reasonably construed as meritocratic, it is rarely the reason anyone becomes a billionaire. Sure, plenty of tech billionaires started off as innovators but the real source of their wealth is capital accumulation and market concentration – that is, taking money they did not rightfully earn.

It is entirely reasonable to argue that no matter how vociferously billionaires claim to be deserving of their wealth, the obscene excess of their fortunes cannot be justified on merit. This begs another question: is meritocracy such a good thing in the first place? On face value, it seems entirely reasonable that the best person should get the job and that people who put in more effort should get more rewards. Billionaires are undoubtedly happy to agree with this logic when they attempt to justify appropriating a gigantic share of the world's wealth. It is helpful, here, to consider the origin of the term 'meritocracy'. This is a word of very recent origin, coined by British sociologist Alan Fox in 1956. Today it is common for meritocracy to be portrayed as a righteous and desirable way that society should be organized but that assessment is a complete U-turn from what Cox had to say.

The word 'meritocracy' first appears in an article called 'Class and Equality', published in the journal *Socialist Commentary* in 1956.[56] The article was only three pages long, but it argued convincingly that while meritocracy might claim to be the high road from class oppression to equality, this was, in fact, a chimera. For Fox, meritocracy was simply a new class system that replaced birthright with talent as the basis of inequality. Meritocracy did nothing to foster equality; it simply changed who was at the top of an unequal system. Fox was nothing if not satirical. What was especially undesirable was that meritocracy championed:

> [A] society in which the gifted, the smart, the energetic, the ambitious and the ruthless are carefully sifted out and helped towards their destined positions of dominance, where they proceed not only to enjoy the fulfillment [*sic*] of exercising their natural endowments but also to receive a fat bonus thrown in for good measure.[57]

The problem is that meritocracy does not remove social inequality; it just changes the basis on which people are unequal.

Fox may have coined the term 'meritocracy' but it became better known through the publication in 1958 of Michael Young's satirical book *The Rise of the Meritocracy, 1870–2033: An Essay on Education and Equality*.[58] Like Fox, Young was far from a fan of meritocracy. The book, written by a fictional sociologist, imagines a Britain in 2033 that had become entirely meritocratic.

> Today we frankly recognize that democracy can be no more than aspiration, and have rule not so much by the people as by the cleverest people; not an aristocracy of birth, not a plutocracy of wealth, but a true meritocracy of talent.[59]

Meritocracy was achieved by providing the best education to the brightest young people, irrespective of their class and family backgrounds. Merit, in this new world, was understood as IQ plus effort, and those who had the most of it ruled the roost. No longer would a highly intelligent and hard-working person born into a lower-class family remain in the lower classes. They would be educated for greatness and responsibility and hoisted up the social ladder in accordance with their merit. This is a society where one's place in the social hierarchy was determined by one's place in the intellectual hierarchy. If a person is in a lower class, it is not because they were born into a particular family, it is because they are actually inferior!

In 2033, nepotism and inheritance were eliminated as the basis of class reproduction. For Young, the meritocratic future is entirely dystopian. Sieved and sifted through the education system, the kids were streamed so that, from an early age, the brightest and the best could be cultivated into a new upper class of meritocratic rulers. Such equality of opportunity leads deliberately to inequality of outcomes. The problem is that meritocracy does not abate inequality. Quite the contrary, it provided a moral justification for a different structure of inequality. This was the dominant political philosophy in Young's dystopian future and is also dominant for today's billionaires.

What can be learned from Young is that if we focus entirely on debating whether billionaires deserve their riches based on an assessment of their merit, then only one half of the myth of meritocracy is being considered. The other, and indeed more potent half, is to ask if meritocracy is a worthy political ideal in the first place. Assuming for a moment that all billionaire wealth is earned on merit, is it the case that all is well in the world and that justice has been achieved? Young says no. The problem is not so much that billionaires represent a failure of meritocracy, but that meritocracy is a failure of an idea. Meritocracy is appealing when opposed to the feudal idea of economic distribution based on birthright, but it is much less appealing when compared to democracy, even though meritocracy is often erroneously conflated into the idea of democracy. This political alignment of meritocracy and democracy is a deeply flawed assumption. Political philosopher Michael J. Sandel calls it the 'tyranny of merit'.[60]

For Sandel, the idea of merit-based wealth is a convenient way for the wealthy and successful to morally justify their positions at the top of society's economic ladder. After all, surely all is well in the moral universe if those who flourish do so because they are worthy, just like the idea that those who are good will go to heaven. Even more conveniently, in the meritocratic mindset, great wealth is virtuous; it is the reward for the superior exercise of individual freedom, the taking of opportunities and the embrace of personal responsibility. Notably, meritocracy is very much not about equality. It is premised on mobility – people moving up and down the ladder of wealth and success, depending on how well they exercise their talents and abilities. This leads Sandel to conclude that:

> Allocating jobs and opportunities according to merit does not reduce inequality; it reconfigures inequality to align with ability. But this reconfiguration creates a presumption that people get what they deserve. And the presumption deepens the gap between rich and poor.[61]

Even more worrying is that meritocracy is not based on hard work and talent alone. It also must be the case that the talents one has are both rare and command value in the economy. If, for example, one has special talents as a schoolteacher, billionaire status is not likely to ensue. If a person's talents are for playing casino capitalism on the stock market, there is much more likelihood of wealth flowing their way. Extreme talent and demanding work can be the case in both professions. Nevertheless, stockbrokers generally earn a great deal more money than teachers. This situation should surely not be taken to imply that stockbrokers are more virtuous than school teachers. Meritocracy is unfair because talents are valued differently. To be born with and have the opportunity to develop talents that command monetary value is to be lucky, in a similar manner to the lord of the manor in feudal times who was lucky on account of his birthright. This is not equality. At best, meritocracy results in class mobility on relatively arbitrary grounds – a person from humble beginnings can become a stockbroker, for example. A new elite emerges based on the ability to create wealth but it is still an elite and a new unequal social hierarchy is born. Just like a feudal hierarchy, it is arbitrary and not based on any justifiable moral grounds. In Sandel's words, the 'aristocracy of inherited privilege has given way to a meritocratic elite that is now as privileged and entrenched as the one in replaced'.[62] Billionaires are among their ranks.

Claims about the self-made status of billionaires vary greatly. For some, despite the growth of inequality having come alongside the expansion of billionaire fortunes, the myth of meritocracy stubbornly maintains that billionaires are meritoriously self-made.

It also maintains that the meritocracy that enabled them to become rich is a good thing. Some claim that as many as 70 per cent of billionaires are self-made, like Bezos, Zuckerberg and Adani. Even those who inherited money, like Arnault, are praised for taking the wealth handed down to them and growing it exponentially.[63] Of all the 'global high-net-worth individuals', a minority of just 8.5 per cent entirely inherited their wealth.[64] Billionaires are all lauded for being visionary and audacious risk-takers who learn from their mistakes, manage their time well and build empires through people.[65]

As reviewed earlier, others claim that the very idea of the self-made billionaire is bogus, with the real process of billionaire wealth creation coming from a combination of inheritance, the exploitation of workers, subsidies from government and tax avoidance.[66] Arguing over whether billionaires are self-made is all well and good, but the shared value that underlies the very debate is that if their wealth were self-made then it would all be okay because that is meritocratic. Cracking the myth of the meritorious billionaire requires this blind adherence to the belief in the virtue of meritocracy to be overruled. If democracy is both a political system and a way of life that values equality, then it directly opposes meritocracy. The political alignment of meritocracy with democracy that was ushered in around much of the world in the 1990s is both a cause and a political justification for inequality. Meritocracy knows no solidarity or community; it is every person for themselves. Shared prosperity and care for the well-being of all citizens is an anathema to meritocracy. In place of meritocracy's survival of the fittest ethos, the promise of democracy is that all can survive and flourish. This is a promise worth remembering and trying to keep.

6

The Myth of the Vigilante Billionaire

On 1 November 2021, David Beasley, Director of the United Nations' World Food Programme (UNWFP), made a provocative, if not seemingly obvious, claim. He stated that the world hunger crisis could be significantly abated if the billionaires contributed a small fraction of their enormous net worth to the cause. Too many nations are 'knocking on famine's door', Beasley explained, citing COVID-19 and the climate crisis as explanatory factors.

Beasley threw down the gauntlet to the mega-rich, naming Jeff Bezos and Elon Musk in his plea: '$6 billion to help 42 million people that are literally going to die if we do not reach them. It is not complicated,' Beasley explained. That amount was just 2 per cent of Musk's total wealth at the time.[1] Musk was provoked. Exuding apparent petulance, he took to Twitter to respond to Beasley's plea. In front of his 65.4 million Twitter followers, Musk exclaimed: 'If WFP [the UN World Food Programme] can describe on this Twitter thread exactly how US$6B will solve world hunger, I will sell Tesla stock right now and do it.' Later he added '[b]ut it must be open source accounting, so the public sees precisely how the money is spent'.[2]

The UN is a coalition of 193-member states set up in the aftermath of the Second World War. When it was first established in 1945, its two principal pledges were to end 'the scourge of war' and reinvigorate 'faith in fundamental human rights'.[3] By 1948, this was cemented with the signing of the UN's Universal Declaration of Human Rights, Article 25 of which asserts that: 'Everyone has the right to a standard of living adequate for the health and well-being of himself [*sic*] and of his family, including food, clothing, housing and medical care.'[4]

Founded in 1961, the UNWFP, which Beasley was leader of in 2021, exists precisely because the right to food – the right not to suffer, or even die, of hunger – is not universally available to all people in the world. Quite the contrary, the UN recognizes that 'one in nine people worldwide still do not have enough to eat'.[5] This is an ongoing struggle in an era where food insecurity is escalating globally. The COVID-19 pandemic, together with political conflict and climate change, have collectively intensified the problem, putting the goal of ending malnutrition and hunger by 2030 in jeopardy. Children are especially at risk. Put simply, the funds available to deal with this terrible problem are inadequate to address the worsening situation.[6]

In 2020, the UNWFP was awarded the Nobel Peace Prize for 'its efforts to combat hunger, promote peace in conflict-affected areas, and prevent the use of hunger as a weapon of war and conflict'.[7] Commenting on the accolade, then German Chancellor Angela Merkel said '[i]f there is a deserving organisation then this is certainly one of them. The people there do incredible work helping others and therefore I am very pleased about the awarding of this Nobel Peace Prize.'[8]

No such generosity of spirit was evident from Musk. Instead, he was content to question both the authority and the transparency of the UN, demeaning the UNWFP's sixty-year legacy in the momentary unleashing of a tweet. Musk did not even seem to have spent the time to read Beasley's statement. Musk's offhand tweet claimed that Beasley had said that the US$6 billion would end world hunger – but that is not what he said. Beasley challenged Musk's response, tweeting: 'Headline not accurate. $6B will not solve world hunger, but it WILL prevent geopolitical instability, mass migration and save 42 million people on the brink of starvation.'[9]

In any case, just days later, Beasley responded to Musk's challenge, providing a detailed plan of exactly how the money would be used. The total bill would be US$6.6 billion. The bulk of this, US$3.5 billion, would be spent on the food itself and delivering it to the places where it was needed. Where functioning markets existed, US$2 billion would go to vouchers and cash to buy food. A sum of

US$700 million would be spent on the in-country management of the programme and the final US$400 million on overall operations. The plan detailed the countries that would receive the assistance and how it would be phased to ensure the most critical needs would be met first.[10]

Musk never responded and the UNWFP received no donations from him. What can explain Musk's behaviour? Political historian Jill Lepore argues that Musk represents a particular form of capitalism. She calls it 'Muskism'. Muskism is akin to feudalism in that, as Lepore explains, '[i]t's like there are these lords and the rest of us are the peasantry, and our fates are in their hands because they know best'. Reflecting more generally on the power of those enthralled by Muskism, Lepore adds:

> These are mere mortals like the rest of us. They put their pants on one leg at a time and then they go out and they try to gain power and subvert ordinary people's ability to control their own lives.[11]

Interrupting the genuine and well-informed plea for help to address hunger and suffering illustrates how power can be exercised. To make matters worse, Musk commands an army of followers and fans who see him as an out-of-this-world visionary who can make even his wildest dreams come true.[12] Musk's fans are called 'Musketeers'. Musk is exemplary in demonstrating billionaire political morality, justifying his political interference based on what he sees as the results that can be generated through his wealth, imagination and know-how. Journalist and billionaire watcher Whizy Kim sums it up as follows:

> Casting himself as a figure pushing the progress of humanity forward has been central to Musk's popularity, his power, and even his business success. He has also capitalized on the idea that a billionaire's intelligence is seen as commensurate with their extreme financial success: Musk must be able to see and know things the rest of us couldn't because he's run several companies that have made him the richest man in the world.[13]

The case of the Musk–Beasley feud serves as an illustrative introduction of the myth of the vigilante billionaire. In common parlance, the term 'vigilante' refers to a person who takes the law into his (usually) or her own hands. A vigilante typically sees their personal morality as superior to that which is inscribed in society's laws and enacted through its institutions. Moreover, vigilantes believe that individual action taken outside of the functioning of the police and judiciary is the only way justice can be achieved. The vigilante's moral certainty is so strong that they believe it to be superior to any socially organized rules or norms. With this unwavering confidence in their own convictions, vigilantes use whatever powers they have to ensure what they think is right is enforced. The classic vigilante usually achieves this through brute force – either by an individual or by a loosely organized group of citizens.

Popular culture is a prime location where vigilantes are presented as heroes who single-handedly ensure that justice is done when society has failed. Vigilantes come in many forms. Superheroes like Batman and Superman have vigilante characteristics. Robin Hood is a classic vigilante seeking justice for the poor by stealing from the rich. Zorro, the Lone Ranger, Mad Max, Van Helsing and even the Teenage Mutant Ninja Turtles – all vigilantes. While each of these characters are seen as heroes, the vigilante is an ambivalent figure who can alternatively be praised for his (again, they are usually men) heroism or condemned for his anti-social lawlessness. One of the most terrible periods of vigilantism occurred in the United States following the Civil War. Between 1882 and 1968, the Confederate states that lost the war witnessed scenes where almost 5,000 people – mainly Black men – were murdered at the hands of vigilante lynch mobs. Commonly, lynching resulted from the victim having done something that was not illegal but offended the morality of the vigilantes. In the Southern United States, it was about controlling African Americans and ensuring their ongoing oppression. A young Black man touching a White woman on the arm was enough to create a race riot.[14]

There is a whole genre of vigilante films, perhaps the most famous of which is *Death Wish*, originally released in 1974 and starring tough-guy character actor Charles Bronson. It was remade in 2019 with action-hero star Bruce Willis. In both cases, the plot is simple and faithful to the vigilante genre. It goes like this: the family of

Paul Kersey, a regular and peaceful middle-aged man, are violently attacked during a home robbery. Despite the police investigating the attacks, there is little progress in catching the culprits. Angry and frustrated, Kersey takes up arms, roaming the city, hunting and killing criminals.

Film studies researcher Gregory Frame explains that *Death Wish*, like many other vigilante movies, is based on the premise that society is under a moral threat and that the authorities who are meant to protect all citizens – the government, the law, the police – have failed in their duty. In the wake of this crisis, one person (generally a White man) emerges as a saviour who can achieve justice in a way that organized society has so wantonly failed. He does so by the strength of his moral certainty, steely determination, and physical power. This is the same cultural logic that Donald Trump used to goad voters into believing that his singular will and convictions could solve all the problems facing regular American citizens. Political and social institutions played no part when considering how America's problems might be addressed. 'I and I alone can fix it,' he proclaimed when he accepted the nomination as the Republican presidential candidate on 21 July 2016.[15] In making this statement, Trump took on a deeply messianic tone. Placing himself above other mortals on a pedestal of god-like sovereignty, his words appeared to paraphrase the biblical verse from Isaiah: 'I, am the Lord; and beside me there is no saviour.'[16]

As Frame goes on to explain, there is a distinctly gendered and racial element to the cultural ideal of the vigilante. He elaborates that 'the vigilante film has long been understood as a reactionary response to the perception that the supremacy of White men in American society is under threat',[17] and that the acts of a single heroic figure can restore a just society. As others fester in the space between moral panic and bureaucratic inefficiency, a hero rises to save the day, the ills of society being no match for his powerful and individualistic masculinity. The fantasy of the vigilante reflects a deep-seated distrust of authority, coupled with an extreme prizing of individuality. The vigilante is like the stereotypical man on a white horse from cowboy films. He would arrive at a scene of rampant Wild West injustice, making everything right before he turned to ride away into the sunset.

What does this all have to do with Elon Musk? Unlike *Death Wish*'s Paul Kersey, Musk is not a violent avenger who seeks justice through the barrel of a gun. However, what is similar is the cultural logic of vigilantism that runs through Musk's reaction to the UNWFP. With Musk, the injustice that needs to be fought is not violent street crime but world hunger; the weapon is not a firearm but money; the inefficient bureaucracy is not the police, it is the UN; the hero is not a middle-class White man but a billionaire one.

What Kersey and Musk do have in common is a distinct disrespect for the efficacy of formal, socially sanctioned authority or rule-based due process. In the case of Paul Kersey, it is a belief that the police and the judiciary are failed institutions – they are not able to achieve justice for the victims they are meant to protect. In Musk's case, it is an apparent belief that an international organization like the UN cannot use funds to effectively address world hunger. In both instances, the vigilante solution lies in the conviction that the power of the individual is that which is a better servant of justice than organized social institutions. In any case, Musk only played the vigilante role up to a point, backing off before making any commitments or taking any action.

What the Musk–Beasley feud showed is that Muskism is billionaire vigilantism *par excellence*. Musk represents a very particular form of capitalism that has no respect for the law, believing that the masters of industry should also be the masters of the world, unencumbered by stuffy bureaucrats trying to stymie their pursuit of greatness. The vigilante billionaire is above the law or at least desires to be and believes that he deserves to be. 'It's a kind of unchecked capitalism that insists that the government really has no role in the regulation of economic activity,' Jill Lepore explains. It doesn't end there. The fantasy of Muskism is that the superhero entrepreneur is not just making a lot of money, he is also capable of single-handedly saving the world from what would otherwise be a terrible fate. We are in the realm of science fiction here. Lepore reports:

> One of the things that's distinctive about Musk, in the sense that he's the best at this, is depicting your product as saving humanity. This also became a thing in Musk's really early years. So even the Twitter bid, in Musk's language, is somehow about saving civilization ... Musk presents himself as a messiah.[18]

When Musk made his high-profile bid to purchase Twitter, his rhetoric was extreme. Was Twitter a good investment? Sure. But that is only a small part of it. In April 2022, Musk became Twitter's largest shareholder when he bought US$3 billion-worth of the social media company's stock. Taking to Twitter himself, he did not crow about his business acumen. Instead, he tweeted: 'given that Twitter serves as the de facto public town square, failing to adhere to free speech principles fundamentally undermines democracy. What should be done "Is a new platform needed?"' He had previously claimed the democratic credential of being a 'free speech absolutist'.[19] His idea was to remove the restrictions that Twitter had in place to prevent people from posting what might be perceived as hateful comments, targeted attacks, conspiracy theories and suchlike. This was precisely the policy that, less than a year earlier, saw then President Donald Trump ousted from Twitter 'due to the risk of further incitement of violence' after his Twitter activity posts about the storming of the US Capitol in January 2021 showed support for the riots.[20]

When he heard about Musk's Twitter purchase, comedian Seth Myers quipped 'with money like that you could do something about poverty, or climate change, or world hunger'.[21] But no, Musk claimed that he would protect the democratic way of life itself. Under his leadership, Twitter will become a 'platform for free speech around the globe', he proselytized, adding that freedom of speech is 'a societal imperative for a functioning democracy'.[22] All of this talk of democracy is great clickbait for vigilante image making but is not consistent with Musk's actual behaviour. When Musk lays off workers at his multi-billion-dollar electric vehicle company Tesla, he gets them to sign agreements binding them legally not to say anything bad about the company – it is what they call a 'non-disparagement clause'. It reads like this:

> You agree not to disparage Tesla, the Company's products, or the Company's officers, directors, employees, shareholders and agents, affiliates and subsidiaries in any manner likely to be harmful to them or their business, business reputation or personal reputation.[23]

That certainly does not seem like the work of a self-proclaimed 'free speech absolutist'. Trying to control what journalists and other public commentators say about his businesses and personal affairs is another one of Musk's long-held practices.[24]

Coming back to the altercation with Beasley and the UNWFP, Musk's vigilante ethos belies a schism between the power afforded to the extremely wealthy and the powerless plea of the hungry, as defended by the UN. Of course, what Musk does with his own money is entirely his own business, even if his wealth is bolstered by the minimal income tax that he pays.[25] Still, for Musk to ask Beasley for a description of how the UNWFP would spend the money and then ignore the entirely reasonable response is another matter altogether. Musk also ignored Beasley's public offer to meet him to discuss the plan and open his books.[26] In the end, it all amounted to little more than a Twitter spat between the two men, with Musk failing even to respond when his own demands were answered. Musk talked the vigilante talk, but he did not take one step on the vigilante walk. In the balance, world hunger remained unchanged and people died. Also unchanged was the massive fortune that Musk controlled. It appeared that Musk's riches meant that he did not need to be accountable even for his stated commitments.

Beasley said at the time:

> For him [Musk] to even enter into this conversation is a game-changer because simply put, we can answer his questions, we can put forth a plan that's clear ... Any and everything he asks, we would be glad to answer. I look forward to having this discussion with him because lives are at stake.[27]

Musk, by all accounts, did not feel any responsibility for the demands he issued. There was no discussion. Perhaps this was one of the tweets that he posted, as he once claimed, that was written when he 'was literally on the toilet'.[28]

What does this all say about the myth of the vigilante billionaires? The thinking of philosopher Giorgio Agamben is helpful in addressing this question.[29] Agamben does not dwell on billionaires or vigilantes in his work but he has a lot to say about how power operates in society. Agamben focuses on political dictators and the methods they use to harness and exercise personal power outside the law. What differentiates democratic power from totalitarian power,

Agamben elaborates, is the idea of the 'state of exception'. A state of exception refers to a political transformation where a single ruler declares that the laws do not apply to them – it is the 'suspension of the juridical order itself'.[30]

When the law is suspended, the leader is no longer a citizen elected to office but becomes the sovereign. Wielding supreme and unaccountable power, the sovereign is not so much a democratic ruler but more like a monarch in the days before democracy. The state of exception suspends the normal democratic process so that one person can make (or not make, as with Musk and the UNWFP) decisions on any basis they wish without recourse to socially mandated rules. The sovereign dictator effectively decrees that the exceptional circumstances that they face demand, out of necessity, that they take personal control rather than them being subject to democratic procedure or institutionally mandated limits on their authority. Sovereign dictatorship ensues. The sovereign has the capacity 'to command, to forbid, to allow, to punish',[31] and hence the law does not apply to them.

In contrast to the individual sovereignty of a dictator, democracy is built on the idea of popular sovereignty: the insistence that the 'people' are collectively the ones who are ultimately responsible for self-rule. The organization of democracy through elected governments and the separation of powers between the legislature, judiciary and executive are all part of how the idea of popular sovereignty is implemented in practice. Central to this is the 'rule of law' whereby all citizens, including people in positions of political power and the wealthy, are subject to the same laws. This is foundational to democratic justice.

None of this means anything to the individual sovereign who declares a 'state of exception' where the laws no longer apply to him (yes, it is usually a man). Instead, he and he alone decides what to do, unencumbered by any collectively agreed rules regarding how society is governed. Society is merely an obstacle to the exercise of personal political morality. Most worryingly is how the demand for sovereignty without recourse to the rule of law can increasingly become the norm rather than the exception, with the ideals of democracy lying in tatters along the way. The ruler effectively becomes the king. This is the desire of the vigilante billionaire – to be a law unto himself, accountable to no one.

The ideas of sovereignty and the state of exception is not just a matter of politics, limited to the Napoleons, Mussolinis and Hitlers, or even George W. Bushes, of history. It is also a cultural fantasy many people aspire to, even if it is perennially out of their reach. This fantasy consists of being entirely self-sufficient, unaccountable to authority and free to act as one pleases without interference or concession to society. But to think this way breaks the fundamental social contract that required, inevitably, for everyone (but the hermit) to live with other people.

Philosopher Thomas Hobbes declared almost 350 years ago that without a social contract where people ceded some of their liberty to an organized government for the common good,[32] life would be 'solitary, poor, nasty, brutish and short'.[33] Without an agreement as to how people in a society live together, Hobbes claimed, there would always be a danger from those people who take 'pleasure in contemplating their own power in the acts of conquest'.[34] The founder of modern political philosophy, Hobbes feared what might happen if social order were to collapse into an everyone-for-themselves state of chaos. Hobbes' thinking marked the advent of the idea of the social contract: that people must give up some of their freedoms and the pursuit of their desires to live together without conflict.

What does this all mean for vigilante billionaires? When Musk challenged the UNWFP, he was not just asking a simple question about how they might use his money. Instead, he was asserting (although in this case not exercising) his power as an individual outside of the democratic social contract. The implication was that, based on his extreme wealth, if he chose to exercise the power that his billions bestowed on him, he would do so in a way that made him answerable to no one. It would be the same case if he chose not to exercise that power. Anyone can decide to not give their own money charitably to help the world's hungry. It is just that for most people, while contributions are important, the power of one individual ability to do anything about it is infinitesimal. Anyone can dream of being a sovereign but without the resources to enact sovereign power, that remains but a vain pipe dream. The difference with billionaires like Musk is that they command extraordinary resources and that comes with enormous power.

In what has been described as a 'golden age for billionaires', there has been a rapid surge in inequality, led by a small minority who have managed to sequester ever-increasing amounts of the world's bounty.[35] Economic inequality is a scourge on the world, leaving many hungry, homeless and without access to healthcare, but what makes this even worse is the political implications of the growing billionaire class. In particular, the worry is that as billionaires strive for sovereignty, they do so as vigilantes. Just like *Death Wish's* Paul Kersey, they take the law into their own hands and, in so doing, usurp the social and democratic institutions that offer the promise of equality, freedom and solidarity of all people.

The rule of law, as a defining feature of free and equal society, means nothing to the vigilante. Instead, personal moral convictions trump socially agreed rules – this is how billionaire morality works. The vigilante enforces their own rules based on the power that they have available to them, irrespective of whether that enforcement is legal or illegal. In 2021, Musk was named *Time* magazine's 'Person of the Year'.[36] *Time* said that Musk was a man who 'aspires to save our planet', describing his character as a 'clown, genius, edgelord, visionary, industrialist, showman, cad'. They fall just short of calling him a vigilante.

Musk being *Time's* Person of the Year happened at the height of the COVID-19 pandemic. Never mind acknowledging the heroic achievements of the vaccine scientists who helped tame the deadly spread of COVID worldwide or on the frontline. Forget the frontline medical staff who risked their own lives caring for the sick. *Time* promoted a billionaire who once blurted out 'the coronavirus panic is dumb'. When quizzed on the plague of sickness and death the virus might cause, Musk cavalierly responded, 'everybody dies'.[37] *Time* did not draw attention to this. Instead, they endorsed Musk not only as 'the richest private citizen in history' but also as the man who successfully 'bends government and industry to the force of his ambition'. Bending government? Is the ability to manipulate the elected representatives of a nation's citizens something to be proud of? That is a matter of judgement but it points precisely to the myth of the vigilante billionaire. Society's laws are nothing but an encumbrance to the realization of personal excellence and moral superiority and must be manipulated out of shape to realize the singular vision of the private sovereign.

All people hold the right to express their views and seek to change the laws of the land and how it is governed. Resistance and dissent are themselves fundamental, if not primary, democratic rights.[38] At one level, this is the purpose of having a political system based on elected governments such that the people can resist and depose their rulers through collective and peaceful political action. It is also the basis of the revisability of the law and freedom of speech. But those are not the democratic values in place when the ultra-rich rise above society's rules in the pursuit of a personal vision. When that happens, it is not the exercise of democratic rights but their abuse. Despite the inequality and abuse of power that billionaires are associated with, many billionaires have become celebrities who are to be put on a pedestal as role models of achievement and excellence. Billionaires represent an ideal that regular people can only aspire to as they struggle through everyday life's practical and financial challenges. There is an inherent irony here, especially when those who represent inequality are idolized by those whose share of the world's riches is dwindling.

A study by psychologists Jesse Walker, Stephanie Tepper and Thomas Gilovich found that when people hear about individuals who have become ultra-rich, they generally believe that they deserve every penny of their incredulous wealth.[39] This belief holds even when those same people believe that the gross and widening inequalities in the world are unjust. It is the humanization of the individual billionaire that wins out over the inequality that all the billionaires represent. Hearing the heroic stories of the philanthropic generosity of Gates, Buffett, Bezos and the like might just convince people that hard work and entrepreneurial spirit got billionaires to the top of the pile and that they are deserving of their excessive wealth.

The Musk–Beasley debacle serves as an illustrative example to introduce the myth of the vigilante billionaire but the problem extends much further than that. Looking beyond the charismatic appeal of the celebrity tycoon reveals not only how deep and wide this phenomenon is but also how it threatens the whole promise of democracy as both a way of life and a means through which society can be organized around fundamental principles of freedom, equality and social solidarity. The expansion of vigilante billionaires heralds the dangerous rise of a new plutocracy – a system where political power is held by the very rich purely based on their wealth.

Professor of Politics at Cambridge University Helen Thompson explains how the world today is in an 'age of plutocracy' that has been developing since the 1980s and the early maturation of neoliberal government policies. As discussed in previous chapters, these policies, spearheaded by Margaret Thatcher in the UK and Ronald Reagan in the US, demonstrated a new enthusiasm for unfettered capitalism being let loose in a system of globalized corporate deregulation. Along the way, labour power, especially organized labour, was weakened. Inequalities started to rise globally as international corporations and wealthy individuals were able to avoid tax in new and more effective ways, even as tax rates were being progressively reduced in many countries anyway. This increased concentration of wealth, more and more free from state regulation, was a recipe for plutocratic expansion.[40]

Author and political journalist Anand Giridharadas is incisive and straightforward when he argues that Musk's first attempt to purchase Twitter in 2022 was the 'perfect marriage for an age of plutocracy'. Giridharadas' analysis suggests that:

> The plutocrats have already rigged the economy. That's just the first step. Then you take some of the spoils and reinvest it in buying even more political influence, so that political inequality can help keep economic inequality yawning. You buy up media or social media platforms and thus can help rig the discourse in your favor, taking control of the tools used by regular people to fight back. You venture, as Mr. Musk did, to a TED conference and, without much pushback, to brand yourself as a kind of public intellectual, a thought leader, a visionary, and thereby in many people's minds you became a sage, not a robber baron.[41]

This is a paradigm case of the myth of the vigilante billionaire in that it is a direct attempt to use economic power to gain political power and claim social leadership. Even more extreme, it seeks to position the billionaire as a new type of plutocratic statesman whose grand vision can save the world in a way that democratic politicians have failed. Whether it be Musk taunting Beasley about world poverty or saving democracy through a takeover of Twitter, the core political morality is the same: the rich get to call the political shots and no government can or should stop them. The vigilante billionaire rises above the law as a new sovereign. Whereas once political power was based on the assumption of the divine right of kings, for the vigilante billionaire it is money that is god and it is the possession of that money that makes him the new king.

Musk exemplifies one incarnation of the myth of the vigilante billionaire but the variations on this myth do not start and end with him. If anything, Musk is relatively idiosyncratic, if not extreme, in his willingness to allow his personal convictions to change the course of the world. Another manifestation of the plutocratic elite, this time en masse, can be found in the Alpine town of Davos. There one can find a whole swag of vigilante kings huddled together.

Driving two hours south-east from Zurich Airport, going around Lake Zurich and climbing until you are about 1,500 metres above sea level, you reach Davos, the highest town in the Alps. In the early 1900s, Davos was best known as a health spa where tuberculosis sufferers would retire to breathe the crisp mountain air that promised to cure them of their deadly lung infection. Dubbed a 'mecca for consumptives', Davos' popularity continued to grow through the twentieth century and not just for the sick. The well-heeled gathered there for holidays, relaxing in the spas and sanatoriums and enjoying the hospitality of what had become a fashionable location for a high-class getaway.[42]

Things started to change in 1971 when Klaus Schwab and Hilde Stoll convened the first meeting of the European Management Symposium, later renamed the WEF. Today, the town of Davos is synonymous with what has become perhaps the most high-profile and influential meeting on the global political calendar. In its 50-year life, the annual meeting has been the site of some momentous historical events. In 1990, just two months after the fall of the Berlin Wall, it was at the Davos Forum that West German Chancellor Helmut Kohl met with East German Prime Minister Hans Modrow. Two years later, in 1992, the Davos meeting was the first time South Africa's President F.W. de Klerk met with the head of the African National Congress Nelson Mandela outside South Africa.[43]

Fast forward to 2019 and Davos is where 16-year-old climate activist Greta Thunberg told the world:

> Our house is on fire. I am here to say, our house is on fire … At places like Davos, people like to tell success stories. But their financial success has come with an

unthinkable price tag. And on climate change, we have to acknowledge we have failed. All political movements in their present form have done so, and the media has failed to create broad public awareness.[44]

The inclusion of the WEF in major political events all seems grist for the mill for an organization that expresses the explicit belief that 'progress happens by bringing together people from all walks of life who have the drive and the influence to make positive change'.[45] What exactly is the idea behind this 'positive change' that will be made in the Swiss Alpine wonderland? It is all about Klaus Schwab's vision of what he calls 'stakeholder capitalism'.[46] Capitalism should not just be all about the short-term profits that further enrich already wealthy shareholders, Schwab claims.

The capitalism that Schwab endorses is one where the prime movers of the global economy do not just ride roughshod over the world pursuing an unquenchable thirst for more and more lucre. Under stakeholder capitalism, economic activities must be:

> protected and guided, to ensure the overall direction of economic development is beneficial to society, and no [economic] actors can free ride on the efforts of others [… and …] all those who have a stake in the economy can influence decision making. Moreover a system of check and balances exists, so that no one stakeholder can become or remain overly dominant.[47]

This all seems well and good. It promises a feel-good win–win situation where capitalists can continue to make profits but everyone else will benefit, too. One does not have to scratch far beneath the surface to realize that the idyll of stakeholder promise is not what it seems. When it comes to Schwab's Davos shindig, it is quite clear that some 'stakeholders' are more equal than others. Davos has a hyper-exclusive guest list of 2,000 people. In January 2020, the last meeting before the COVID-19 pandemic, 119 of those on the list were billionaires. Their collective worth was US$500 billion. To put those numbers in perspective, twice as many billionaires were attending as there were heads of state.[48] In 2023, there were 116 billionaires at the Forum, even though

Russian billionaires were excluded because of the war in Ukraine and Chinese billionaires were still not travelling internationally because of a resurgence of COVID cases in China. Only 52 heads of state turned up that year.[49]

As the Davos festivities unfold, billionaires get to feed at the trough with CEOs, politicians and do-gooding celebrities. That is very far from being representative of the stakeholders of world capitalism. *Forbes Magazine* reports that there are 2,755 billionaires in the world.[50] The global population is just about 8 billion people. A quick calculation yields that if billionaires were considered to be a 'stakeholder group', then they are over-represented at Davos by a factor of up to 200,000. Smiley stakeholder rhetoric aside, Davos is the preserve of elite power where money buys influence. Proportionally few women go either – just 22 per cent of the guest list in 2019 was female.[51] This rose miserably to 24 per cent for the 2020 meeting, with no breakdown released for 2022,[52] and no data made available for 2023. The following year, 2024, saw a slight increase to 28 per cent.[53]

It would appear that rich men are the ones holding the reins of stakeholder capitalism. To be clear, when the Davos 'leaders' proselytize about stakeholder capitalism, the faint smell of democracy that comes with the chesty rhetoric is deceptive. The Davos manifesto may well state that corporations *should* pay tax, be intolerant to corruption, ensure human rights and insist on fair markets.[54] Still, the question is left open about the realization of such noble ideals. One thing for sure, at Davos, is a belief that corporations might change their profit-hungry spots and become engines of social justice has nothing to do with the idea of popular sovereignty, democratic governance or the rule of law. In all cases, the market is the answer, regulation is the enemy and corporations are in charge. Any stakeholder benevolence coming out of Davos is entirely at the discretion of the powerful, should they choose of their own free will to express their billionaire munificence.

The 'Davos manifesto' makes it abundantly clear who is the boss, and it is not the people:

> Business leaders now have an incredible opportunity. By giving stakeholder capitalism concrete meaning, they can move beyond their legal obligations and uphold

their duty to society. They can bring the world closer to achieving shared goals, such as those outlined in the Paris climate agreement and the United Nations Sustainable Development Agenda. If they really want to leave their mark on the world, there is no alternative.[55]

The key phrase here is 'if they really want to'. Despite all the climate-loving, pro-social and community-friendly words that large corporations and their billionaire bosses want to engage in, they will do it in a way that is 'beyond their legal obligations'. Vigilantism is in the air – the stakeholder corporation operates outside of the law. This is an obligation not to the social contract embedded in law and custom and upheld by the representatives of the people, it is an obligation purely to the idiosyncratic machinations of one's own conscience.

With such a gathering of the well-heeled in-crowd of the power elite, it is hardly surprising that an organization that claims to be 'accountable to all parts of society' with 'moral and intellectual integrity' has come under criticism. Global Convenor of the activist group Fight Inequality Alliance, Jenny Ricks, makes the point that Davos is an entirely 'unaccountable space' and to think that the discussions and pronouncements that go on there are a replacement for actual policies is a dangerous chimera. The real problems facing people around the world today – from energy affordability to economic inequality – are not going to be solved at Davos, Ricks argues. This is so because the radical changes that are required to address fundamental national and global inequalities are not in the interests of the global elite. Wealth redistribution and economic justice are threats to a billionaire class wanting to hold on to its supreme social position. Ricks shows that more fundamental questions need to be asked:

Policy choices made by governments and international institutions throughout the pandemic have fallen woefully short of protecting people from the impact of multiple crises. Spiralling inflation, sky-rocketing energy bills and fuel prices, as well as high and still rising food prices, spelled disaster for so many. But the richest few, who continued to increase their wealth in the past two years, are still benefitting from the crisis. As a result, questions are being raised on the morality of an economic system that has failed to help the masses and instead supercharged inequality during a global health emergency.[56]

If anything, Davos is the most potent international symbol of the vigilante billionaire as a new breed of law-free plutocrat. This character comes in the form of the much maligned 'Davos Man', nothing if not the anti-hero prototype of the mythical vigilante billionaire.

The epithet 'Davos Man' is generally credited to political scientist and Harvard Professor Samuel P. Huntington. However, the actual term he issued in his 1996 book, *The Clash of Civilizations and the Remaking of World Order*,[57] was 'Davos people'. Huntington was referring to 'businessmen, bankers, government officials, intellectuals and journalists ... who generally share beliefs in individualism, market economics, and political democracy'. Davos people are the elite power holders who 'control virtually all international institutions, many of the world's governments, and the bulk of the world's economic and military capabilities'.[58]

In identifying the Davos people, Huntington's concern was with how the minority globalized cosmopolitan elite that ran the global political and economic institutions were increasingly out of touch with most people in the world. The international group of 'globalizing elites' Huntington argued, lived in a 'sociocultural bubble' in which they had developed their own culture, values and language of 'global speak'. This language, above all else, is the language of global business:

> All these globalising organisations, and not just the multinational corporations, operate in a world defined by 'expanding markets', the need for 'competitive advantage', 'efficiency', 'cost-effectiveness', 'maximising benefits and minimising costs', 'niche markets', 'profitability' and 'the bottom line.' They justify this focus on the grounds that they are meeting the need of consumers all over the world. That is their constituency ... the national citizen gives way to the global consumer.[59]

The 'Davos Men', or 'gold-collar workers' as they have been called, have little respect for the boundaries between nations or the priorities of myopic state politicians. The world is the oyster of the Davos Man who cuts himself off from those unlike him.

The Davos Man who flourished in the economic boom of globalization and corporate deregulation is still very much alive today. The Global Financial Crisis of 2008–2009 made him stronger. He seized the climate crisis as a business opportunity. He profited handsomely from the new online markets created by the COVID-19 pandemic. Davos Men were among the heads of the companies Oxfam called the 'pandemic profiteers' who saw their profits soar as the world suffered a health and financial crisis. Meanwhile, the likes of Microsoft, Johnson & Johnson, Facebook, Pfizer and Visa raked in billions of dollars of excess profit amid accusations of price gouging and wanton market exploitation.[60] The Davos Man has one overarching loyalty and it is to himself.

Not all Davos Men are billionaires, but so many billionaires are Davos Men. *New York Times* journalist Peter S. Goodman convincingly argues that COVID-19 served to jet-propel inequality to new extremes as the Davos billionaires strutted their stakeholder-loving credentials in public while accelerating their quest for wealth centralization behind the scenes. Leaving rampant political populism, poverty, hunger and illness in their wake, the cosmopolitan ultra-rich never had it so good.

What Davos Men and their billionaire subset also have in common is a particular image of masculinity – what might be called 'Davos masculinity' – and it is propelled by a vigilante mystique where personal conscience triumphs over democratically decided frameworks, these being a mere encumbrance to greatness. What are the characteristics of Davos masculinity? Globalization's specific effects on masculinity must be considered to answer this question. After all, the Davos Man is, if nothing else, a citizen of the world not beholden to the limitations of any established cultures. His status as an international cosmopolitan gives the Davos Man an air of vigilante cool as he swans around in designer-branded 'business casual' attire. The laws of any single country are merely an impediment to his manly greatness, a morally superior greatness too potent to allow pesky rules and laws to get in his way. Lawyers are important, to be sure, but their value comes from finding ways to circumvent the law, not giving advice on how to follow it.

The masculinity of the Davos Man is a variant of what sociologist Raewyn Connell calls 'hegemonic masculinity'. The Greek word *hegemon* refers to a supreme leader, although the more general notion of hegemonic in politics denotes a form of cultural domination that is supported and reinforced through processes of socialization and education. Hegemonic masculinity is the culturally dominant form of masculinity that represents, for better or worse, an ideal of masculinity. There are many ways to be a man, with masculinities coming in many different forms. Hegemonic masculinity is, however, one that is especially dominant. Conventionally, hegemonic masculinity has been associated with aggressiveness, competitiveness, alpha-male dominance, stoicism and rugged independence. No room for sissies, cry-babies and Mummy's boys in the world of 'real men'. The 'real man' is a go-getter whose drive for success knows no bounds. The world is there for the taking and nothing and no one will stand in the way of the male action hero.

As is the case with vigilantes, government regulation is the special enemy of the Davos Man's right to independence and moral superiority. In the battlefield of the market where the Davos Men fight it out to see who is the most powerful, interference by bothersome regulations is an anathema to the right to free competition. Governments become cast in the misogynistic image of the 'nanny state' which, like an overprotective grandmother, smothers the natural freedom that should be a young man's right. The might of the Davos Man does not need to seek refuge behind apron strings. Well, at least not unless it benefits them.

The Davos Man represents a particular variety of hegemonic masculinity that reaches its full vigilante potential in its billionaire form. Davos masculinity emerged out of what Connell identified as 'transnational business masculinity',[61] as it began to form in the 1980s and 1990s. The growing role of corporations in society coupled with economic globalization yielded a new form of hegemonic manhood that was incubated in multinational corporations and financial markets. Here masculinity itself became globalized as a new form of male domination in the form of the entrepreneur who was self-starting, independent and creative, as well as not reliant on the state for his personal success. This new man came in the form of 'business executives who operate in global markets, and the political executives who interact (and in many contexts, merge) with them'.[62]

He did not need to prove himself through brute physical force as his forebears did but rather through the power of the capitalist institutions that he led.

The catalyst for the creation of new transnational business masculinity was economic globalization and the prevalence of the multinational corporation that came with it. The new managers were affluent and had direct access to power through their work. Unlike their conservative forebears, the new breed also supported a socially progressive political stance, believing in gender equity, endorsing multiculturalism and rejecting homophobia. Heterosexuality was no longer mandatory to be considered a 'man' and concern for the aesthetic of one's own body and clothing was important.[63]

Davos masculinity has grown and adapted to a borderless world of endless possibilities. Economist Lourdes Beneria explains the characteristics of the Davos Men with incisive insight.[64] She describes the Davos Man as the rational economic man who has gone global. This is the character for whom everything is apprehended in terms of weighing costs and benefits for personal gain, including the patronizing tipping of one's hat to needy stakeholders. The morality of Davos masculinity is simple, Beneria expounds, and despite his softened edges, competition remains core to his male identity. For the Davos Man, the global economy is a jungle in which only the fittest and most manly will survive. Failure is bankruptcy and if a Davos Man were to succumb to such weakness, then it would be an appropriate punishment for his impotent performance in the manly playing field of the global marketplace. Being a winner means being market driven and efficient, beating the competition in the playground games of the international economy.

The market in which the Davos Man operates is the public sphere where values such as 'human cooperation, empathy, and collective well-being' are out of place in the male-dominated competitive economic arenas.[65] These are arenas where selfishness, individualism and hardness are themselves held up as virtues. When women are admitted, they risk being co-opted into the masculine mould of the rational economic man, albeit in a woman's body. For women to be successful in the world of transnational business masculinity, they must, according to former Facebook Chief Operating Officer Sheryl Sandberg, 'lean in'. In Sandberg's 2013 *New York Times* bestselling book of that name, *Lean In*,[66] she advocated that if women wanted to take an equal place in the corridors of corporate power, they needed to shake off the barriers that existed in their consciousness by being ambitious, assertive and demanding. The idea of leaning in is intensely individualistic, with women told that if they adopt the behaviours of men – indeed, Davos Men – then they could take their rightful place at the top table.

This is not to say that none of the men who go to Davos care about women. The problem, as political economist Juanita Elias has described,[67] is that the Davos Man's approach to addressing 'women's issues' reflects his own steadfast individualism. When matters such as the gender pay gap, lack of representation and outright discrimination are considered, they are stripped down to questions of individual opportunity rather than a collectively political struggle. Women are an investment that will yield returns in the market-driven world of the Davos Men. Elias concludes that 'there is an inevitability about the way in which gender issues are instrumentalized in order to link women's empowerment and gender equality straightforwardly to economic growth and competitiveness'.[68]

The Davos Man is by no means a macho brute or John Waynesque gritty tough guy of a previous era. Quite the contrary, while distinctly masculine in his competitiveness and self-confidence, today's Davos Man is smart, sophisticated and deeply engaged in moral and political issues. The Davos Man has added to transitional business masculinity a concern for deploying his resources and talents towards environmental and social goals. Arguably, this redirection escalated in the aftermath of the Global Financial Crisis of 2008– 2009. If the crisis was blamed on big corporations and their financiers – and the men who ran them – then this image of masculinity needed to be cleaned up. Since the Global Financial Crisis, the Davos rhetoric has moved from focusing just on economic growth and global development to a new penchant for the environment and social causes.

In analysing the WEF's official communications, sociologists Shawn Pope and Patricia Bromley found that the 2010s saw a 'social awakening'. The reinvigorated Davos Man now preaches equality, champions environmentalism and proselytizes about social inclusion.[69] None of the original characteristics of the new business masculinity were dropped; they were just augmented with a broader remit – those characteristics could be deployed not just to solve business problems but to solve society's problems as well. This encroachment of business and market solutions on all problems remains central to the political morality of the billionaire class. It is a corporate takeover of the sociopolitical sphere.

As well as market-based gender equality, the Davos Man cares about climate change, supports Black Lives Matter, abhors the crude roughness of toxic masculinity and shudders at the vulgarity of strong-man political populism. All these things are problems to be solved through individual leadership and the market mechanism. The values of the Davos Man remain unchanged. He is all out for win–win solutions where any problem in the world can be solved without compromising the Holy Grail of shareholder value. Sure, stakeholders are important but the shareholder is a stakeholder, too. Stop global warming? We must do it, so long as shareholders benefit. Address gender pay inequality? Yes, so long as it improves the bottom line. Eradicate the crime of modern slavery? Absolutely, and it will be a new source of competitive advantage. The common denominator for all solutions is that they are corporate based and entail minimal government interference through legislation.

Former Australian Prime Minister Scott Morrison's approach to climate change is a telling example of the withdrawal of government and reliance on the private sector to solve public problems. In late 2021 at the UN Climate Change Conference, Morrison had become something of an international pariah for his lukewarm climate policies.[70] Climate Action International called out Australia's 'breathtaking climate ineptitude', adding that 'Scott Morrison and his band of merry fossil fools either failed to sign up to a progressive phase-out pledge or made an announcement that was better suited to an oil, gas and coal convention.'[71]

The criticism was that while developed countries were setting ambitious goals for decarbonization, Australia was branded a 'climate laggard' for weak targets and a refusal to end coal-powered electricity.[72] Lord Deben, Chair of the UK Climate Change Committee, had this to say to Australians:

> What was so disappointing for us is the way it appeared
> your prime minister really doesn't understand the urgency
> of what we have to do … That's difficult for Australia,
> but Australia really has to get on with it, just like every

other country ... Nations around you will disappear
beneath the sea because that's what is going to happen to
the South Pacific ... As it gets worse for everyone else,
people are simply not going to be prepared to trade with
countries that don't meet the same standards.[73]

Morrison is no member of the vigilante billionaire class. He was the
political foot servant to that class, always eager to promote the mantra
of small government, the munificence of free enterprise and the
virtues of reducing taxation for the rich. In Australia in the aftermath
of his embarrassment at the UN Climate Change Conference,
Morrison addressed the Victorian Chamber of Commerce and
Industry with a new angle on his climate change rhetoric:

Just as the animal spirits of enterprise have worked
together with scientists and technologists to change the
world in the past ... I am more than convinced they hold
the answer to solving the challenge of a decarbonised
economy. We believe climate can be ultimately solved by
'can-do capitalism' not 'don't do governments' seeking
to control peoples' lives.[74]

When Morrison talked of the 'animal spirits of enterprise', he was
making a relatively obscure reference to a term originally used by
the massively influential twentieth-century economist John Maynard
Keyes. It was back in 1936, in his book *The General Theory of
Employment, Interest, and Money*,[75] that Keynes used the term 'animal
spirits' to refer to the spontaneous impulse to act and make decisions.
This form of enterprise, for Keynes, is not governed by rational
calculation and assessment but by feelings of confidence and hope
– an 'innate urge to activity'.[76]

Morrison got this all wrong, using the idea of the animal
spirits to equate the entrepreneur with some kind of natural man
pursuing his desires in the competitive jungle of the marketplace.
The animalistic entrepreneur gets things done by fighting it out
in the entrepreneurial playground of what Morrison called 'can-
do capitalism'. By contrast, Morrison deprecated government as
not possessing the same manly instincts of the capitalist. Morrison's
image of 'can't do government' is the direct opposite of go-getting

capitalist action hero. He feminizes government and then uses that femininity to condemn it as weak and ineffectual.

The macho can-do capitalist that Morrison kneels to is the image of the vigilante billionaire-cum-Davos superhero. It is on account of this image that the vigilante billionaire can duck and weave from the ogre of legislation and regulation. Such limitations are the realm of the ordinary mortal, not the vigilante billionaire. Who would want nettlesome bureaucratic rules and laws to get in the way of the caring bravery and ambition of the can-do animal spirit? Sociologists Mona Danner and Gay Young explain that '[t]he creed of "Davos Man" is that the key to allowing global markets to work naturally is to minimize state intervention',[77] unless, of course, that intervention is to the benefit of corporations. This conviction that the state's power needs to be restricted so that the benefits of capitalism can be realized is precisely the same unreflective neoliberal dogma that Morrison was evincing.

Danner and Young go on to explain that the Davos Man is part of a global elite that retains the masculine trait of control and domination, who achieves this, however, through the market mechanism and capital accumulation. For the Davos Man, whatever the problem, the liberated market is the solution. The Davos Men control the institutions of the global economy, institutions which are themselves masculine in character:

> These institutions ... are masculine in two senses: on the one hand, men (or, more precisely, a small number of elite, white, Western men) dominate these institutions, and their views and interests prevail; on the other hand, such institutions serve as sites where particular notions of masculinity are created, maintained and legitimated in the context of ongoing global processes. Global social institutions, then, are places in which a particular form of globally dominant masculinity is forged and exercised.[78]

This new form of masculinity retains the inherent patriarchy of its older variants coupling it with the core masculine values of individualism and competitiveness. The Davos Man is an 'action hero' strutting the world stage, solving wicked problems and profiting handsomely along the way. The Davos Man is powerful and in control.

The character of the Davos Man represents a moralization of capitalist wealth. In his book *Davos Man: How the Billionaires Devoured the World*,[79] Peter S. Goodman, the economics correspondent of *The New York Times*, chronicles how billionaire tycoons such as Amazon's Bezos, Blackstone Group's Stephen Schwarzman, Salesforce's Marc Benioff, JPMorganChase's Jamie Dimon and BlackRock's Larry Fink champion billionaire philanthropy and stakeholder capitalism as the solution to the world's social, environmental and economic woes, while never reneging on their commitment to building their own wealth and that of their shareholders. The billionaires have done this, Goodman avers, not just through business acumen or economic exploitation but by 'warping the workings of democracy'.[80] This has been achieved by the neoliberal con trick that insists against logic and facts that corporate and market deregulation coupled with tax cuts for corporations and the wealthy will lead to shared prosperity and social progress.[81] Davos Men can only save the world if they operate above the laws that have stymied progress in the past.

The Davos Man is not just a man of great wealth but is also one who proclaims his own moral superiority. This is how he differs from the rich elite of the past. Goodman explains that the Davos Man presents as a conscientious globalist who maintains that his personal success is a precondition for social progress. In Goodman's assessment, this renders him as 'a predator who attacks without restraint, perpetually intent on expanding his territory and seizing the nourishment of others, while protecting himself from reprisal by posing as a symbiotic friend to all'.[82]

That the Davos Man can cure the world's ills with his free market and high-tech solutions is a far too convenient narrative to drown out the realities of the inequalities he perpetuates. When Kenyan political activist Njoki Njehu went to Davos to protest against billionaires, what she experienced was:

> a gathering of elites looking to put a smiley face on the inequality crisis and the climate emergency. Off-camera, they network and make deals. On camera, they talk about the need to reverse climate change or the long-running

rise in global inequality, then finish their champagne and take their limo to their private jet back home.[83]

Adding to this, she also observed an absence of discussion of how tax reform and revitalized government might be part of any solution. The Davos Man alone was the solution rising above bureaucratic inefficiency with style, panache and determination. Njehu evinces a democratic alternative fuelled by public demand for justice. 'People are tired and angry from all of this hypocrisy, of billionaires and CEOs gathering in Davos to fight inequality in their name, when in reality, these same billionaires and CEOs directly cause their misery,'[84] she argues. The Davos Man is the problem, not the solution.

The growth of Davos is pretty much synchronous with the expansion of the number of billionaires in the world. What better a place to use the warm-sounding rhetoric of stakeholder capitalism to stake a claim for world power, leaving heads of state and politicians in the wake. In championing his self-gratifying morality, the enemy of the Davos Man is government regulation – nothing should interfere with exercising his manly freedom. This is the man who respects no bounds to the realization of his greatness and for whom the imposed limits of a regulated global economy are an obstacle for achieving not only his greatness but also his magnanimity.

Between Muskism's ideal of the self-styled billionaire superhero and the Davos Man's new breed of corporate saviourism, there is the myth of the vigilante billionaire. This is a myth that represents a very sophisticated way to simultaneously moralize extreme wealth and promote the value of a world increasingly ruled by billionaires and for billionaires. Amid all this, the democratic promise of equality is cast asunder. The vigilante billionaire is the rich man who, unsatisfied with mere wealth seeks power in extreme forms, ultimately wanting nothing less than to rule the world. If the myths of the good billionaire are not usurped maybe one day the billionaires will be the bosses of everything.

7

Reasons for Hope

In Turin in 1988, the great liberal philosopher Isaiah Berlin was awarded the first Senator Giovanni Agnelli International Prize 'for the ethical dimension in advanced societies'. To mark the occasion, Berlin delivered an address entitled 'The Pursuit of the Ideal',[1] in which he reflected on the political forces that had shaped the twentieth century. Chief among these forces, Berlin argued, were the 'ideological storms' that had led to 'totalitarian tyrannies of both right and left'. Whether it be the state socialisms of Joseph Stalin's USSR and Mao Zedong's People's Republic of China or the fascist dictatorships of Adolf Hitler's Germany and Benito Mussolini's Italy, extreme and uncompromising political positions had manifested in oppressive political autocracies dedicated to creating an ideal society.

For Berlin, state totalitarianism begins with the belief in a utopian image of the perfect society. Whether that society is the communist end of history presaged by a proletarian revolution or the righteous rule of a superior Aryan race, it starts with a desire for perfection and ends with the use of force to implement the ideal model in political practice. In each case, there lies an underlying belief that the leader knows what is best for everyone – they have access to the 'truth' in a manner that others do not. The mentality of the utopian dictator is described by Berlin as follows:

> Since I know the only true path to the ultimate solution
> of the problem of society, I know which way to drive
> the human caravan; and since you are ignorant of what
> I know, you cannot be allowed to have liberty of choice
> even within the narrowest limits, if the goal is to be

140

reached. You declare that a given policy will make you happier, or freer, or give you room to breathe; but I know that you are mistaken, I know what you need, what all men need; and if there is resistance based on ignorance or malevolence, then it must be broken and hundreds of thousands may have to perish to make millions happy for all time.[2]

The tragic outcome of the politics informed by such utopian hubris is a century that will be remembered for the death and suffering it produced in the revolutionary wars, gas chambers, genocidal massacres, political assassinations, gulags and concentration camps that were used in pursuit of some utopian ideal or other. Utopia never arrived, anywhere. To humanity's disgrace, the outcome was quite the opposite.

The beginning of the dominance of neoliberalism as a political, economic and social doctrine, including the opening of China and Russia to global economic markets, coincided with the time Berlin wrote his essay. In this new era, especially in liberal-democratic countries, the liberalism Berlin promoted was translated into reducing state intervention in people's lives, especially economic life. The mechanisms used to achieve this were tax reduction on corporations and individuals, the privatization of public corporations, market deregulation, removal of tariffs, weakening trade unions and lowering public spending. Along with these massive reforms, distrust in government and the valuing of freedom from state intrusion formed the central political justification of Western globalization. Despite promises to the contrary, a chief result of neoliberalism has been growing economic inequality whereby the spoils of economic growth accrued disparately to the wealthy few: the billionaires who have been the subject of this book.[3] If the extremities of state power marred the twentieth century, the twenty-first century has shaped up to be marred by the extremities of economic power, represented by the growing ranks of billionaires. Billionaires are a global phenomenon, skewed across the world between China, the United States, India, the United Kingdom, Germany and beyond.[4]

Berlin's vision of liberalism is very different from what has occurred through the neoliberal era. Contrary to Berlin's hopes, the economic injustice that has resulted from neoliberal reforms is an outcome akin to his concern that: '[b]oth liberty and equality are among the primary goals pursued by human beings through many centuries; but total liberty for wolves is death to the lambs'.[5] The situation today is one where billionaires behave like wolves, appropriating the world's wealth for themselves while others struggle, suffer or even die. The balance between freedom and equality is way off-kilter, with excessive freedom (especially freedom within the global economy) resulting in gross inequality. Berlin feared that the concentration of political power among dictator ideologues in the twentieth century was leading to the erosion of liberty. In the twenty-first century, the fear is that the concentrations of economic power among billionaires is leading to the erosion of even the hope of equality. This book illustrates how visibility of this shift in the locus of power has been obfuscated by the cultural valorization of the billionaires; the very people who both epitomize and reap the material benefits of the growing catastrophe of economic inequality.

The idea of this book was never to offer knock-out solutions to the vast global problem of billionaire wealth, global economic inequality or the anti-democratic exercise of power by the ultra-wealthy. To claim to be able to do so would fall victim to the same absurd heroic pretensions with which billionaires are so often portrayed and portray themselves. No self-assured messianic vigilante is going to appear to solve all the world's problems once and for all. So, what is to be done? Heed can be taken from Berlin by not looking for a single ideologically driven master plan to fix everything and deliver a real-life utopia in the here and now. History tells us that such a cure would be worse than the disease. The history of the twentieth century has shown that bending the world to meet the ideal imaginings of a single vision for the future is, at best, hubris. At worst, it is tyranny. This is a history that can be learned from. Making progress will not arrive on the heels of any single person devising a blueprint for a perfect world. If there is to be progress towards equality and if prosperity is to be more fairly shared, it will not come at the hands of a single know-it-all crusader who develops a master plan to save the world.

The promise of progress lies in fostering a shared political conviction and building consensus across differences, with people working together for new democratic possibilities where the wealth created in the world is put to work for the benefit of all of humanity rather than being stockpiled by the elite few. Progress entails ensuring that all people have access to opportunities to succeed, that markets are inclusive and competitive, that education and reskilling are available to all, that taxation systems are used to ensure fair economic distribution,[6] and that business serves society rather than the other way around. We are a long way from that when companies like Jeff Bezos' Amazon have more lobbyists in the US capital than the total number of US senators.[7] That is not reason to give up. Pursuing economic justice does not require a singular master plan that claims to provide the solution to the world's woes, once and forever. The ebb and flow of political progress comes from pragmatic coalitions working together across differences for the common good, making progress one step at a time. Political solidarity for the pursuit of equality is required if the sad legacy of neoliberalism and its billionaires is to be overcome. Fortunately, the collective work is alive and well across the globe, and this offers reasons for hope.

The date 17 September 2011 was pivotal. That was when, near Zuccotti Park in New York's Lower Manhattan, a group of protestors started what was intended to be a week-long 'sit-in' in Wall Street, in the heart of the Financial District. The location was carefully chosen; they were protesting the vast economic inequality created by a globally financialized US. The protestors communicated their case on the then young social media site Twitter, tweeting with the hashtag #OccupyWallStreet. News spread like wildfire, and Zuccotti Park ended up being not only occupied by thousands of people but also broadcast as headline news across the world. The New York Police arrested 200 protestors and forced the rest to vacate Zuccotti Park on 15 November, but the protest did not end there.[8]

The Wall Street protest struck a chord in the US, with more protests erupting in almost 100 different cities from Chicago to Houston, Austin, Tampa and San Francisco and beyond. The movement was soon global, with Occupy sites rising across Europe, Asia and Australasia. The driving slogan of the movement was 'we are the 99%', reflecting how the wealthiest of the world's people – the top 1 per cent – may be in control of the political and economic system but it is the vast democratic majority who has the rightful claim on that power.

US President Barack Obama expressed sympathy:

> I think it expresses the frustrations the American people
> feel, that we had the biggest financial crisis since the Great
> Depression, huge collateral damage all throughout the
> country … and yet you're still seeing some of the same
> folks who acted irresponsibly trying to fight efforts to
> crack down on the abusive practices that got us into this
> in the first place.[9]

The Wall Street protest lasted only 59 days, with most other protest
sites around the world closed down within a few months after that.
It is safe to say that Occupy yielded little direct political change
during the heady days of late 2011. The revolution that some hoped
it would spawn did not happen. Corporatocracy was not overthrown
and a new global era of social democracy did not dawn in the heat
of that moment.[10] The fact is that economic inequality got worse
in the years after the protests.

To suggest that Occupy failed, however, is wrong. Occupy was
not just a movement of disruption, it reset contemporary political
discourse when it comes to equality.[11] The bodies assembled in the
occupation of streets and squares across the world made a difference.
They were an embodied symbol of both the failure and the promise
of democracy. The slogan, 'we are the 99%', said it all. Activist Jamie
Kelsey–Fry captured it when he argued that:

> [Occupy] changed the dialogue, making it okay for
> anybody to say the economic system was corrupt or
> the bankers got bailed out and we got sold out. That
> no longer became something that the left wing says. Or
> people with degrees in politics. It became ordinary for
> people from all walks of life to be saying that.[12]

Through the Occupy movement, as the world was awakened to
the realities of inequality, the bogus lie of trickle–down economics
had been laid bare as a con trick by the rich and for the rich.
The movement did not end (or even improve) inequality, that is a
longer project, but it did put inequality on the political agenda and
it remains there still. City University of New York researchers Ruth

Milkman, Stephanie Luce and Penny Lewis describe Occupy as the 'midwife for a new generation of progressive political activists'. Left-wing politics enjoyed a resurgence, whether in the US through Senator Bernie Sanders or in the UK through former leader of the Labour Party, Jeremy Corbyn. Occupy was also the forerunner to other global social movements powered through social media and became the inspiration for new activists around the world.[13]

A significant legacy of the Occupy movement was that democratic socialist ideas that had become taboo since the fall of the Berlin Wall in 1989 re-entered mainstream political discourse, no longer dismissed as the whimsical pipe dreams of the 'loony left'. Unequal distribution of wealth, class struggle and the failures of capitalism got back on the agenda. In an era of neoliberal triumphalism, that was no small achievement. Nobel Prize-winning economist Joseph Stiglitz has argued that Occupy drew attention to the serious limits of corporate capitalism and how capitalist economies around the world were serving the interests of only a vast minority.[14]

In the US, the Fight for $15 Fair Wage movement started less than a year after the Zuccotti Park occupation. Their stated purpose is:

> We're changing the rules of the game to ensure ALL workers get the dignity and respect they deserve. For too long, rich CEOs and corporations have held all the power. It's time to hold them accountable.[15]

The $15 in the title is a reference to 200 fast-food workers stopping work to demand the right to unionize and to have their pay increased to US$15 per hour. That was in 2012, and today the movement is active in 300 cities across six continents. Fighting underpayments of low-wage workers, the movement has led to the minimum wage being increased to US$15 in 12 US states, benefiting 26 million workers. Commenting on their achievements, Service Employees International Union president Mary Kay Henry said, 'The key accomplishment was that the Fight for $15, which was led by black, brown and immigrant workers all across the country, taught all workers that when you join together you can make changes in your jobs and in your lives.'[16]

The Fight for $15 movement is also credited with inspiring a new wave of union activism and support, with post-Occupy millennial workers demanding better pay and conditions by exercising their right to organize in staunchly anti-union businesses such as Starbucks and Amazon. Political commentator Michael Levitin assesses that the Occupy movement was the starting point that:

> revived the labor movement … and reinvented activism, birthing a new culture of protest that put the fight for economic and social justice at the forefront of a generation. Far from a passing phenomenon, Occupy inaugurated an era of political change in which the demands of the majority continue to grow louder and more focused … they issued a singular demand that was all of the demands: Justice. Fairness. Equality.[17]

Occupy was an inspiration for the most effective political protests that followed it: #MeToo, Black Lives Matter and the 2017 Women's Marches against Trump all drew on the Occupy playbook.[18] It is safe to say that Occupy led to the creation of a new generation of politicized young people to a level that had not been seen since the 1960s. The realities of economic inequality and the promise of economic justice are central. Indeed, inequality is one of the major political issues today – it is a crisis and it is on the agenda. Recall, for example, US Congresswoman Ocasio-Cortez, strolling down the red carpet at the prestigious Met Gala at the Metropolitan Museum of Art's Costume Institute in New York City in 2021 wearing a glorious white dress emblazoned with red letters that read: 'tax the rich'.[19]

Ocasio-Cortez was referencing the 'tax the rich' movement, which has mounted a sustained, if not loosely coordinated, campaign to use progressive taxation to create a more equal distribution of wealth and income. In many ways, this is a movement to roll back the economic freedoms given to the rich through the neoliberal era. There is precedent. At the end of the Second World War, the maximum marginal income tax rate in the UK was 97.5 per cent. In the US, it was 94 per cent. By the mid-2020s, those rates had fallen to 45 per cent in the UK and 37 per cent in the US. Across all advanced democratic nations, top tax rates have fallen and inequality has increased. Comparing 1981 to 2019, the average maximum inheritance tax dropped from 51 to 37 per cent, with personal income tax down from 30 to 16 per cent. In the same period, the share of income commanded by the highest paid 10 per cent went from 33 to 40 per cent.[20] The rich never had it so good.

The call to combat inequality by using the tax system to distribute wealth and income more fairly has been issued loud and clear in recent years. Economist Thomas Piketty has been one of the most convincing and widely heard voices on this topic. In 2013, Piketty published *Le capital au XXIe siècle* in French,[21] with the English translation coming out the following year as *Capital in the Twenty-First Century*.[22] Across a sprawling 750 pages, Piketty provided a far-reaching explanation of economic inequality since the 1700s, focusing especially on Europe and the US. Inequality is caused by unfettered capitalism, Piketty concludes, and only through state intervention can the slide to greater and greater economic injustice be reversed. Without such intervention, democracy itself is in jeopardy of collapsing under the pressure of the runaway capitalism that has created today's new generation of billionaires. For this to be addressed, capitalism must be controlled by democracy and harnessed for shared prosperity. In Piketty's words:

> Capitalism and market forces are very powerful in producing wealth and innovation. But we need to ensure that these forces act in the common interest. We want capitalism and market forces to be the slave of democracy rather than the opposite. Market forces and capitalism by themselves aren't sufficient to ensure the common good and to limit the concentration of wealth at levels that are compatible with democratic ideals. We need to make sure that we use these forces in a way that's consistent with our common interests and, in particular, the interests of disadvantaged groups. Ultimately, that's a matter of political choices and political institutions.[23]

Piketty refers to the current economic system as 'patrimonial capitalism', where wealth is concentrated with the minority of the population and where this system reproduces itself through wealth inheritance across generations. Socially, this creates a new class system that divides the haves from the have-nots based on the unequal distribution of extreme wealth across generations. What should be done? If the goal is the preservation of democracy and the fairer distribution of wealth, Piketty argues that there needs to be a combination of investment in public education and the implementation of a progressive income tax and a new global wealth tax.[24] The intended result is an increase in the wealth held by the lower and middle classes both through earnings and economic redistribution. That is the only way, Piketty argues, that capitalism can serve the common good.

Despite being a lengthy, dense and scholarly book, *Capital in the Twenty-First Century* struck a chord in 2014. In the wake of Occupy Wall Street, public awareness about economic inequality was riding high. Piketty's book explained why this had happened and proposed how it could be fixed. The book leapt onto *The New York Times* Best Seller list, quickly climbing to the number one spot. Demand for the book was so high that Amazon sold out, leading Piketty's publisher, Harvard University Press, to rush to print more copies. They had not even contemplated the success of the book, vastly underestimating the public and political discontent over growing inequality. Suddenly Piketty was a celebrity economist, with an eager audience who wanted to listen to his message about how a fairer world was possible.[25] Politicians took heed, too. Piketty served as a special advisor to the Labour Party in the UK in 2015 and 2016.[26] He joined French presidential candidate Benoît Hamon's campaign team in 2017, on a platform of fighting inequality. Piketty's ideas directly informed US Senator Elizabeth Warren's progressive tax proposals in 2019.[27]

Across the world, the political lesson from Piketty's work was that the expansion of inequality across the globe was not inevitable. It is a political choice. The problem was that in the wake of the global neoliberal reforms ushered in from the 1980s, the liberal-democratic world had, deliberately or otherwise, chosen inequality. Economic inequality is not an accident of history, it is the direct result of decisions made through public policy and embedded in the zeitgeist that saw injustice as either acceptable, necessary or unavoidable.

The problem of inequality, as represented in extremity by the very existence of the billionaire class, is a political problem that, to date, the world's politicians have not had the will to address head on, although there are welcome signs of that changing. Joseph Stiglitz puts this down to poorly functioning democracies where wealth buys political influence to maintain the unequal status quo through tax policies favouring the wealthy. This is made even worse when members of the billionaire class control the media, with magnate Rupert Murdoch's media empire serving as a case in point of pushing the view that increasing taxes on the wealthy will inhibit economic growth.[28] Stiglitz explains that:

> With the right reforms, democracies can become more inclusive, more responsive to citizens, and less responsive to the corporations and rich individuals who currently hold the purse strings. But salvaging our politics also will require equally dramatic economic reforms. We can begin to enhance the wellbeing of all citizens fairly ... only when we leave neoliberal capitalism behind and do a much better job at creating the shared prosperity that we acclaim.[29]

The growing awareness of the unjust damage done by global inequality was made even more concrete in 2015, when the United Nations released its Sustainable Development Goals. Adopted by all member countries of the United Nations, these goals set out a 'call to action to end poverty, protect the planet and improve the lives and prospects of everyone, everywhere'.[30] Setting a deadline of 2030, the United Nations gave its member states 15 years to achieve the goals related to poverty, inequality, climate change, environmental degradation, peace and justice. The official declaration read:

> We are meeting at a time of immense challenges to sustainable development. Billions of our citizens continue to live in poverty and are denied a life of dignity. There are rising inequalities within and among countries. There are enormous disparities of opportunity, wealth and power ... We will seek to build strong economic foundations for all our countries. Sustained, inclusive and sustainable economic growth is essential for prosperity. This will only be possible if wealth is shared and income inequality is addressed.[31]

At the UN Summit in New York in September 2023, world leaders were called to account for the lack of progress in achieving the goal to end global inequality. Heads of states of the world's richest countries back-pedalled on their failures. German Chancellor Olaf Scholz admitted that 'the progress we wanted for the whole world in the fight against poverty and for better coexistence has become slower'. French Foreign Minister Catherine Colonna condemned Russia for exacerbating food shortages by blowing up Ukrainian grain stores. Her president, Emmanuel Macron, did not even show up to the gathering. Neither did British Prime Minister Rishi Sunak, China's Xi Jinping or Russia's Vladimir Putin.[32] The opening of the UN General Assembly's high-level meeting was an occasion for Secretary-General António Guterres to tell the world's leaders that 'we seem incapable of coming together to respond' to the existential crisis facing the planet.[33]

Earlier, in September 2023, a group of 300 economists, millionaires and politicians wrote a letter to the G20 Summit in Delhi, the G20 being a forum for economic cooperation among the world's 20 largest economies.[34] Bluntly titled 'G20 Leaders Must Tax Extreme Wealth', the letter implored G20 member states to increase taxes on the world's ultra-rich. It argued that the massive concentration of wealth among the world's richest people was threatening both political stability and human rights, blaming policy makers who had progressively reduced taxation rates for decades. The question was about political will:

> Our political choices allow ultra-wealthy individuals to continue to use tax shelters and enjoy preferential treatment to the extent that, in most countries in the world, they pay lower tax rates than ordinary people ... Across the world, people are desperate for change. Public polls in all G20 countries show overwhelming support for political action to curb inequality and tax extreme wealth.[35]

Oxfam has similarly called on the world's governments to curtail billionaire wealth and power. Oxfam advocates for 'breaking up monopolies, empowering workers by supporting living wages, unionization, and paid sick and family leave, taxing corporations and the superrich, and embracing public services'. By its estimation, a billionaire wealth tax could raise US$1.8 trillion per annum that could be invested in public services and climate change mitigations such that everyone could benefit from the wealth produced by the world.[36] The world's politicians have failed to make any significant commitment to addressing inequality that is suffered across the globe. Despite this, there is hope in the rising chorus of voices demanding changes that will remedy the realities of economic injustice. In the twenty-first century, the aftermath of the Occupy movement has witnessed a growing public demand to do just that. The failure of governments to take decisive action to solve the problems is palpable but the pressure to do so continues to grow. There are also counter-pressures to prevent action and the myths of the good billionaire that have been the subject of this book stand as a direct obstacle to the types of changes that people the world over support. The moralization of the billionaire class is the de facto moralization of inequality and vigilance is needed in combatting the injustice of that inequality if that is to be made right. If billionaires are thought of as righteous, heroic, generous and meritoriously deserving of their immense wealth, then there is no reason to change. A false lesson from believing these myths is that to be poor or destitute is one's own individual responsibility. Another false lesson is that if those with great wealth choose to use some of it to solve public problems, then others should be grateful for their magnanimity rather than critical of the system that produced it. Both lessons imply that forcing the fair distribution of wealth through economic policy and drastic reforms would seem downright immoral.

Using political means to address inequality is generally considered a policy position associated with those of a progressive or left-wing political persuasion. This is indeed the case with the examples of Jeremy Corbyn in the UK, Benoît Hamon in France and Bernie Sanders and Elizabeth Warren in the US, all demonstrating the political importance of equality. The issue is broader than the spectrum of political differences drawn between right and left, however. Billionaire power is political as much as it is economic, and the dangers testified to in this book are not just of the unequal distribution of wealth and income but also of a resurgent plutocracy. With plutocracy in ascendence, the very system of liberal-democratic government that enables political differences between left and right to exist in the first place might just fade away, replaced by a neofeudalism where the owners of the world's capital rule all. Some may be benevolent, some may not, but either way the world is at their mercy.

Does inequality matter? According to research done by the OECD,[37] not only has economic inequality been on the rise over the past 30 years but this has also been matched by stagnant or worsening social mobility. In this same period, people's concern about inequality has risen. The OECD suggests that 'reforms to reduce deep-seated economic inequalities in outcomes and opportunities require wide public support'. Following public support, policies can be developed and implemented to improve people's economic opportunities and to redistribute income and wealth. The answer to the problem of inequality is not to wait patiently for the billionaire class to exercise their good-hearted benevolence for the benefit of society. Inequality represented by billionaire excess is a political problem that needs a political solution. Around the world, despite growing awareness and concern about inequality, governments have been reluctant, in many cases stubbornly resistant, to engage in the redistributive and equality policies required to do anything about it.[38] Meanwhile, the problem is worsening.

In making a small contribution to addressing the growing political unease about the inequalities produced by neoliberalism, this book has sought to undermine the myths of the good billionaires. It is hoped that this is a contribution to the much larger political project of developing the political will to address inequality in the name of shared prosperity. That is the project, conducted in solidarity for justice and equality, that can instigate and achieve real reform. The continually growing awareness of the scourge of inequality and the obscenity of wealth concentration is cause for hope that things can change.

To imagine a future that overcomes the injustices of the present demands a politics of hope; not a utopian hope for a perfect future but the motivation that arises from a shared desire for things to be different, for them to be better. The growing awareness of, and activism against, the economic inequalities of which billionaires are an extreme symptom is a source of such collective hope. This is hope without naiveté, however, and certainly without the expectation that a saviour will arise from the mist to magically fix everything. The world has been on an accelerated trajectory of inequality for decades and the powerful forces of wealth that desire to keep it that way are significant and ubiquitous. Change is not easy, neither is hoping for change.

Blaming individual billionaires for the problem of inequality is easy and all too obvious. That gives them too much credit. Billionaires are a symptom of the problem, not the creators of it. The ability of particular individuals to accrue such obscene amounts of wealth is a result of them being able to exploit a political and economic system that has set the world up for economic injustice. Blaming individuals, no matter how arrogant, privileged or entitled they are is a distraction from the real task of changing the system that created them. Individual people come and go through the ebb and flow of life. It is systems that exist beyond any individual that have entrenched inequality and created a world where a vast minority of people hoard wealth and power.

The tragedy of the past 40 years of the neoliberal experiment has been the loss of faith in a collective project of progress towards shared prosperity and equality. Globalization from the West has not been about embracing a world where all can prosper. It has created a winner-takes-all system that prizes individual achievement. This has worked and the winners continue to take more and more of what the world's wealth can offer, casting the promise of democracy and equality asunder along the way. The salt in the wounds is that this system that is geared for the benefit of the few rather than the many presents itself as just and righteous, as if some people deserve the lavish excess of wealth at the expense of those who do not. Such are the myths of the good billionaire.

But the demand for change is also increasingly pervasive as a new generation emerges unwilling to accept the harsh realities and injustices of economic inequality. There are many parts to the solution, ranging from market reform, taxation policy, to public education. Above all of that is the need for a resurgent hope in the democratic promises of freedom, equality and solidarity. Unlike inequality itself, hope is not an existential reality, it is a political choice to believe that the condition of the world can and should be more just. Without an idea of a future that is better than the present there can be no renewed political imagination that will take action for progress.

Political hope is not an individual matter, its force emerges from solidarity across differences as people around the world realize that economic inequality is not only undesirable but that it is also not inevitable. Political choices made decades ago set the world on the current trajectory where billionaire power increasingly trumps popular will. Political choices are also what will alter that trajectory. The growing number of voices around the world calling for a new politics of equality are testament to the possibility that those choices can be made, if only the collective political will to do so continues to develop. Collective political will – the will of the people – is the centrepiece of democracy, both as a model of government and as a political ideal. So long as power continues to accrue to an increasingly large billionaire class, the world is on a road away from democracy, returning to the plutocracy and feudalism that deserves to be kept in the past. Being fooled by the myths of the good billionaire is fuel in the engine of this terrible journey.

Notes

Acknowledgements

[1] Rhodes, C. (2021) 'The AFR's 2021 Rich List shows we're not all in this together', *The Conversation*, [online] 28 May, Available from: https://theconversation.com/the-afrs-2021-rich-list-shows-were-not-all-in-this-together-161738.

[2] Rhodes, C. (2022) 'Is woke capitalism the new trickle-down economics?', *Common Dreams*, [online] 23 January, Available from: https://www.commondreams.org/views/2022/01/23/woke-capitalism-new-trickle-down-economics.

[3] Rhodes, C. (2022) 'Billionaire activism reveals the failure of Australian democracy', *Independent Australia*, [online] 25 February, Available from: https://independentaustralia.net/politics/politics-display/billionaire-activism-reveals-the-failure-of-australian-democracy,16087.

[4] Rhodes, C. (2022) 'Patagonia's radical business move is great – but governments, not billionaires, should be saving the planet', *The Guardian*, [online] 20 September, Available from: https://www.theguardian.com/commentisfree/2022/sep/20/patagonia-billion-dollar-climate-initiative-philanthropy.

[5] Clarke, P. and Rhodes, C. (2023) 'Is it ethical to be a billionaire?', ABC Radio, *Nightlife*, [online] 20 April, Available from: https://www.abc.net.au/radio/programs/nightlife/is-it-ethical-to-be-a-billionaire/102249938.

[6] Rhodes, C, Frank, N. and Friel, S. (2023) 'SavingTheWorld', Ep 5, Myths of the Good Billionaire, YouTube, [online], Available from: https://www.youtube.com/watch?v=Z5hIyYkYkf0.

Foreword

[1] Interview with Richard Edelman, in Bakan, J. (2020) *The New Corporation: How 'Good' Corporations Are Bad for Democracy*, London: Penguin Random House, p 116.

[2] Interview with Edelman, in Bakan, *The New Corporation*, pp 127–128.

[3] Bakan, *The New Corporation*; Bakan, J. (2004) *The Corporation: The Pathological Pursuit of Profit and Power*, Los Angeles, CA: Free Press.

[4] Slobodian, Q. (2018) *Globalists: The End of Empire and the Birth of Neoliberalism*, Cambridge: Cambridge University Press.

5   See Campbell, P.S. (2013) 'Democracy v. concentrated wealth: in search of a Louis D. Brandeis quote', 16 *Green Bag* 2D 251 (Spring), University of Louisville School of Law Legal Studies Research Paper Series No. 2014-11, [online], Available from: http://www.greenbag.org/v16n3/v16n3_articles_campbell.pdf.

6   See, for example, Slobodian, Q. (2018) 'Trump, populists and the rise of right-wing globalization', *The New York Times*, 22 October.

7   See Bakan, *The New Corporation*, pp 135–143.

Preface

1   Moreno, J.E. (2023) 'Elon Musk proposes "cage match" with Mark Zuckerberg', *The New York Times*, [online] 22 June, Available from: https://www.nytimes.com/2023/06/22/business/musk-zuckerberg-cage-match.html.

2   Carey, A. (2023) 'Mark Zuckerberg mocks Twitter owner Elon Musk with first tweet in 11 years', *news.com.au*, [online] 8 July, Available from: https://www.news.com.au/technology/online/social/mark-zuckerberg-mocks-twitter-owner-elon-musk-with-first-tweet-in-11-years/news-story/aef3efcb5f663c90c2388c73b4decbe8.

3   TMZ (2023) 'MARK ZUCKERBERG, ELON MUSK: ITALIAN GOVERNMENT OFFER ... Fight Like True Gladiators ... At The Colosseum!', [online] 29 June, Available from: https://www.tmz.com/2023/06/29/elon-musk-mark-zuckerberg-mma-fight-colosseum-rome-italian-government-dana-white-ufc/.

4   Musk, E. quoted in Milmo, D. (2022) 'How "free speech absolutist" Elon Musk would transform Twitter', *The Guardian*, [online] 14 April, Available from: https://www.theguardian.com/technology/2022/apr/14/how-free-speech-absolutist-elon-musk-would-transform-twitter.

5   Musk, E. quoted in Dean, G. (2022) 'Read the letter Elon Musk sent Twitter's chairman outlining his "best and final offer" to buy the company', *Business Insider*, [online] 14 April, Available from: https://www.businessinsider.com/read-elon-musk-takeover-offer-letter-twitter-chairman-bret-taylor-2022-4?r=US&IR=T.

6   Zuckerberg, M. in Wagner K. and Swisher, K. (2017) 'Read Mark Zuckerberg's full 6,000-word letter on Facebook's global ambitions', *Vox*, [online] 16 February, Available from: https://www.vox.com/2017/2/16/14640460/mark-zuckerberg-facebook-manifesto-letter.

7   Christensen, M.B., Hallum, C., Maitland, A., Parrinello, Q. and Putaturo, C. (2023) *Survival of the Richest: How We Must Tax the Super-Rich Now to Fight Inequality*, Oxford: Oxfam.

8   Riddell, R., Ahmed, N., Maitland, A., Lawson, M. and Taneja, A. (2024) *Inequality Inc.: How Corporate Power Divides Our World and the Need for a New Era of Public Action*, Oxford: Oxfam.

9   See, for example, Giridharadas, A. (2020) *Winners Take All: The Elite Charade of Changing the World*, New York, NY: Penguin; Mazzucato, M. (2018) *The Value of Everything: Making and Taking in the Global Economy*, New York, NY:

Public Affairs; and Stiglitz, J.E. (2020) *People, Power, and Profits: Progressive Capitalism for an Age of Discontent*, New York, NY: W.W. Norton.

10 Thatcher, M. (1975) 'Britain can win', *News of the World*, 22 September (emphasis added).

11 Reagan, R. (1983) 'Remarks at the National Conference of the National Federation of Independent Business', *Ronald Reagan Presidential Library and Museum* website, [online] 12 June, Available from: https://www. reaganlibrary.gov/archives/speech/remarks-national-conference-national-federation-independent-business (emphasis added).

12 Ostry, J.D., Loungani, P. and Furceri, D. (2016) 'Neoliberalism: oversold?', *Finance and Development*, 53(2): 38–41.

13 Chackraborty, A. (2016) 'You're witnessing the death of neoliberalism from within', *The Guardian*, [online] 31 May, Available from: https:// www.theguardian.com/commentisfree/2016/may/31/witnessing-death-neoliberalism-imf-economists.

14 Philp, C. quoted in Duggan, J., (2022) *iNews*, [online] 24 September, Available from: https://inews.co.uk/news/minister-denies-mini-budget-gamble-that-benefits-rich-hits-out-at-politics-of-envy-1876715.

15 UN (2023) 'Goal 10: reduce inequality within and among countries', *United Nations* website, [online] 9 July, Available from: https://www.un.org/sustainabledevelopment/inequality/.

16 Piketty. T. cited in Chancel, L., Piketty, T., Saez, E. and Zucman, G. (2021) *World Inequality Report 2022*. Paris: World Inequality Lab, p 234.

17 *Tax the Rich* website, [online], Available from: https://unrigoureconomy. com/campaigns/tax-the-rich/.

18 De Leo, A. (2024) 'The 15 best eat-the-rich movies, ranked', *Collider*, [online] 14 January, Available from: https://collider.com/the-menu-best-eat-the-rich-social-commentary-movies/.

19 Le Guin, U.K. (2014) 'Speech in acceptance of the National Book Foundation Medal for Distinguished Contribution to American Letters', *Ursula K. Le Guin* website, [online], Available from: https://www.ursulak leguin.com/nbf-medal.

Chapter 1

1 Gates, B. (2022) *How to Prevent the Next Pandemic*, New York, NY: Knopf.

2 Gates, *How to Prevent the Next Pandemic*, p 21.

3 Gates, B. (2021) *How to Avoid a Climate Disaster*, New York, NY: Knopf.

4 Hammond, A.C.R. (2020) 'Heroes of progress, pt. 50: Bill Gates', *Human Progress* website, [online] 5 August, Available from: https://www. humanprogress.org/heroes-of-progress-pt-50/.

5 BBC (2021) 'Bill and Melinda Gates Foundation: what is it and what does it do?', *BBC News*, [online] 4 May, Available from: https://www.bbc.com/news/world-us-canada-56979480.

6 Bill and Melinda Gates Foundation (2022) 'Homepage', *Bill and Melinda Gates Foundation* website, [online], Available from: https://www.gates foundation.org/ [Accessed 10 July 2022].

7 Luckerson, V. (2018) '"Crush them": an oral history of the lawsuit that upended Silicon Valley', *The Ringer*, [online] 18 May, Available from: https://www.theringer.com/tech/2018/5/18/17362452/microsoft-antitrust-lawsuit-netscape-internet-explorer-20-years.

8 Stoller, M. (2022) 'Microsoft brings a cannon to a knife fight', *BIG*, [online] 19 January, Available from: https://mattstoller.substack.com/p/microsoft-brings-a-cannon-to-a-knife?s=r.

9 CFI (2022) 'Microsoft Antitrust Case', *Corporate Finance Institute* website, [online] 25 February, Available from: https://corporatefinanceinstitute.com/resources/knowledge/strategy/microsoft-antitrust-case/.

10 Jackson, T.P. quoted in Stein, T. (1999) 'Microsoft ruled a monopoly / court finds firm abused its power', *SFGate*, [online] 6 November, Available from: https://www.sfgate.com/news/article/Microsoft-Ruled-a-Monopoly-Court-finds-firm-2899336.php.

11 Naughton, J. (2020) 'Let's not forget, Bill Gates hasn't always been the good guy ...', *The Guardian*, [online] 29 August, Available from: https://www.theguardian.com/commentisfree/2020/aug/29/lets-not-forget-bill-gates-hasnt-always-been-the-good-guy.

12 Hofman, M. (2015) 'Young Bill Gates was an angry office bully', *GQ*, [online] 28 October, Available from: https://www.gq.com/story/young-bill-gates-was-an-angry-office-bully.

13 Fox, E.J. (2016) 'Bill Gates admits he was a nightmare boss', *Vanity Fair*, [online] 1 February, Available from: https://www.vanityfair.com/news/2016/02/bill-gates-admits-he-was-a-nightmare-boss.

14 Carr, A. (2021) 'Bill Gates's carefully curated geek image unravels in two weeks', *Bloomberg*, [online] 21 May, Available from: https://www.bloomberg.com/news/articles/2021-05-21/bill-gates-s-carefully-curated-dad-geek-image-unravels-in-two-weeks#xj4y7vzkg.

15 Foley, S. (2011) 'Gates is a ruthless schemer, says his Microsoft co-founder', *The Independent*, [online] 31 March, Available from: https://www.independent.co.uk/tech/gates-is-a-ruthless-schemer-says-his-microsoft-cofounder-2257843.html.

16 Foley, 'Gates'.

17 Wayt, T. (2021) 'Bill Gates was an office bully who opposed diversity efforts, report claims', *New York Post*, [online] 29 June, Available from: https://nypost.com/2021/06/29/bill-gates-was-an-office-bully-who-opposed-diversity-efforts-report-claims/.

18 Klawe, M. cited in Bentley-York, J. (2021) '"Bully" Bill Gates shouted and swore at Microsoft staff and "thinks usual rules don't apply to him", insiders claim', *The US Sun*, [online] 30 June, Available from: https://www.the-sun.com/news/3187946/bill-gates-shouted-swore-staff-insiders-claim/#:~:text=BILL%20Gates%20has%20been%20branded,'t%20apply%20to%20him.%E2%80%9D.

19 Gates, B. quoted in Umoh, R. (2018) 'Early in his career, Bill Gates memorized the license plates of every employee to keep tabs on them', *CNBC Make It*, [online] 25 April, Available from: https://www.cnbc.

com/2018/04/25/bill-gates-memorized-microsoft-employees-license-plates-to-track-them.html.

20 Hofman, 'Young'.

21 Bentley-York, '"Bully"'.

22 Spolsky, J. (2006) 'My first BillG Review', *Joel on Software*, [online] 16 June, Available from: https://www.joelonsoftware.com/2006/06/16/my-first-billg-review/.

23 *The New York Times* (2020) 'Best sellers: hardcover non-fiction', [online] 7 March, Available from: https://www.nytimes.com/books/best-sellers/2021/03/07/hardcover-nonfiction/.

24 Gates, B. quoted in *BER* (2019) 'The merits and drawbacks of philanthrocapitalism', *Berkeley Economic Review*, [online] 14 March, Available from: https://econreview.berkeley.edu/the-merits-and-drawbacks-of-philanthrocapitalism/.

25 Maslow, A.H. (1966) *The Psychology of Science: A Reconnaissance*, South Bend, IN: Gateway Editions, p 16.

26 LaFranco, R., Chung, G. and Peterson-Withorn, C. (2024) 'Forbes World's Billionaires List: the richest in 2024', *Forbes*, [online], Available from: https://www.forbes.com/sites/chasewithorn/2024/04/02/forbes-worlds-billionaires-list-2024-the-top-200/ [Accessed 5 April 2024].

27 LaFranco, R. and Peterson-Withorn, C. (2023) 'Forbes World's Billionaires List: the richest in 2022', *Forbes*, [online], Available from: https://www.forbes.com/billionaires/ [Accessed 8 July 2023].

28 Gates, B. quoted in Huddleston Jr., T. (2022) 'Bill Gates plans to give away "virtually all" his $113 billion—here's the impact that could actually have', *CNBC*, [online] 15 July, Available from: https://www.cnbc.com/2022/07/15/bill-gates-plans-to-give-away-virtually-all-his-113-billion-fortune.html.

29 Huet, N. and Paun, C. (2017) 'Meet the world's most powerful doctor: Bill Gates', *Politico*, [online] 4 May, Available from: https://www.politico.eu/article/bill-gates-who-most-powerful-doctor/.

30 Curtis, M. (2016) *Gated Development – Is the Gates Foundation Always a Force for Good?*, London: Global Justice Now, p 10.

31 Reich, R.M. (2016) 'Repugnant to the whole idea of democracy? On the role of foundations in democratic societies', *PS: Political Science & Politics*, 49(3): 466–472.

32 Plato (375 BCE/1955) *The Republic*, London: Penguin.

33 James I (1609/2013) 'James I's Speech before Parliament March 21, 1609', in B. MacArthur (ed.), *The Penguin Book of Historical Speeches* [online], London: Penguin, n.p.

34 Cawthorn, D. (2017) *Philosophical Foundations of Leadership*, London: Routledge, pp 41–50.

35 Brown, W. (2015) *Undoing the Demos: Neoliberalism's Stealth Revolution*, New York, NY: Zone Books, pp 202–203.

36 Gates, B. quoted in Bae, H. (2015) 'Bill Gates' 40th anniversary email: goal was "a computer on every desk"', *CNN Business*, [online] 6 April, Available

from: https://money.cnn.com/2015/04/05/technology/bill-gates-email-microsoft-40-anniversary/.

37 TBS Report (2020) 'The ballad of Bill Gates' billions', *The Business Standard*, [online] 29 December, Available from: https://www.tbsnews.net/feature/wealth/ballad-bill-gates-billions-178171.

38 Bowman, A. (2012) 'The flip side to Bill Gates' charity billions', *New Internationalist*, [online] 1 April, Available from: https://newint.org/features/2012/04/01/bill-gates-charitable-giving-ethics.

39 Esmark, A. (2020) *The New Technocracy*, Bristol: Policy Press.

40 Jung, C.G. (1959) *The Archetypes of the Collective Unconscious*, London: Routledge.

41 Jung, *The Archetypes*, p 262.

42 Jung, *The Archetypes*, p 4.

43 Roesler, C. (2012) 'Are archetypes transmitted more by culture than biology? Questions arising from conceptualizations of the archetype', *Journal of Analytical Psychology*, 57(2): 223–246.

44 McGoey, L. (2016) *No Such Thing as a Free Gift: The Gates Foundation and the Price of Philanthropy*, London: Verso.

Chapter 2

1 Peterson-Withorn, C. (2024) 'Forbes' 38th Annual World's Billionaires List: facts and figures 2024', *Forbes*, [online] 2 April 2024, Available from: https://www.forbes.com/sites/chasewithorn/2024/04/02/forbes-38th-annual-worlds-billionaires-list-facts-and-figures-2024/?sh=7fc99a8843a6.

2 Forbes (2024) 'The world's real-time billionaires', *Forbes*, [online], Available from: https://www.forbes.com/real-time-billionaires [Accessed 7 April 2024].

3 Moskowitz, D. (2021) 'The 10 richest people in the world', *Investopedia*, [online] 8 December, Available from: https://www.investopedia.com/articles/investing/012715/5-richest-people-world.asp.

4 Niemietz, B. (2022) 'The 10 richest people added more than $400 billion to their worth in 2021', *Yahoo! News*, [online] 2 January, Available from: https://news.yahoo.com/10-richest-people-added-more-004800162.html.

5 Forbes (2023) 'Profile: Francoise Bettencourt Meyers & family', *Forbes*, [online], Available from: https://www.forbes.com/profile/francoise-bettencourt-meyers/?sh=5f8f1b092b06 [Accessed 9 November 2023].

6 Forbes (2024) 'Profile: Francoise Bettencourt Meyers & family', *Forbes*, [online], Available from: https://www.forbes.com/profile/francoise-bettencourt-meyers/?sh=6f56392c2b06 [Accessed 22 April 2024].

7 Forbes (2024) 'The world's real-time billionaires', *Forbes*, [online], Available from: https://www.forbes.com/real-time-billionaires/#6e8bfd673d78 [Accessed 8 April 2024].

8 Tribune News Service (2022) 'Wealth of world's 10 richest ballooned by US$402 billion in 2021', *South China Morning Post*, [online] 2 January, Available from: https://www.scmp.com/news/world/united-states-canada/article/3161831/wealth-worlds-10-richest-ballooned-us402-billion?utm_source=rss_feed.

9   Williams, E. (2024) 'Forbes: these are the world's 16 Black billionaires', *The Atlanta Journal – Constitution*, [online] 2 February, Available from: https://www.ajc.com/news/atlanta-black-history/who-are-the-black-billionaires/PRWODTCBXNHZLLSQTZOHU5Y3B4/.

10   Bloomberg (2022) 'Bloomberg Billionaires Index as at 13 January', *Bloomberg*, [online], Available from: https://www.bloomberg.com/billionaires/ [Accessed 14 January 2024]; Bloomberg (2023) 'Bloomberg Billionaires Index as at 9 November', *Bloomberg*, [online], Available from: https://www.bloomberg.com/billionaires/ [Accessed 9 November 2023].

11   Sandler, R. (2021) 'Inside the trillion dollar tech world', *Forbes*, [online] 10 November, Available from: https://www.forbes.com/sites/rachelsandler/2021/11/10/inside-the-trillion-dollar-tech-factory/?sh=6099e4e64a25.

12   Liu, P. (2024) 'Tech billionaires have added an astonishing $750 billion to their fortunes over the past year', *Forbes*, [online] 2 April, Available from: https://www.forbes.com/sites/phoebeliu/2024/04/02/tech-billionaires-have-added-an-astonishing-750-billion-to-their-fortunes-over-the-past-year/.

13   Popken, B. (2021) 'Elon Musk is now the richest man on the planet, overtaking Jeff Bezos', *NBC News*, [online] 7 January, Available from: https://www.nbcnews.com/business/business-news/elon-musk-now-richest-man-planet-overtaking-jeff-bezos-n1253280.

14   Dhiraj, A.B. (2021) 'French billionaire Bernard Arnault becomes the world's wealthiest man', *CEO World*, [online] 30 May, Available from: https://ceoworld.biz/2021/05/30/french-billionaire-bernard-arnault-becomes-the-worlds-wealthiest-man/.

15   Cai, K. (2021) 'Elon Musk is now the second richest person in the world', *Forbes*, [online] 20 August, Available from: https://www.forbes.com/sites/kenrickcai/2021/08/20/richest-person-in-world-elon-musk-jeff-bezos-bernard-arnault/.

16   Bloomberg (2023) 'Bloomberg Billionaires Index as at 9 November', *Bloomberg* [online], Available from: https://www.bloomberg.com/billionaires/ [Accessed 9 November 2023].

17   Jackson, J. (2021) 'Elon Musk trolls Jeff Bezos after surpassing him as world's richest person', *Newsweek*, [online] 29 September, Available from: https://www.newsweek.com/elon-musk-trolls-jeff-bezos-after-surpassing-him-worlds-richest-person-1633948

18   Staff Writer (2020) 'How long does it take to count to a billion?', *Reference* website, [online] 7 April, Available from: https://www.reference.com/world-view/long-count-billion-c1f1fc3ab57aebb.

19   EHD (2022) 'Grasping large numbers', *The Endowment for Human Development* website, [online], Available from: https://www.ehd.org/pdf/large%20numbers.pdf [Accessed 15 January 2022].

20   OECD (2023) 'Income', *OECD* website, [online], Available from: https://www.oecdbetterlifeindex.org/topics/income/ [Accessed 9 November 2023].

21   Dolan, K.A. (2021) 'Forbes' 35th Annual World's Billionaires List: facts and figures 2021', *Forbes*, [online] 6 April, Available from: https://www.forbes.

com/sites/kerryadolan/2021/04/06/forbes-35th-annual-worlds-billionaires-list-facts-and-figures-2021/?sh=6397c2c15e58.

22 LaFranco, R., Chung, G. and Peterson-Withorn, C. (2024) 'Forbes World's Billionaires List: the richest in 2022', *Forbes*, [online], Available from: https://www.forbes.com/sites/chasewithorn/2024/04/02/forbes-worlds-billionaires-list-2024-the-top-200/ [Accessed 5 April 2024].

23 Riddell, R., Ahmed, N., Maitland, A., Lawson, M. and Taneja, A. (2024) *Inequality Inc: How Corporate Power Divides Our World and the Need for a New Era of Public Action*, Oxford: Oxfam.

24 Salked, A. (2023) 'How long does it take tech CEOs to earn your salary?', *SimpleTexting* website, [online] updated 26 April, Available from: https://simpletexting.com/tech-ceo-salary/ [Accessed 9 November 2023].

25 Mushtaque, A. (2023) 'Average salary in each state in US', *Yahoo! Finance*, [online] 26 July, Available from: https://finance.yahoo.com/news/average-salary-state-us-152311356.html.

26 Office of National Statistics (2023) 'UK house price index: June 2023', *Office of National Statistics* website, [online] released 16 August, Available from: https://www.ons.gov.uk/economy/inflationandpriceindices/bulletins/housepriceindex/june2023.

27 Pringle, E. (2023) 'It takes a $650,000-a-year income to reach America's top 1%', *Forbes*, [online] 15 July, Available from: https://fortune.com/2023/07/14/what-salary-do-you-need-to-earn-to-be-in-top-1-percent-us-state-connecticut-new-york/.

28 Wealth-X (2022) 'About us', *Wealth-X* website, [online], Available from: https://www.wealthx.com/about-us/ [Accessed 16 January 2022].

29 Imberg, M., Shaban, M and Warburton, S. (2021) *Billionaire Census 2021*, New York, NY: Wealth-X.

30 Imberg, M., Shaban, M and Warburton, S. (2023) *Billionaire Census 2023*, New York, NY: Wealth-X.

31 Imberg, Shaban and Warburton, *Billionaire Census 2021*, p 10.

32 Imberg, Shaban and Warburton, *Billionaire Census 2021*, p 13.

33 Imberg, Shaban and Warburton, *Billionaire Census 2021*, p 20.

34 Ocasio-Cortez, A. in *Now This* (2020) 'AOC calls out billionaires at MLK day event', Twitter, [online] 24 January, Available from: https://twitter.com/nowthisnews/status/1220439307636355078.

35 Rhodes, C. and Bloom. P. (2016) 'Apple and Ireland are betting on "Nation Inc" and a world of shareholder citizens', *The Conversation*, [online] 6 September, Available from: https://theconversation.com/apple-and-ireland-are-betting-on-nation-inc-and-a-world-of-shareholder-citizens-64956.

36 Floyd, D. (2021) 'Explaining the Trump tax reform plan', *Investopedia*, [online] 28 September, Available from: https://www.investopedia.com/taxes/trumps-tax-reform-plan-explained/.

37 Trump, D. in Bryan, B. (2017) 'TRUMP: the GOP tax bill is "the rocket fuel our economy needs to soar higher than ever before"', *Business Insider Australia*, [online] 2 November, Available from: https://www.businessinsider.com/trump-gop-tax-plan-reform-bill-details-text-2017-11.

38 Ingraham, C. (2020) '"Trickle-down" tax cuts make the rich richer but are of no value to overall economy, study finds', *The Washington Post*, [online] 23 December, Available from: https://www.washingtonpost.com/business/2020/12/23/tax-cuts-rich-trickle-down/.

39 WSJ (2020) 'The 2017 tax cuts helped companies more than workers', *The Wall Street Journal*, [online] 29 May, Available from: https://www.wsj.com/articles/the-2017-tax-cuts-helped-companies-more-than-workers-11590778957.

40 Hope, D. and Limberg, J. (2020) 'Footing the COVID-19 bill: economic case for tax hike on wealthy', *The Conversation*, [online] 17 December, Available from: https://theconversation.com/footing-the-covid-19-bill-economic-case-for-tax-hike-on-wealthy-151945.

41 Burnette-McGrath, M. (2019) 'Reagan-era economic theory in the Tax Cuts and Jobs Act: trickle-down economics through increased international mobility of certain corporate income', *Florida State University Business Review*, 18: 57–80.

42 Reich, R. (2022) 'Why is trickle-down economics still with us?', *The Guardian*, [online] 10 October, Available from: https://www.theguardian.com/commentisfree/2022/oct/09/why-is-trickle-down-economics-still-with-us.

43 Quiggin, J. (2012) *Zombie Economics*, Princeton, NJ: Princeton University Press.

44 Fink, L. (2022) 'Larry Fink's 2022 letter to CEOs: the power of capitalism', *BlackRock*, [online] 17 January, Available from: https://www.blackrock.com/corporate/investor-relations/larry-fink-ceo-letter.

45 GlobeScan (2023) *Shifting the Narrative in a Polarized World: Analysis of Larry Fink's 11th Annual Letter to CEOs*, London: GlobeScan.

46 Rubio, M. (2021) 'Sen. Marco Rubio: here's how we fight the woke elites running corporate America', *Fox Business*, [online] 23 September, Available from: https://www.foxbusiness.com/politics/america-woke-corporations-sen-marco-rubio.

47 Ghosh, J. (2022) 'The biggest killer of pandemic times: inequality', *Social Europe*, [online] 24 January, Available from: https://www.socialeurope.eu/the-biggest-killer-of-pandemic-times-inequality.

48 Walsh, B. (2019) '"Billionaires should not exist": Bernie Sanders rolls out a plan for a wealth tax', *Barron's*, [online] 24 September, Available from: https://www.barrons.com/articles/billionaires-should-not-exist-bernie-sanders-rolls-out-a-plan-for-a-wealth-tax-51569343144.

49 Sanders, B. (2020) 'Sanders, colleagues introduce tax on billionaire wealth gains to provide health care for all', press release, *Bernie Sanders: US Senator for Vermont* website, [online] 6 August, Available from: https://www.sanders.senate.gov/press-releases/sanders-colleagues-introduce-tax-on-billionaire-wealth-gains-to-provide-health-care-for-all/#:~:text=The%20Make%20Billionaires%20Pay%20Act,million%20applied%20for%20unemployment%20insurance.

50 CNN *New York Times* Debate (2019) 'Sanders calls inequality a "moral and economic outrage"', *The New York Times*, [online] October, Available from: https://www.nytimes.com/video/us/politics/100000006770953/sanders-billionaires.html.

51 Taylor, C. (2023) 'Bernie Sanders calls for income over $1 billion to be taxed at 100%: "people can make it on $999 million"', *Fortune*, [online] 3 May, Available from: https://fortune.com/2023/05/02/bernie-sanders-billionaire-wealth-tax-100-percent/.

52 Russell-Moyle, L. (2019) 'I never expected to go viral just for saying billionaires shouldn't exist', *The Guardian*, [online] 2 November, Available from: https://www.theguardian.com/commentisfree/2019/nov/01/viral-billionaires-super-rich-exist.

53 Picchi, A. (2021) 'Elon Musk to Bernie Sanders after taxing the rich tweet: "I keep forgetting that you're still alive"', *CBS News*, [online] 15 November, Available from: https://www.cbsnews.com/news/elon-musk-bernie-sanders-tweet/.

54 SBS (2021) 'Jeff Bezos slammed after thanking Amazon workers for funding his space flight', *SBS News*, [online] 21 July, Available from: https://www.sbs.com.au/news/article/jeff-bezos-slammed-after-thanking-amazon-workers-for-funding-his-space-flight/busmwowlg.

55 Agarwal, M. (2021) '"You guys paid for all this": Jeff Bezos thanks employees for space trip, gets roasted', *Business Today*, [online] 22 July, Available from: https://www.businesstoday.in/trending/world/story/you-guys-paid-for-all-this-jeff-bezos-thanks-employees-for-space-trip-gets-roasted-302022-2021-07-22.

56 Sainato, M. (2021) '14-hour days and no bathroom breaks: Amazon's overworked delivery drivers', *The Guardian*, [online] 11 March, Available from: https://www.theguardian.com/technology/2021/mar/11/amazon-delivery-drivers-bathroom-breaks-unions.

57 Warren, E. quoted in Zahn, M. (2021) 'Bezos thanks Amazon customers who "paid" for space flight, sparking criticism from Sen. Warren and AOC', *Yahoo! Finance*, [online] 21 July, Available from: https://finance.yahoo.com/news/elizabeth-warren-attacks-amazon-taxes-bezos-space-flight-195411533.html.

58 Murphy, T. (2021) 'Jeff Bezos thanks Amazon workers and customers for making him so rich he can go to space', *Mother Jones*, [online] 20 July, Available from: https://www.motherjones.com/politics/2021/07/jeff-bezos-thanks-amazon-workers-and-customers-for-making-him-so-rich-he-can-go-to-space/?utm_source=twitter&utm_campaign=naytev&utm_medium=social.

59 Blue Origin (2024) 'Blue Origin's mission', *Blue Origin* website, [online], Available from: https://www.blueorigin.com/about-blue [Accessed 19 March 2024].

60 Jones, S. (2021) 'One giant leap for inequality: Jeff Bezos's space joyride is a spectacle of grotesque wealth', *Intelligencer*, [online] 20 July, Available from: https://nymag.com/intelligencer/2021/07/jeff-bezoss-space-trip-is-one-giant-leap-for-inequality.html.

[61] Wu, C. (2021) 'Amazon founder Jeff Bezos blasted after thanking employees for funding his billion-dollar space trip', *Sky News*, [online] 21 July, Available from: https://www.skynews.com.au/world-news/amazon-founder-jeff-bezos-blasted-for-thanking-employees-for-funding-his-billiondollar-space-trip/news-story/c3d30971f42567596999f8bef312ece6.

[62] Fernholz, T. (2018) 'Jeff Bezos explains how his space company will save civilization', *Quartz*, [online] 30 April, Available from: https://qz.com/1266038/jeff-bezos-explains-how-his-space-company-blue-origin-will-save-civilization.

[63] Hansen, S. (2021) 'Richest Americans—including Bezos, Musk and Buffett—paid federal income taxes equaling just 3.4% of $401 billion in new wealth, bombshell report shows', *Forbes*, [online] 8 June, Available from: https://www.forbes.com/sites/sarahhansen/2021/06/08/richest-americans-including-bezos-musk-and-buffett-paid-federal-income-taxes-equaling-just-34-of-401-billion-in-new-wealth-bombshell-report-shows/?sh=1a853fde7fe1.

[64] AAP (2022) 'Mike Cannon-Brookes pulls plug on AGL buy after sweetened takeover bid rejected', *SBS News*, [online] 7 March, Available from: https://www.sbs.com.au/news/article/mike-cannon-brookes-pulls-plug-on-agl-buy-after-sweetened-takeover-bid-rejected/rreo1ij41.

[65] AGL (2020) 'Climate statement and commitments', *AGL Energy* website, [online], Available from: https://www.agl.com.au/content/dam/digital/agl/documents/about-agl/who-we-are/our-company/230217-climate-statement-and-commitments.pdf [Accessed 3 May 2022].

[66] Toscana, N. (2022) 'Mike Cannon-Brookes lodges AGL takeover bid to "accelerate coal exit"', *Sydney Morning Herald*, [online] 20 February, Available from: https://www.smh.com.au/business/companies/brookfield-cannon-brookes-launch-bid-for-agl-to-accelerate-coal-exit-20220220-p59y25.html.

[67] Chanticleer (2022) 'Three megatrends collide in Cannon-Brookes, Brookfield's AGL bid', *The Australian Financial Review*, [online] 20 February, Available from: https://www.afr.com/chanticleer/three-megatrends-collide-in-cannon-brookes-brookfield-s-agl-bid-20220220-p59y33?utm_medium=social&utm_campaign=nc&utm_source=Twitter#Echobox=1645338905.

[68] Dewan, A. (2021) 'Australia is shaping up to be the villain of COP26 climate talks', *CNN World*, [online] 13 September, Available from: https://edition.cnn.com/2021/09/12/australia/australia-climate-cop26-cmd-intl/index.html.

[69] McKee, B. (2021) 'Extinction Rebellion protesters burn Australian flag, label nation a "climate pariah"', [online] 1 November, Available from: https://www.skynews.com.au/australia-news/extinction-rebellion-protesters-burn-australian-flag-label-nation-a-climate-pariah/news-story/bfd72a0f433d1bc0a28eefb02c932725.

[70] Kavita Naidu in Johnson, P. (2021) 'Australia labelled untrustworthy, a climate change "pariah" after stoush with French President, COP26', *ABC News*, [online] 5 November, Available from: https://www.abc.net.

au/news/2021-11-05/australia-morrison-criticised-cop26-coal-macron-stoush-qa/100596086.

71 Morton, A. (2022) 'Coalition spends $31m on ads spruiking efforts to cut greenhouse gas emissions', *The Guardian*, [online] 14 February, Available from: https://www.theguardian.com/media/2022/feb/14/coalition-spends-31m-on-ads-spruiking-efforts-to-cut-greenhouse-gas-emissions.

72 Mike Cannon-Brookes in Parkinson, G. (2018) 'Billionaire blows up again over Coalition's "fair dinkum" power slogan', *Renew Economy*, [online] 1 November, Available from: https://reneweconomy.com.au/billionaire-blows-up-again-over-coalitions-fair-dinkum-power-slogan-38220/.

73 Mike Cannon-Brookes in Kohler, A. (2022) 'Cannon-Brookes: AGL bid as much about software as energy', *Eureka Report*, [online] 24 February, Available from: https://www.eurekareport.com.au/investment-news/cannon-brookes-agl-bid-as-much-about-software-as-energy/151003.

74 Sheldrick, M. (2021) 'Will activist tech billionaires be the superheroes the world needs in the post-Covid world?', *Forbes*, [online] 22 January, Available from: https://www.forbes.com/sites/globalcitizen/2021/01/22/will-activist-tech-billionaires-be-the-superheroes-the-world-needs-in-the-post-covid-world/?sh=606b6faf7526.

75 Johnson, S. (2020) 'Tech giant worth $50 BILLION pays NO Australian tax but says that's fair because of its spending on research – while founder's help for bushfire victims could also turn a profit', *The Daily Mail*, [online] 24 February, Available from: https://www.dailymail.co.uk/news/article-8036277/Atlassian-paid-no-income-tax-despite-making-1billion-one-year.html.

76 Chanthadavong, A. (2020) 'ATO reports IBM continued to avoid paying tax during 2019 financial year', *ZD Net*, [online] 11 December, Available from: https://www.zdnet.com/article/ato-reports-ibm-continued-to-avoid-paying-tax-during-2019-financial-year/#:~:text=The%20company's%20tax%20bill%20came,domiciled%20in%20London%2C%20not%20Australia.

77 Aston, J. (2020) 'Mike Cannon-Brookes doesn't merit being listened to', *The Australian Financial Review*, [online] 23 February, Available from: https://www.afr.com/rear-window/mike-cannon-brookes-doesn-t-merit-being-listened-to-20200223-p543in.

78 Forbes (2024) 'Mike Cannon-Brookes', *Forbes Profile*, [online], Available from: https://www.forbes.com/profile/mike-cannon-brookes/?sh=773040827fd4 [Accessed 22 April 2024].

79 Dunham, W. (2019) 'Billionaire industrialist and conservative donor David Koch dies at age 79', *Reuters*, [online] 23 August. Available from: https://www.reuters.com/article/us-people-david-koch-idUKKCN1VD1D6.

80 Jones, S. (2019) 'David Koch's monstrous legacy', *Intelligencer*, [online] 23 August, Available from: https://nymag.com/intelligencer/2019/08/david-kochs-monstrous-legacy.html.

81 Mayer, J. (2017) *Dark Money: The Hidden History of the Billionaires Behind the Rise of the Radical Right*, Palatine, IL: Anchor Books.

82 Page, B.I., Seawright, J. and Lacombe, M.J. (2018) *Billionaires and Stealth Politics*, Chicago, IL: University of Chicago Press.

83 Hiltzik, M. (2021) 'These 63 billionaires supported Trump, showing the necessity of a wealth tax', *The Los Angeles Times*, [online] 15 January, Available from: https://www.latimes.com/business/story/2021-01-15/u-s-billionaires-trump-presidency.

84 Dawsey, J., Stein, J., Scherer, M. and Dwoskin, E. (2024) 'Many GOP billionaires balked at Jan. 6. They're coming back to Trump', *The Washington Post*, [online] 30 March, Available from: https://www.msn.com/en-us/news/politics/many-gop-billionaires-balked-at-jan-6-they-re-coming-back-to-trump/ar-BB1kKamg.

85 Schouten, F. (2024) 'Republican billionaires rally around Trump for April fundraiser as election – and scramble for cash – heats up', *CNN*, [online] 19 March, Available from: https://edition.cnn.com/2024/03/19/politics/republican-billionaires-trump-fundraiser/index.html.

86 Freedom Foundation (2022) 'You can make a difference', *Freedom Foundation* website, [online], Available from: https://www.freedomfoundation.com/ [Accessed 5 May 2023].

87 Bloomberg (2018) 'Group funded by conservative billionaires launches anti-union campaign following Supreme Court ruling', *The Los Angeles Times*, [online] 28 June Available from: https://www.latimes.com/business/la-fi-freedom-foundation-20180628-story.html.

88 D'Angelo, C. (2019) 'Pro-Trump billionaires continue to bankroll climate denial', *HuffPost*, [online] 27 February, Available from: https://www.huffpost.com/entry/mercers-trump-climate-denial_n_5c76b643e4b0031d9564572e.

89 CO2 Coalition (2023) 'Providing the facts about CO2 and climate change', *CO2 Coalition* website, [online], Available from: https://co2coalition.org/ [Accessed 20 November 2023].

90 Brulle, R.J., Hall, G., Loy, L. and Schell-Smith, K. (2021) 'Obstructing action: foundation funding and US climate change counter-movement organizations', *Climactic Change*, 166(17): 1–7.

91 Horton, H. and Bychawski, A. (2022) 'Climate sceptic thinktank received funding from fossil fuel interests', *The Guardian*, [online] 4 May, Available from: https://www.theguardian.com/environment/2022/may/04/climate-sceptic-thinktank-received-funding-from-fossil-fuel-interests.

92 Kroll, A. (2013) 'Exposed: the dark-money ATM of the Conservative movement', *Mother Jones*, [online] 5 February, Available from: https://www.motherjones.com/politics/2013/02/donors-trust-donor-capital-fund-dark-money-koch-bradley-devos/.

93 Dean, J. (2020) 'Neofeudalism: the end of capitalism?', *Los Angeles Review of Books*, [online] 12 May, Available from: https://lareviewofbooks.org/article/neofeudalism-the-end-of-capitalism/.

Chapter 3

1   Discovery Channel (2002) 'Glenn Stearns', *Discovery Channel* website, [online], Available from: https://www.discovery.com/profiles/glenn-stearns---undercover-billionaire [Accessed 20 June 2022].

2   Zippia (2022) 'Stearns lending company history timeline', *Zippia* website, [online], Available from: https://www.zippia.com/stearns-lending-careers-39638/history/ [Accessed 14 October 2022].

3   Horatio Alger Association (2022) 'Who we are', *Horatio Alger Association* website, [online], Available from: https://horatioalger.org/about-us/history-of-horatio-alger-association/ [Accessed 20 June 2022].

4   Glennstearns.com (2022) 'An investment in America's futures', *Glenn Stearns* website, [online], Available from: https://www.glennstearns.com/philanthropist/horatio-alger [Accessed 20 June 2022].

5   Discovery Channel (2020) '*Discovery* announces second season of "Undercover Billionaire" with three business tycoons vying to make a million-dollar company in just 90 days', *The Futon Critic* website, [online] 19 November, Available from: http://www.thefutoncritic.com/news/2020/11/19/discovery-announces-second-season-of-undercover-billionaire-with-three-business-tycoons-vying-to-make-a-million-dollar-company-in-just-90-days-239014/20201119discovery01/.

6   Adams, J.T. (1931) *The Epic of America*, Boston, MA: Little Brown and Company.

7   Adams, *The Epic of America*, p xix.

8   Adams, *The Epic of America*, p 410.

9   Adams, *The Epic of America*, p xx.

10 Adams, *The Epic of America*, p 415.

11 Adams, *The Epic of America*, p 414.

12 Columbia Business School (2022) 'Leon G. Cooperman '67', *Columbia Business School* website, [online], Available from: https://business.columbia.edu/board-emeriti/people/leon-g-cooperman-67 [Accessed 16 December 2022].

13 Fox, M. (2020) 'Billionaire Leon Cooperman started with nothing: "I had negative net worth"', *CNBC*, [online] 4 November, Available from: https://www.cnbc.com/2020/11/04/billionaire-leon-cooperman-started-with-nothing-i-had-negative-net-worth.html.

14 Forbes (2022) 'Leon G. Cooperman', *Forbes Magazine*, [online], Available from: https://www.forbes.com/profile/leon-g-cooperman/?sh=4f204e9c18f7 [Accessed 5 April 2024].

15 Cooperman, L.G. quoted in Saslow, E. (2022) 'The moral calculations of a billionaire', *The Washington Post*, [online] 30 January, Available from: https://www.washingtonpost.com/nation/2022/01/30/moral-calculations-billionaire/.

16 Smith, A. (1776/1982) *The Wealth of Nations: Books I–III*, London Penguin; and Smith, A. (1776/1999) *The Wealth of Nations: Books IV–V*, London Penguin.

17 Rasmussen, D.C. (2016) 'The problem with inequality, according to Adam Smith', *The Atlantic*, [online] 9 June, Available from: https://www.theatlantic.com/business/archive/2016/06/the-problem-with-inequality-according-to-adam-smith/486071/.

18 Rasmussen, 'The problem'.

19 Smith, *The Wealth of Nations: Books I–III*, p 512.

20 Breuninger, K. (2018) 'Trump claimed he turned a "small" $1 million loan from his father into an empire, *The New York Times* says it was more like $60.7 million in loans', *CNBC*, [online] 2 October, Available from: https://www.cnbc.com/2018/10/02/trumps-small-loan-from-his-father-was-more-like-60point7-million-nyt.html.

21 Alexander, D. (2024) 'Here's how much Donald Trump is worth', *Forbes*, [online] 5 April, Available from: https://www.forbes.com/sites/danalexander/article/the-definitive-networth-of-donaldtrump/?sh=54cc70102a8e.

22 Cillizza, C. (2018) 'The creation myth of the billionaire businessman Donald Trump just imploded', *CNN Politics*, [online] 3 October, Available from: https://edition.cnn.com/2018/10/03/politics/donald-trump-taxes-fred-trump/index.html.

23 Trump, D. quoted in Washington Post Staff (2015) 'Full text: Donald Trump announces a presidential bid', *The Washington Post*, [online] 16 June, Available from: https://www.washingtonpost.com/news/post-politics/wp/2015/06/16/full-text-donald-trump-announces-a-presidential-bid/.

24 King Jr., M.L. (1960/1985) 'The Negro and the American dream', Excerpt from Address at the Annual Freedom Mass Meeting of the North Carolina State Conference of Branches of the NAACP, in C. Carson, T. Armstrong, S. Carson, A. Clay and K. Taylor (eds), *The Martin Luther King, Jr. Papers Project: Volume V: Threshold of a New Decade, January 1959–December 1960*, Berkeley, CA: University of California Press, p 508.

25 King Jr., M.L. (1963/2003) 'I have a dream', Address at March on Washington for Jobs and Freedom, in C. Carson and K. Shepard (eds), *A Call to Conscience: The Landmark Speeches of Martin Luther King, Jr.*, New York, NY: Harper, pp 75–88.

26 Beach, J.M. (2007) 'The ideology of the American dream: two competing philosophies in education, 1776–2006', *Educational Studies*, 41(2): 148–164.

27 Whiting, K. (2022) 'Oxfam: this is what inequality looks like in 2022 – and 6 ways to solve it', *Oxfam* website, [online] 17 January, Available from: https://www.weforum.org/agenda/2022/01/inequality-in-2022-oxfam-report/.

28 Fukuyama, F. (1989) 'The end of history?', *The National Interest*, 16: 3–28, p 3.

29 Thatcher, M. (1985) 'Speech to Conservative Party Conference 11 October 1985', *Margaret Thatcher Foundation* website, [online], Available from: https://www.margaretthatcher.org/document/106145.

30 Thatcher, M. quoted in Sotheby's (2019) 'The man whose powerful critique of socialism influenced Margaret Thatcher', *Sotheby's* website, [online]

12 March, Available from: https://www.sothebys.com/en/articles/this-is-what-we-believe-margaret-thatcher-and-f-a-hayek.

31 Beichman, A. (1974) 'The Conservative Research Department: the care and feeding of future British political elites', *Journal of British Studies*, 13(2): 92–113.

32 Hayek, F.A. (1960) *The Constitution of Liberty*, London: Routledge.

33 Thatcher, M. quoted in Eagle, A. and Ahmed, I. (2018) *The New Serfdom: The Triumph of Conservative Ideas and How to Defeat Them*, London: Biteback.

34 Thatcher, M. (1980) 'Speech to Conservative Women's Conference', *The Thatcher Foundation* website, [online] 21 May, Available from: https://www.margaretthatcher.org/document/104368.

35 Hayek, *The Constitution*.

36 Thatcher, M. (1977) 'Speech to Zurich Economic Society ("The New Renaissance")', *Margaret Thatcher Foundation* website, [online] 14 March, Available from: https://www.margaretthatcher.org/document/103336.

37 Reiff, M.R. (2021) 'Can liberal capitalism survive?', *The GCAS Review*, 1(1): 1–46.

38 Hayek, *The Constitution*, p 39.

39 Jefferies, T. (2015) 'What happened to Thatcher's share ownership dream? It's nowhere near as common as the ex-Tory PM hoped 30 years ago – but does it matter?', *This Is Money* website, [online] 9 October, Available from: https://www.thisismoney.co.uk/money/investing/article-3265284/What-happened-Margaret-Thatcher-s-share-ownership-dream.html.

40 Brewer, M. and Wernham, T. (2022) 'Income and wealth inequality explained in 5 charts', *IFS* website, [online] 9 November, Available from: https://ifs.org.uk/articles/income-and-wealth-inequality-explained-5-charts.

41 Stiglitz, J.E. (2008) 'Is there a post-Washington Consensus consensus?', in N. Serra and J. Stiglitz (eds), *The Washington Consensus Reconsidered: Towards a New Global Governance*, New York, NY: Oxford University Press, pp 41–56.

42 Babb, S. and Kentikelenis, A. (2021) 'People have long predicted the collapse of the Washington Consensus. It keeps reappearing under new guises', *The Washington Post*, [online] 16 April, Available from: https://www.washingtonpost.com/politics/2021/04/16/people-have-long-predicted-collapse-washington-consensus-it-keeps-reappearing-under-new-guises/.

43 Pilotta, J.J. (2016) 'The entrepreneur as hero?', in V. Berdayes and J.W. Murphy (eds), *Neoliberalism, Economic Radicalism, and the Normalization of Violence*, Copenhagen: Springer, pp 37–52.

44 Olen, H. (2022) 'Let's put the myth of the billionaire genius to rest', *The Washington Post*, [online] 11 November, Available from: https://www.washingtonpost.com/opinions/2022/11/11/billionaire-worship-crypto-bankman-fried-musk/.

45 Spencer, H. (1866/1910) *The Principles of Biology*, New York, NY: D. Appleton and Co.

46 Spencer, *The Principles*, p 531.

47 Spencer, H. quoted in Wiltshire, D. (1978) *The Social and Political Thought of Herbert Spencer*, Oxford: Oxford University Press, p 197.

48 Carnegie, A. quoted in Wall, J.F. (1970) *Andrew Carnegie*, Oxford: Oxford University Press, p 381.

49 O'Connell, J. and Ruse, M. (2021) *Social Darwinism*, Cambridge: Cambridge University Press.

50 Carnegie, A. (1889) 'Wealth', *The North American Review*, 148(391): 653–664, 655.

51 Kasiyarno (2014) 'American dream: the American Hegemonic culture and its implications to the world', *Humaniora*, 26(1): 13–21.

52 Scorza, J. (2014) 'Global education and the "American dream"', *University World News*, [online] 30 May, Available from: https://www.universityworldnews.com/post.php?story=20140529110744340.

53 Goldberg, J. (2020) 'Trump: Americans who died in war are "losers" and "suckers"', *The Atlantic*, [online] 4 September, Available from: https://www.theatlantic.com/politics/archive/2020/09/trump-americans-who-died-at-war-are-losers-and-suckers/615997/.

54 Steverman, B. (2022) 'Tax-free inheritances fuel America's new $73 trillion gilded age', *Bloomberg*, [online] 3 February, Available from: https://www.bloomberg.com/news/articles/2022-02-02/what-the-73-trillion-great-wealth-transfer-means-for-america-s-super-rich.

55 Sandler, R. (2021) 'The Forbes 400 Self-Made Score 2021: from silver spooners to bootstrappers', *Forbes*, [online] 5 October, Available from: https://www.forbes.com/sites/rachelsandler/2021/10/05/the-forbes-400-self-made-score-2021-from-silver-spooners-to-bootstrappers/?sh=3b5ebad30c2a.

56 Reich, R. (2022) 'Poverty shaming: why the ultra-wealthy perpetuate the rags-to-riches myth of being "self-made"', *Milwaukee Independent*, [online] 22 September, Available from: https://www.milwaukeeindependent.com/robert-reich/poverty-shaming-ultra-wealthy-perpetuate-rags-riches-myth-self-made/.

57 Reich, R. [@RBReich] (2022) 'The truth behind "self-made" billionaires', [tweet], Twitter, 21 September, Available from: https://twitter.com/rbreich/status/1572299871364976641.

58 Reich, 'The truth'.

59 Musk, E. [@elonmusk] (2022) 'You both an idiot and a liar', [tweet], Twitter, 21 September, Available from: https://twitter.com/elonmusk/status/1572414455681814528.

60 Musk, E. [@elonmusk] (2019) 'He didn't own an emerald mine' [tweet], Twitter, 29 December, Available from: https://twitter.com/elonmusk/status/1211054942192119808.

61 Musk, E. [@elonmusk] 2019) 'This is a pretty awful lie', [tweet], Twitter, 29 December, Available from: https://twitter.com/elonmusk/status/1211071324518531072?lang=en.

62 Clay, H. cited in Paul, H. (2014) *The Myths That Made America*, Bielefeld: transcript Verlag, p 369.

63 Paul, *The Myths*, p 379

64 Paul, *The Myths*, p 395.

65 Nemmers, A. (2022) "'Pay no attention ...'": the self-made man, his fairy godfather, and American meritocracy', *The Journal of American Culture*, 45(2): 198–211.

66 Forbes (2024) 'Profile of Amancio Ortega', *Forbes*, [online], Available from: https://www.forbes.com/profile/amancio-ortega/?sh=6c5311a7116cc [Accessed 22 April 2024].

67 Forbes (2023) 'Profile of Karl Albrecht', *Forbes*, [online], Available from: https://www.forbes.com/profile/karl-albrecht/?sh=6595744ba325 [Accessed 11 July 2023].

68 Forbes (2024) 'Profile of Zhong Huijuan', *Forbes*, [online], Available from: https://www.forbes.com/profile/zhong-huijuan/?sh=67b6c6f0281e [Accessed 22 April 2024].

69 Picchi, A. (2022) 'The world's wealthiest person: how did Elon Musk get so rich?', *CBS News*, [online] 30 September, Available from: https://www.cbsnews.com/news/elon-musk-net-worth-how-did-elon-musk-get-so-rich/.

70 Friedman, M. (1970) 'The social responsibility of business is to increase its profits', *New York Times*, 13 September.

71 Stiglitz, J.E. (2019) 'Is stakeholder capitalism really back?', *Project Syndicate*, [online] 27 August, Available from: https://www.project-syndicate.org/commentary/how-sincere-is-business-roundtable-embrace-of-stakeholder-capitalism-by-joseph-e-stiglitz-2019-08.

72 McNair, K. (2023) 'New bill in Congress would give U.S. teachers a $60,000 minimum wage—these 5 states currently pay teachers best', *CNBC*, [online] 16 March, Available from: https://www.cnbc.com/2023/03/16/best-and-worst-paying-states-for-teachers.html.

73 Wieczner, J. (2018) 'How Tesla's Elon Musk could become the world's richest person without ever getting a paycheck', *Fortune*, [online] 24 January, Available from: https://fortune.com/2018/01/23/tesla-elon-musk-worth-world-richest/.

74 Christophers, B. (2022) *Rentier Capitalism: Who Owns the Economy, and Who Pays for It?*, London: Verso Books.

75 Kalmowitz, A. (2022) 'Tesla will not pay any federal taxes this year despite record profits, stock price', *Jaopnik*, [online] 14 February, Available from: https://jalopnik.com/tesla-will-not-pay-any-federal-taxes-this-year-despite-1848534111?utm_source=twitter&utm_medium=SocialMarketing&utm_campaign=dlvrit&utm_content=jalopnik.

76 Hirsch, J. (2015) 'Elon Musk's growing empire is fueled by $4.9 billion in government subsidies', *Los Angeles Times*, [online] 30 May, Available from: https://www.latimes.com/business/la-fi-hy-musk-subsidies-20150531-story.html.

Chapter 4

1 Huyssen, D. (2019) 'We won't get out of the Second Gilded Age the way we got out of the first', *Vox*, [online] 1 April, Available from: https://www.vox.com/first-person/2019/4/1/18286084/gilded-age-income-inequality-robber-baron.

2 Callahan, D. (2017) *The Givers: Wealth, Power, and Philanthropy in a New Gilded Age*, New York, NY: Vintage.

3 George, H. (1879) *Progress and Poverty*, Vol. 1, New York, NY: D. Appleton and Co., p 7.

4 Clarke, G. (2019) 'The new global governors: globalization, civil society, and the rise of private philanthropic foundations', *Journal of Civil Society*, 15(3): 197–213.

5 Altrata (2022) 'Global philanthropy trends of ultra high net worth individuals', *Altrata* website, [online] 29 November, Available from: https://altrata.com/articles/global-philanthropy-trends-of-ultra-high-net-worth-individuals.

6 Kaltmeier, O. (2019) 'Invidious comparison and the new global leisure class: on the refeudalization of consumption in the Old and New Gilded Age'. *Forum for Inter-American Research*, 12(1): 9–42.

7 Di Mento, M. (2024) 'Philanthropy 50', *The Chronicle of Philanthropy*, [online] 4 March, Available from: https://www.philanthropy.com/article/the-philanthropy-50/#id=browse_2023.

8 Forbes Wealth Team (2022) 'From Warren Buffett to newcomer Jeff Bezos, the nation's most generous billionaires have given away a collective $169 billion in their lifetimes—and are still richer than ever', *Forbes*, [online] 19 January, Available from: https://www.forbes.com/sites/forbeswealthteam/2022/01/19/americas-top-givers-2022-the-25-most-philanthropic-billionaires/?sh=764e4d9b3a6c.

9 Watson, R.W. (2022) 'Asia's 2022 heroes of philanthropy', *Forbes*, [online] 5 December, Available from: https://www.forbes.com/sites/ranawehbe/2022/12/05/asias-2022-heroes-of-philanthropy/.

10 Business Desk (2022) 'Gautam Adani becomes 5th richest person in the world; know his net worth', *News 18*, [online] 25 April, Available from: https://www.news18.com/news/business/gautam-adani-becomes-5th-richest-person-in-the-world-know-his-net-worth-5048701.html.

11 Watson, 'Asia's 2022 heroes'.

12 Perkins, M. and Obrecht, C. (2023) 'Pledge letter', *Giving Pledge* website, [online], Available from: https://givingpledge.org/pledger?pledgerId=427 [Accessed 31 July 2023].

13 Watson, 'Asia's 2022 heroes'.

14 Collins, C., Flannery, H., Ocampo, O. and Thomhave, K. (2020) *The Giving Pledge at 10: A Case Study in Top Heavy Philanthropy*, An IPS Inequality Briefing Paper, Washington, DC: Institute for Policy Studies.

15 The Giving Pledge (2023) 'A commitment to philanthropy', *The Giving Pledge* website, [online], Available from: https://givingpledge.org/ [Accessed 31 July 2023].

16 Bekiempis, V. (2022) 'Bill Gates pledges to donate "virtually all" of $113bn fortune to his foundation', *The Guardian*, [online] 16 July, Available from: https://www.theguardian.com/us-news/2022/jul/15/bill-gates-billions-fotune-donate-foundation.

17 Bill and Melinda Gates Foundation (2024) 'Foundation fact sheet', *Bill and Melinda Gates Foundation* website, [online], Available from: https://www.gatesfoundation.org/about/foundation-fact-sheet [Accessed 22 April 2024].

18 Collins, Flannery, Ocampo and Thomhave, *The Giving Pledge at 10*.

19 Collins, Flannery, Ocampo and Thomhave, *The Giving Pledge at 10*.

20 McCormick, E. (2022) 'Patagonia's billionaire owner gives away company to fight climate crisis', *The Guardian*, [online] 15 September, Available from: https://www.theguardian.com/us-news/2022/sep/14/patagonias-billionaire-owner-gives-away-company-to-fight-climate-crisis-yvon-chouinard.

21 Reuters (2022) 'Here's why Patagonia's billionaire founder Yvon Chouinard is giving away his company', *Reuters*, [online] 15 September, Available from: https://nypost.com/2022/09/15/patagonia-founder-yvon-chouinard-to-give-away-his-company/.

22 Chouinard, Y. cited in Conn, C. (2022) 'Patagonia chair: "We are turning capitalism on its head by making the earth our only shareholder"', *Fortune*, [online] 15 September, Available from: https://fortune.com/2022/09/14/patagonia-chair-we-are-turning-capitalism-on-its-head-by-making-the-earth-our-only-shareholder-charles-conn/.

23 Deleon, J. (2023) 'What Patagonia teaches us about building a brand that lasts', *Highsnobiety* website, [online], Available from: https://www.highsnobiety.com/p/patagonia-brand-history-highsnobiety-book/ [Accessed 22 August 2023].

24 Gallagher, B. (2017) '"Uncommon clothes for uncommon people": a brief history of Patagonia', *Grailed* website, [online] 1 December, Available from: https://www.grailed.com/drycleanonly/patagonia-history?curator=FashionREDEF.

25 Neate, R. (2022) 'Yvon Chouinard – the "existential dirtbag" who founded and gifted Patagonia', *The Guardian*, [online] 16 September, Available from: https://www.theguardian.com/global/2022/sep/15/yvon-chouinard-the-existential-dirtbag-who-founded-and-gifted-patagonia.

26 Chiu, A. (2022) '5 things to know about Patagonia's unusual history of activism', *The Washington Post*, [online] 22 September, Available from: https://www.washingtonpost.com/climate-solutions/2022/09/15/patagonia-chouinard-environmental-activism-climate/.

27 *1% For the Planet* website, [online], Available from: https://www.onepercentfortheplanet.org/ [Accessed 16 July 2023].

28 Neate, 'Yvon Chouinard'.

29 Patagonia (2022) 'Patagonia's next chapter: Earth is now our only shareholder', *Patagonia Works* website, [online] 14 September, Available from: https://www.patagoniaworks.com/press/2022/9/14/patagonias-next-chapter-earth-is-now-our-only-shareholder.

[30] Chouinard, Y. (2023) 'Earth is now our only shareholder', *Patagonia* website, [online], Available from: https://www.patagonia.com.au/pages/ownership [Accessed 17 July 2023].

[31] IRS (2023) 'Types of organizations exempt under Section 501(c)(4)', *Internal Revenue Service (IRS)* website, [online], Available from: https://www.irs.gov/charities-non-profits/other-non-profits/types-of-organizations-exempt-under-section-501c4 [Accessed 21 July 2023].

[32] Erskine, M. (2022) 'Yvon Chouinard and the Patagonia Purpose Trust—what is it and will it work?', *Forbes*, [online] 16 September, Available from: https://www.forbes.com/sites/matthewerskine/2022/09/16/yvon-chouinard-and-the-patagonia-purpose-trust-what-is-it-and-will-it-work/?sh=4dd388222deb.

[33] Patagonia, 'Patagonia's next chapter'.

[34] Chang, R.J. (2023) 'Here's who fell off Forbes' 2023 billionaires list', *Forbes*, [online] 5 April, Available from: https://www.forbes.com.au/news/billionaires/heres-who-fell-off-forbes-2023-billionaires-list/.

[35] Gelles, D. (2022) 'Billionaire no more: Patagonia founder gives away the company', *The New York Times*, [online] 14 September, Available from: https://www.nytimes.com/2022/09/14/climate/patagonia-climate-philanthropy-chouinard.html.

[36] Forbes (2024) 'Gina Rinehart', *Forbes*, [online], Available from: https://www.forbes.com/profile/gina-rinehart/?sh=2dab4eaa2db7 [Accessed 24 April 2024].

[37] McCrann, T. (2022) 'Rinehart keeps quietly bidding', *The Herald-Sun*, republished on *Hancock Prospecting* website, [online] 27 February, Available from: https://www.hancockprospecting.com.au/rinehart-keeps-quietly-bidding/#:~:text=Its%20ownership%2C%20by%20the%20by,is%20built%20on%20iron%20ore [Accessed 25 July 2023].

[38] *Gina Rinehart* website, [online], Available from: https://www.ginarinehart.com.au/biography/ [Accessed 16 July 2023].

[39] Butler, B. (2021) 'Australia's biggest landholder is Gina Rinehart, controlling 9.2m hectares', *The Guardian*, [online] 17 May, Available from: https://www.theguardian.com/australia-news/2021/may/17/australias-biggest-landholder-is-gina-rinehart-controlling-92m-hectares.

[40] Tasker, S.-J. (2017) 'Gina Rinehart: the iron lady behind a long list of philanthropy', *The Australian*, [online] 12 January, republished on *Hancock Prospecting* website, [online], Available from: https://www.hancockprospecting.com.au/wp-content/uploads/2017/02/Gina-Rinehart-the-iron-lady-behind-a-long-list-of-philanthropy.pdf [Accessed 25 July 2023].

[41] Thompson, B. (2023) 'Rinehart gives away millions to workers in birthday raffle', *The Australian Financial Review*, [online] 7 February, Available from: https://www.afr.com/wealth/people/rinehart-giving-away-millions-to-workers-in-birthday-raffle-20230206-p5cid5.

[42] Triple M (2022) 'Netball Australia on the brink of financial ruin', *Triple M* website, [online] 17 June, Available from: https://www.triplem.com.au/story/netball-australia-on-the-brink-of-financial-ruin-201346.

[43] Netball Australia (2022) 'Hancock prospecting invests in the Origin Australian Diamonds', *Netball Australia* website, [online] 29 September, Available from: https://netball.com.au/news/hancock-prospecting-invests-origin-australian-diamonds.

[44] Tu, J. (2023) 'Donnell Wallam named NAIDOC Sportsperson of the Year', *Women's Agenda*, [online] 4 July, Available from: https://womensagenda.com.au/latest/donnell-wallam-named-naidoc-sportsperson-of-the-year/.

[45] Leschinski, J. (2023) 'Lang Hancock's Solution to the "Aboriginal Problem" (1984)', YouTube, [online] 18 July, Available from: https://www.youtube.com/watch?v=pMaRuk6pGOc.

[46] McGregor, R. (1997) *Imagined Destinies: Aboriginal Australians and the Doomed Race Theory, 1880–1939*, Melbourne: Melbourne University Press.

[47] Anon (1912) 'A dying race', *The West Australian*, 8 April, excerpt quoted in Clark, D. (2019) 'Racism and social Darwinism', *The Carrolup Story* website, 29 January, [online], Available from: https://www.carrolup.info/racism-and-social-darwinism/.

[48] Healing Foundation (2023) 'Who are the Stolen Generations?', *Healing Foundation* website, [online], Available from: https://healingfoundation.org.au/resources/who-are-the-stolen-generations/ [Accessed 19 July 2023].

[49] Whiteman, H. (2022) 'Billionaire dumps Australia netball team in dispute over father's racist comments', *CNN*, [online] 24 October, Available from: https://edition.cnn.com/2022/10/23/sport/australia-netball-rinehart-diamonds-sponsorship-spt-intl-hnk/.

[50] NITV (2022) 'Netball Australia chair goes amid mining sponsorship standoff with players', *SBS*, [online] 17 October, Available from: https://www.sbs.com.au/nitv/article/netball-australia-chair-steps-down-amidst-mining-sponsorship-saga/917qnldnq.

[51] Wang, J. (2022) 'Calls for Gina Rinehart to apologise for father's racist comments after $15m Netball Australia funding withdrawal', *news.com.au*, [online] 25 October, Available from: https://www.news.com.au/sport/netball/calls-for-gina-rinehart-to-apologise-for-fathers-racist-comments-after-15m-netball-australia-funding-withdrawal/news-story/d76711a478e974bb3c840e9a01771430.

[52] Staff Writers (2022) 'Indigenous netball star Donnell Wallam left "devastated" by Hancock Prospecting bombshell', *Fox Sports*, [online] 24 October, Available from: https://www.foxsports.com.au/netball/indigenous-netball-star-donnell-wallam-left-devastated-by-hancock-prospecting-bombshell/news-story/f863470a24ad055a1cb6ebfb99eae95c.

[53] Hancock Prospecting (2022) 'Hancock Prospecting public statement regarding Netball Sponsorship', *Hancock Prospecting* website, [online] 22 October, Available from: https://www.hancockprospecting.com.au/prospecting-public-statement-regarding-netball-sponsorship/.

[54] Hancock Prospecting (2022) 'Hancock statement on sports organisations and recent media', *Hancock Prospecting* website, [online] 22 October, Available from: https://www.hancockprospecting.com.au/hancock-statement-on-sports-organisations-and-recent-media/.

55 Mundine, A. quoted in McCarthy, J. (2022) 'How a stupid comment by this wealthy old man 40 years ago is still a lesson for us all', *New Daily*, [online] 25 October, Available from: https://thenewdaily.com.au/opinion/2022/10/25/hancock-indigenous-comment/.

56 Rinehart, G. cited in The Australian (2016) 'Gina Rinehart: Donald Trump shows us the way to succeed', *The Australian*, [online] 23 November, Available from: https://www.theaustralian.com.au/nation/gina-rinehart-donald-trump-shows-us-the-way-to-succeed/news-story/aa2b6328aad9b557e164b4d7fa75f0fa.

57 Bucci. N. (2022) 'Gina Rinehart pictured at Donald Trump's campaign launch in Instagram photobomb', *The Guardian*, [online] 17 November, Available from: https://www.theguardian.com/business/2022/nov/17/gina-rinehart-donald-trump-2024-presidential-election-campaign-launch-eric-trump-instagram.

58 Palmer, M. (2019) 'The too small female list of Trump/Morrison dinner invitees', *Women's Agenda*, [online] 23 September, Available from: https://womensagenda.com.au/latest/the-too-small-female-list-of-trump-morrison-dinner-invitees/.

59 Kitney, D. (2016) 'Gina Rinehart: Donald Trump shows us the way to succeed', *The Australian*, [online] 23 November, Available from: https://www.theaustralian.com.au/nation/gina-rinehart-donald-trump-shows-us-the-way-to-succeed/news-story/.

60 Mauss, M. (1924/1990) *The Gift: The Form and Reason for Exchange in Archaic Societies*, trans. W.D. Halls, London: Routledge.

61 Mauss, *The Gift*, p 65.

62 Mauss, *The Gift*, p 70.

63 Andreoni, J. (1990) 'Impure altruism and donations to public goods: a theory of warm glow giving', *The Economic Journal*, 100(401): 464–477.

64 Andreoni, J. (1989) 'Giving with impure altruism: applications to charity and Ricardian equivalence', *Journal of Political Economy*, 97(6): 1447–1458.

65 Vallely, P. (2020) 'How philanthropy benefits the super-rich', *The Guardian*, [online] 8 September, Available from: https://www.theguardian.com/society/2020/sep/08/how-philanthropy-benefits-the-super-rich.

66 Kramer, P. cited in Spiegel (2010) 'German millionaires criticize Gates' "Giving Pledge"', *Spiegel International*, [online] 10 August, Available from: https://www.spiegel.de/international/germany/negative-reaction-to-charity-campaign-german-millionaires-criticize-gates-giving-pledge-a-710972.html.

67 Vallely, 'How philanthropy benefits the super-rich'.

68 Forbes (2023) 'Profile: Jeff Bezos', *Forbes*, [online], Available from: https://www.forbes.com/profile/jeff-bezos/ [Accessed 1 August 2023].

69 AP (2022) 'Amazon founder Jeff Bezos says he will give away most of his fortune', *ABC News*, [online] 14 November, Available from: https://www.abc.net.au/news/2022-11-15/jeff-bezos-says-he-will-give-away-most-of-his-fortune/101653710.

70 Fung, B. (2022) 'Exclusive: Jeff Bezos says he will give most of his money to charity', *CNN*, [online] 14 November, Available from: https://edition.cnn.com/2022/11/14/business/jeff-bezos-charity/index.html.

71 Kim, W. (2023) 'What does it mean to give away a $118 billion fortune?', *Vox*, [online] 27 January, Available from: https://www.vox.com/recode/23553730/jeff-bezos-philanthropy-giving-pledge-charity.

72 Kim, 'What does it mean to give away a $118 billion fortune?'.

73 Davis, S. (2021) 'Philanthropy: tool of the capitalist system', *Left Voice*, [online] 6 February, Available from: https://www.leftvoice.org/philanthropy-tool-of-the-capitalist-system/.

74 Maclean, M., Harvey, C., Yang, R. and Mueller, F. (2021) 'Elite philanthropy in the United States and United Kingdom in the new age of inequalities', *International Journal of Management Reviews*, 23(3): 330–352.

75 Maclean, Harvey, Yang and Mueller, 'Elite philanthropy', p 330.

76 OECD (2020), *Taxation and Philanthropy*, OECD Tax Policy Studies, No. 27, Paris: OECD Publishing.

77 Oxfam (2022) 'Do the rich pay their fair share?' *Oxfam* website, [online] 15 November, Available from: https://www.oxfamamerica.org/explore/stories/do-the-rich-pay-their-fair-share/.

78 Eisinger, J., Ernsthausen, J. and Kiel, P. (2021) 'The secret IRS Files: trove of never-before-seen records reveal how the wealthiest avoid income tax', *ProPublica*, [online] 8 June, Available from: https://www.propublica.org/article/the-secret-irs-files-trove-of-never-before-seen-records-reveal-how-the-wealthiest-avoid-income-tax.

79 McCaffery, E.J. (2002) *Fair Not Flat: How to Make the Tax System Better and Simpler*, Chicago, IL: University of Chicago Press.

80 Mangan, D. (2016) 'Trump brags about not paying taxes: "That makes me smart"', *CNBC*, [online] 26 September, Available from: https://www.cnbc.com/2016/09/26/trump-brags-about-not-paying-taxes-that-makes-me-smart.html.

81 Kredell, M. (2021) '"Buy, borrow, die" gains new life', *USC Gould School of Law* website, [online] 30 August, Available from: https://gould.usc.edu/about/news/?id=4887.

82 McCaffery, E.J. (2016) 'Taxing wealth seriously', *University of Southern California Law School Legal Studies Working Paper Series*, Paper 202.

83 Osnos, E. (2023) 'The Getty Family's Trust issues', *The New Yorker*, [online] 16 January, Available from: https://www.newyorker.com/magazine/2023/01/23/the-getty-familys-trust-issues.

84 Conesa, E. (2023) 'France's ultra-rich pay less tax, new study confirms', *Le monde*, [online] 6 June, Available from: https://www.lemonde.fr/en/politics/article/2023/06/06/france-s-ultra-rich-pay-less-tax-new-study-confirms_6029311_5.html.

85 Advani, A., Summers, A. and Tarrant, H. (2022) 'Who are the super-rich? The wealth and connections of the Sunday Times Rich List', *CAGE Policy Briefing No. 37*, July.

86 Oxfam (2023) 'Inequality and poverty: the hidden costs of tax dodging', *Oxfam* website, [online], Available from: https://www.oxfam.org/en/inequality-and-poverty-hidden-costs-tax-dodging [Accessed 18 August 2023].

87 Oxfam (2023) 'Richest 1% grab nearly twice as much new wealth as rest of the world put together', *Oxfam* website, [online] 16 January, Available from: https://www.oxfam.org.uk/media/press-releases/richest-1-grab-nearly-twice-as-much-new-wealth-as-rest-of-the-world-put-together/.

88 Germain, J. (2021) 'Billionaires barely pay taxes – here's how they get away with it', *Teen Vogue*, [online] 15 October, Available from: https://www.teenvogue.com/story/why-billionaires-dont-pay-taxes.

89 Bishop. M. and Green, M. (2008) *Philanthrocapitalism: How the Rich Can Save the World*, London: Bloomsbury.

90 Bishop and Green, *Philanthrocapitalism*, pp 2–3.

91 Clinton, B. (2008) 'Foreword', in Bishop and Green, *Philanthrocapitalism*, pp vii–viii.

92 Bishop and Green, *Philanthrocapitalism*, p 6.

93 McGoey, L. (2021) 'Philanthrocapitalism and the separation of powers', *Annual Review of Law and Social Science*, 17: 391–409, p 391.

94 McGoey, L. (2016) *No Such Thing As a Free Gift: The Gates Foundation and the Price of Philanthropy*, London: Verso.

Chapter 5

1 Robehmed, N. (2019) 'At 21, Kylie Jenner becomes the youngest self-made billionaire ever', *Forbes*, [online] 5 March, Available from: https://www.forbes.com/sites/natalierobehmed/2019/03/05/at-21-kylie-jenner-becomes-the-youngest-self-made-billionaire-ever/?sh=602934ee2794.

2 Jenner, K. cited in Duboff, J. (2015) 'Kylie Jenner's lip kit sells out, ruptures internet', *Vanity Fair*, [online] 30 November, Available from: https://www.vanityfair.com/style/2015/11/kylie-jenner-lip-kit-sells-out.

3 Ilchi, L. (2019) 'A timeline of Kylie Jenner's beauty brand', *Women's Wear Daily*, [online] 20 November, Available from: https://wwd.com/fashion-news/fashion-scoops/how-kylie-jenner-turned-kylie-cosmetics-beauty-empire-into-1-billion-dollar-business-1203374667/.

4 Daas, R. (2022) 'Cosmetics empire to luxury rides: a look at Kylie Jenner's net worth', *Lifestyle Asia*, [online] 12 December, Available from: https://www.lifestyleasia.com/ind/culture/people/kylie-jenner-net-worth-explained/.

5 Dolan, K.A. (2018) 'Here's what Forbes means by self-made: from bootstrappers to silver spooners', *Forbes*, [online] 13 July, Available from: https://www.forbes.com/sites/kerryadolan/2018/07/13/heres-what-forbes-means-by-self-made-from-bootstrappers-to-silver-spooners/?sh=55b5fe311ca3.

6 Bitsky, L. (2022) 'The Kardashian-Jenner family tree: a complete guide for keeping up', *news.com.au*, [online] 22 March, Available from: https://pagesix.com/article/kardashian-jenner-family-tree/.

7   Chappet, M.-C. (2021) 'Why are we still keeping up with the Kardashians?', *Harper's Bazaar*, [online] 19 March, Available from: https://www.harpersbazaar.com/uk/culture/culture-news/a35876944/keeping-up-with-the-kardashians-final-series/.

8   Sharma, N.T. (2022) 'The Kardashians have accumulated a mind-boggling 1.2 billion followers on Instagram – here is how the famous family brilliantly used their social media influence to create successful business empires', *Luxury Launches*, [online] 29 January, Available from: https://luxurylaunches.com/celebrities/kardashian-family-social-media-influence.php.

9   Shennan, R. (2022) 'Why are the Kardashians famous?', *National World*, [online] 29 April, Available from: https://www.nationalworld.com/news/people/why-kardashians-famous-who-reality-tv-family-stardom-explained-3675198.

10 Robehmed, 'At 21'.

11 Roberts, D. (2020) 'The radical moral implications of luck in human life', *Vox*, [online] 17 February, Available from: https://www.vox.com/platform/amp/science-and-health/2018/8/21/17687402/kylie-jenner-luck-human-life-moral-privilege.

12 Jenner, K. quoted in Ahlgrim, C. (2019) 'Kylie Jenner insists she is "self-made" because her parents "cut her off at the age of 15"', *Insider*, [online] 20 February, Available from: https://www.insider.com/kylie-jenner-says-she-is-self-made-paper-interview-2019-2.

13 *Cambridge Dictionary* (2023) 'Momager', in *Cambridge Dictionary*, Cambridge: Cambridge University Press, [online], Available from: https://dictionary.cambridge.org/dictionary/english/momager [Accessed 27 February 2023].

14 Dhami, A. (2022) 'Momager Kris Jenner is mixing something up with Kylie Cosmetics', *ITP Live*, [online] 6 September, Available from: https://itp.live/news/momager-kris-jenner-is-mixing-something-up-with-kylie-cosmetics.

15 Beacom, B. (2019) 'Billionaire Kylie Jenner is not a great role model for young women', *The Herald*, [online] 7 March, Available from: https://www.heraldscotland.com/opinion/17481872.billionaire-kylie-jenner-not-great-role-model-young-women/.

16 KcKim, J.K. in Rosenstein, R. (2017) 'Kylie Jenner just settled a lawsuit with one Instagram', *Harper's Bazaar*, [online] 25 January, Available from: https://www.harpersbazaar.com/beauty/news/a20109/kylie-jenner-makeup-lawsuit/.

17 Wilford, D. (2023) 'Miley, Kim, Kylie Jenner top list of most-searched nepo babies', *Toronto Sun*, [online] 21 February, Available from: https://torontosun.com/entertainment/celebrity/miley-kim-kylie-jenner-top-list-of-most-searched-nepo-babies.

18 Noah, T. (2023) 'Stop whining about celebrity nepotism', *TNR*, [online] 30 January, Available from: https://newrepublic.com/article/170264/stop-whining-celebrity-nepotism.

19 Maher, D. (2022) 'Nepo babies: 14 celebrities with famous parents', *Harper's Bazaar*, [online], Available from: https://harpersbazaar.com.au/celebrities-who-are-nepotism-babies/ [Accessed 14 February 2023].

[20] Jones, N. (2022) 'An all but definitive guide to the Hollywood nepo-verse', *New York*, [online] 19 December, Available from: https://www.vulture.com/article/hollywood-nepotism-babies-list-taxonomy.html.

[21] Kato, B. (2023) 'Kim Kardashian is top "nepo baby" of all with $1.8B – see who else ranks', *New York Post*, [online] 12 January, Available from: https://nypost.com/2023/01/12/top-nepo-baby-is-kim-kardashian-with-1-8b-see-who-else-ranks/.

[22] Wooldridge, A. (2021) *The Aristocracy of Talent: How Meritocracy Made the Modern World*, London: Penguin.

[23] Wooldridge, 'The Aristocracy of Talent'.

[24] Depp, L.-R. cited in Massabrook, N. (2023) 'Are they "nepo babies"? These celebrity kids have spoken out about nepotism', *US Weekly*, [online] 24 April, Available from: https://www.usmagazine.com/celebrity-news/pictures/nepo-babies-celebrity-kids-whove-spoken-out-about-nepotism/.

[25] Paltrow, G. cited in Massabrook, 'Are they "nepo babies"?'.

[26] Clance, P.R. and Imes, S.A. (1978) 'The imposter phenomenon in high achieving women: dynamics and therapeutic intervention', *Psychotherapy: Theory, Research & Practice*, 15(3): 241–247, p 241.

[27] Kolhatkar, S. (2023) 'Nepo babies and the myth of the meritocracy', *CounterPunch*, [online] 6 January, Available from: https://www.counterpunch.org/2023/01/06/nepo-babies-and-the-myth-of-the-meritocracy/.

[28] Kolhatkar, 'Nepo babies'.

[29] Kambhampaty, A.P. and Issawi, D. (2022) 'What is a "nepotism baby"?', *The New York Times*, [online] 2 May, Available from: https://www.nytimes.com/2022/05/02/style/nepotism-babies.html.

[30] Simmel, G. (1906) 'The sociology of secrets and of secret societies', *American Journal of Sociology*, 11(4): 441–498, p 486.

[31] Simmel, 'The sociology of secrets', p 486.

[32] Simmel, 'The sociology of secrets', p 487.

[33] Hobbes, M. (2019) 'The "glass floor" is keeping America's richest idiots at the top', *HuffPost*, [online] 15 October, Available from: https://www.huffpost.com/entry/the-glass-floor-is-keeping-americas-richest-idiots-at-the-top_n_5d9fb1c9e4b06ddfc516e076.

[34] Reim, G. (2014) 'Michael Dell's son raises $585K for new dating app', *Builtin ATX*, 10 November.

[35] Forbes (2023) 'Michael Dell', *Forbes*, [online], Available from: https://www.forbes.com/profile/michael-dell/?sh=2050d8966ce0 [Accessed 3 March 2023].

[36] Nguyen, B. and Delouya, S. (2023) 'Michael Dell's nepo babies: how the family of the billionaire computer mogul is making moves in the tech industry', *Business Insider*, [online] 12 January, Available from: https://www.businessinsider.com/michael-dell-nepo-baby-billionaire-family-children-brother-wife-tech-2023-1.

[37] Weiss, V. (2014) 'Zach Dell pushing dating app sans billionaire dad's money', *Jewish Business News*, [online] 24 July, Available from: https://

jewishbusinessnews.com/2014/07/24/zach-dell-pushing-dating-app-sans-billionaire-dads-money/.

38 Bell, Z. in Nguyen and Delouya, 'Michael Dell's nepo babies'.

39 Reeves, R.V. and Howard, K. (2013) 'The glass floor: education, downward mobility and opportunity hoarding', *Centre on Children and Families at Brookings*, [online] November, Available from: https://www.brookings.edu/wp-content/uploads/2016/06/glass-floor-downward-mobility-equality-opportunity-hoarding-reeves-howard.pdf; see also Hobbes, 'The "glass floor"'.

40 Harding, L. (2016) 'What are the Panama Papers? A guide to history's biggest data leak', *The Guardian*, [online] 5 April, Available from: https://www.theguardian.com/news/2016/apr/03/what-you-need-to-know-about-the-panama-papers.

41 Wintour, P. (2001) 'Meritocracy at heart of Blair's new "big idea"', *The Guardian*, [online] 9 February, Available from: https://www.theguardian.com/politics/2001/feb/08/uk.election2001.

42 Blair, T. cited in White, M. (2001) 'Party politics: Blair sets out his faith', *The Guardian*, [online] 15 May, Available from: https://www.theguardian.com/politics/2001/may/14/election2001.uk.

43 Blair, T. cited in White, 'Party politics'.

44 Blair, T. cited in Littler, J. (2018) *Against Meritocracy: Culture, Power and Myths of Mobility*, London: Routledge, p 86.

45 Chambers, E.G., Foulon, M., Handfield-Jones, H., Hankin, S.M. and Michaels III, E.G. (1998) 'The war for talent', *The McKinsey Quarterly*, 3: 44–57.

46 Chambers et al, 'The war for talent', p 46.

47 Tannock, S. (2009) 'Global meritocracy, nationalism and the question of whom we must treat equally for educational opportunity to be equal', *Critical Studies in Education*, 50(2): 201–211.

48 Brown, P. and Tannock, S. (2009) 'Education, meritocracy and the global war for talent', *Journal of Education Policy*, 24(4): 377–392.

49 Ramaswamy, V. (2023) 'Why I'm running for president', *The Wall Street Journal*, [online] 21 February, Available from: https://www.wsj.com/articles/why-im-running-for-president-c4a8ea7.

50 Tsipras, A. quoted in Hellenic News of America (2023) 'SYRIZA "will create infrastructures of trust, meritocracy, accountability & transparency"', says Tsipras, *Hellenic News of America*, [online] 1 March, Available from: https://hellenicnews.com/syriza-will-create-infrastructures-of-trust-meritocracy-accountability-transparency-says-tsipras/.

51 Audi, A. (2022) 'Meritocracy is a myth in Brazil', *The Brazilian Report*, [online] 19 October, Available from: https://brazilian.report/society/2022/10/19/meritocracy-fallacy-inequality/.

52 Sakmud, M. quoted in FMT Reporters (2023) 'Lack of meritocracy among top reasons why Malaysians migrate', *FMT*, [online] 21 February, Available from: https://www.freemalaysiatoday.com/category/nation/2023/02/21/lack-of-meritocracy-among-top-reasons-why-malaysians-migrate/.

53 Littler, *Against Meritocracy*.
54 Jacobs, D. (2015) 'Extreme wealth is not merited', *Oxfam Discussion Papers*, Oxford: Oxfam International.
55 Jacobs, 'Extreme wealth', p 27.
56 Fox, A. (1956) 'Class and equality', *Socialist Commentary*, May, 11–13.
57 Fox, 'Class and equality', p 13.
58 Young, M. (1958) *The Rise of Meritocracy 1870–2033: An Essay on Education and Equality*, London: Penguin.
59 Young, *The Rise of Meritocracy*, p 21.
60 Sandel, M.J. (2020) *The Tyranny of Merit: What's Become of the Common Good?*, London: Penguin.
61 Sandel, *The Tyranny of Merit*, p 117.
62 Sandel, *The Tyranny of Merit*, p 166.
63 Mint (2023) '70% of billionaires are self-made and only 30% legacy', *mint* website, [online] 22 March, Available from: https://www.livemint.com/news/india/70-of-billionaires-are-self-made-and-only-30-legacy-11679479214477.html.
64 Clifford, C. (2019) 'Nearly 68% of the world's richest people are "self-made," says new report', *CNBC*, [online] 26 September, Available from: https://www.cnbc.com/2019/09/26/majority-of-the-worlds-richest-people-are-self-made-says-new-report.html.
65 Dimitropoulou, A. (2022) 'What makes a successful self made billionaire', *CEOWorld Magazine*, [online] 21 July, Available from: https://ceoworld.biz/2022/07/21/what-makes-a-successful-self-made-billionaire/.
66 Reich, R. (2022) 'The truth behind "self-made" billionaires', *Robert Reich* website, [online], Available from: https://robertreich.org/post/695958318007664640 [Accessed 15 July 2023].

Chapter 6

1 McSweeney, E. and Pourahmadi, A. (2021) '2% of Elon Musk's wealth could help solve world hunger, says director of UN food scarcity organization', *CNN Business*, [online] 1 November, Available from: https://edition.cnn.com/2021/10/26/economy/musk-world-hunger-wfp-intl/index.html.
2 Cited in Vega, N. (2021) 'Elon Musk tweets he is willing to spend $6 billion to fight world hunger—on one condition', *CBBC*, [online] 1 November, Available from: https://www.cnbc.com/2021/11/01/elon-musk-tells-un-food-chief-hell-spend-6-billion-to-fight-hunger.html.
3 Sengupta, S. (2019) 'What is the United Nations? Its history, its goals and its relevance', *The New York Times*, [online] 24 September, Available from: https://www.nytimes.com/2019/09/24/world/americas/what-is-the-united-nations.html.
4 United Nations (1948) 'Universal Declaration of Human Rights', *United Nations* website, [online], Available from: https://www.un.org/en/about-us/universal-declaration-of-human-rights [Accessed 4 December 2021].

5   UNWFP (2021) 'Mission', *United Nations World Food Programme* website, [online], Available from: https://www.wfp.org/overview [Accessed 4 December 2021].

6   Zaracostas, J. (2021) 'Hope for nutrition summit as global hunger spikes', *The Lancet*, 398(10316): 2061–2062.

7   The Nobel Peace Prize (2021) 'World Food Programme (WFP): facts', *The Nobel Prize* website, [online], Available from: https://www.nobelprize.org/prizes/peace/2020/wfp/facts/ [Accessed 4 December 2021].

8   In BBC (2020) 'Nobel Peace Prize: UN World Food Programme wins for efforts to combat hunger', *BBC News*, [online] 9 October, Available from: https://www.bbc.com/news/world-54476569.

9   ABC News (2021) 'Elon Musk offers $US6 billion to UN World Food Programme if it can prove it'll end world hunger', *ABC News*, [online] 2 November, Available from: https://www.abc.net.au/news/2021-11-02/elon-musk-un-food-programme-world-hunger/100588926.

10 UNWFP (2021) 'WFP's plan to support 42 million people on the brink of famine', *United Nations World Food Programme* website, [online] 3 November, Available from: https://www.wfp.org/stories/wfps-plan-support-42-million-people-brink-famine.

11 Lepore, J. in Illing, S. (2021) 'Elon Musk's imaginary world', *Vox*, [online] 6 December, Available from: https://www.vox.com/vox-conversations-podcast/2021/12/6/22809704/vox-conversations-elon-musk-jill-lepore-the-evening-rocket.

12 Bradshaw, H. (2021) 'The Elon Musk effect: how to build an army of passionate followers', *Medium*, [online] 2 July, Available from: https://medium.com/illumination/the-elon-musk-effect-how-to-build-an-army-of-passionate-followers-35d08e6d9805.

13 Kim, W. (2022) 'Elon Musk fans can't handle the truth', *Vox*, [online] 13 July, Available from: https://www.vox.com/recode/23207361/elon-musk-twitter-narrative-billionaire.

14 Jones, J. (2021) 'The serious and growing danger of vigilantism', *The Hill*, [online] 29 November, Available from: https://thehill.com/opinion/criminal-justice/583282-the-serious-and-growing-danger-of-vigilantism/.

15 Leonnig, C.D. and Rucker, P. (2021) *I Alone Can Fix It: Donald J. Trump's Catastrophic Final Year*, London: Bloomsbury.

16 King James Bible (2001) Isaiah 43:11, Copenhagen: Holybooks, p 435.

17 Frame, G. (2021) 'Make America hate again? The politics of vigilante geriaction', *Journal of Popular Film and Television*, 49(3): 168–180, p 169.

18 Lepore, J. in NPR (2022) 'What Elon Musk's Twitter bid says about "extreme capitalism"', *NPR*, [online] 18 April, Available from: https://www.npr.org/transcripts/1093318919.

19 Musk, E. cited in O'Brien, T.L. (2022) 'Why Elon Musk just spent $4b buying a big chunk of Twitter', *Sydney Morning Herald*, [online] 5 April, Available from: https://www.smh.com.au/business/companies/why-elon-musk-just-spent-4b-buying-a-big-chunk-of-twitter-20220405-p5aati.html.

NOTES

20 Guardian staff (2021) 'Twitter says Trump ban is permanent – even if he runs for office again', *The Guardian*, [online] 10 February, Available from: https://www.theguardian.com/us-news/2021/feb/10/trump-twitter-ban-permament-social-media.

21 Meyer, S. in Yeo, A. (2022) 'Seth Meyer unpacks what Elon Musk's Twitter acquisition means for democracy', *Mashable*, [online] 28 April, Available from: https://mashable.com/video/seth-meyers-elon-musk-twitter.

22 Musk, E. in Hawkins, J. and Walsh, M.J. (2022) 'What will Elon Musk's ownership of Twitter mean for "free speech" on the platform?', *The Conversation*, [online] 27 April, Available from: https://theconversation.com/what-will-elon-musks-ownership-of-twitter-mean-for-free-speech-on-the-platform-181626.

23 Kolodny, L. (2022) 'Elon Musk says he wants free speech, but his track record suggests otherwise', *CNBC*, [online] 25 April, Available from: https://www.cnbc.com/2022/04/25/elon-musk-and-free-speech-track-record-not-encouraging.html.

24 Kolodny, L. 'Elon Musk says he wants free speech'.

25 Eisinger, J., Ermsthausen, J. and Kiel, P. (2021) 'The secret IRS files: trove of never-before-seen records reveal how the wealthiest avoid income tax', *ProPublica*, [online] 8 June, Available from: https://www.propublica.org/article/the-secret-irs-files-trove-of-never-before-seen-records-reveal-how-the-wealthiest-avoid-income-tax.

26 Weisbrod, K. (2021) 'Warming trends: Elon Musk haggles over hunger, how warming makes birds smaller and wings longer, and better glitter from nanoparticles', *Inside Climate News*, [online] 20 November, Available from: https://insideclimatenews.org/news/20112021/warming-trends-elon-musk-hunger-birds-amazon-dont-look-up/.

27 In CNN (2021) 'UN reveals how $9 billion of Elon Musk's money could stop world hunger', *9News*, [online] 19 November, Available from: https://www.9news.com.au/world/un-responds-to-elon-musk-world-hunger-challenge/b7222110-dab5-4d8d-bd31-b362f3ce6013.

28 Musk, E. quoted in Wayt, T. (2022) 'Too Musk information: Elon says he tweets from the toilet', *New York Post*, [online] 14 April, Available from: https://nypost.com/2022/04/14/elon-musk-reveals-when-he-most-often-posts-on-twitter/.

29 Agamben, G. (2005) *State of Exception*, Chicago, IL: University of Chicago Press.

30 Agamben, *State of Exception*, p 4.

31 Agamben, *State of Exception*, p 37.

32 Hobbes, T. (1651/2008) *Leviathan: Or the Matter, Forme and Power of a Commonwealth, Ecclesiasticall and Civil*, Oxford: Oxford University Press.

33 Hobbes, *Leviathan*, XIII.

34 Hobbes, *Leviathan*, XIII.

35 Kennedy, S. (2021) 'What Piketty's Lab discovered', *Bloomberg*, [online] 7 December, Available from: https://www.bloomberg.com/news/newsletters/

2021-12-07/what-s-happening-in-the-world-economy-billionaires-got-richer-amid-pandemic.

36 Time (2021) '2021 Person of the Year', *Time Magazine*, [online] 14 December, Available from: https://time.com/person-of-the-year-2021-elon-musk/.

37 Musk, E. quoted in McFall-Johnsen, M. (2020) 'Elon Musk promoted coronavirus misinformation for months. Then his own infection kept him out of SpaceX's astronaut launch', *Business Insider*, [online] 26 November, Available from: https://www.businessinsider.com/elon-musk-promoted-coronavirus-misinformation-then-tested-positive-2020-11.

38 Santos, J.-A. (2009) 'The basis of the right to resistance in the legal thought of Arthur Kaufmann', *Archiv für Rechts- und Sozialphilosphie*, 95(3): 352–358.

39 Walker, J., Tepper, S.J. and Gilovich, T. (2021) 'People are more tolerant of inequality when it is expressed in terms of individuals rather than groups at the top', *Proceedings of the National Academy of Sciences*, 118(43): 1–9.

40 Thompson, H. (2022) *Disorder: Hard Times in the 21st Century*, Oxford: Oxford University Press.

41 Giridharadas, A. (2022) 'Elon Musk is a problem masquerading as a solution', *The New York Times*, [online] 26 April, Available from: https://www.nytimes.com/2022/04/26/opinion/elon-musk-twitter.html.

42 Piatti, B. (2020) 'The German doctor who created Davos', *House of Switzerland* website, [online] 13 January, Available from: https://houseofswitzerland.org/swissstories/history/german-doctor-who-created-davos [Accessed 4 January 2022].

43 Gallagher, B. (2020) 'A look at Davos through the years', *The New York Times*, [online] 19 January, Available from: https://www.nytimes.com/2020/01/19/business/davos-world-economic-forum.html?auth=login-google1tap&login=google1tap.

44 Thunberg, G. (2019) 'Address at World Economic Forum: our house is on fire', *Iowa State University Archives of Women's Political Communication*, [online] 25 January, Available from: https://awpc.cattcenter.iastate.edu/2019/12/02/address-at-davos-our-house-is-on-fire-jan-25-2019/.

45 WEF (2022) 'Our mission', *World Economic Forum* website, [online], Available from: https://www.weforum.org/about/world-economic-forum [Accessed 4 January 2022].

46 Schwab, K. (2021) *Stakeholder Capitalism: A Global Economy That Works for Progress, People and Planet*, Hoboken, NJ: Wiley.

47 Schwab, *Stakeholder Capitalism*, p 173.

48 Rogers, T.N. (2020) '119 billionaires, 53 heads of state, and an $8.3 million security bill: a look at Davos by the numbers', *Business Insider*, [online] 22 January, Available from: https://www.businessinsider.com/davos-by-the-numbers-billionaires-private-jets-security-bill-2020-1.

49 Loffhagen, E. (2024) 'Davos 2024: what is it, who is attending, and why is it controversial?', *The Standard*, [online] 16 January, Available from: https://www.standard.co.uk/news/world/what-is-davos-2024-world-economic-forum-politicians-billionaires-criticism-b1053239.html.

50 Dolan, K.A., Wong, J. and Peterson-Withorn, C. (2021) 'Forbes World's Billionaire List: the richest in 2021', *Forbes*, [online], Available from: https://www.forbes.com/billionaires/ [Accessed 6 January 2022].

51 Rogers, '119 billionaires'.

52 Shendruk, A. (2022) 'Who's at Davos 2022?', *Quartz*, [online] 24 May, Available from: https://qz.com/2168596/whos-at-davos-2022/.

53 Reuters (2024) 'Heard in Davos: what we learned from the WEF in 2024', *Reuters*, [online] 20 January, Available from: https://www.reuters.com/world/heard-davos-what-we-learned-wef-2024-2024-01-19/.

54 WEF (2022) 'The Davos manifesto', *World Economic Forum* website, [online], Available from: https://www.weforum.org/the-davos-manifesto [Accessed 6 January 2022].

55 Schwab, K. (2019) 'Why we need the "Davos Manifesto" for a better kind of capitalism', *World Economic Forum* website and *Project Syndicate*, [online] 1 December, Available from: https://www.weforum.org/agenda/2019/12/why-we-need-the-davos-manifesto-for-better-kind-of-capitalism/.

56 Ricks, J. (2022) 'Davos is dead', *Aljazeera*, [online] 23 May, Available from: https://www.aljazeera.com/opinions/2022/5/23/davos-is-dead.

57 Huntington, S.P. (1996) *The Clash of Civilizations and the Remaking of World Order*, New York, NY: Simon and Schuster.

58 Huntington, *The Clash of Civilizations*, p 57.

59 Huntington, S.P. (2004) 'Dead souls: the denationalization of the American elite', *The National Interest*, 75: 5–18, p 8.

60 Oxfam (2020) 'Pandemic profiteers exposed', *Oxfam* website, [online] 22 July, Available from: https://www.oxfam.org/en/press-releases/pandemic-profiteers-exposed-report.

61 Connell, R.W. (1998) 'Masculinities and globalization', *Men and Masculinities*, 1(1): 3–23.

62 Connell, 'Masculinities', p 16.

63 Connell, R.W. and Wood, J. (2005) 'Globalization and business masculinities', *Men and Masculinities*, 7(4): 347–364.

64 Beneria, L. (1999) 'Globalization, gender and the Davos Man', *Feminist Economics*, 5(3): 61–83.

65 Beneria, 'Globalization', p 72.

66 Sandberg, S. (2013) *Lean In: Women, Work, and the Will to Lead*, New York, NY: WH Allen.

67 Elias, J. (2013) 'Davos woman to the rescue of global capitalism: postfeminist politics and competitiveness promotion at the World Economic Forum', *International Political Sociology*, 7(2): 152–169.

68 Elias, 'Davos woman', p 166.

69 Pope, S. and Bromley, P. (2022) 'Who is "Davos Man" today?', *LSE Business Review*, [online] 10 May, Available from: https://blogs.lse.ac.uk/businessreview/2022/05/10/who-is-davos-man-today/.

70 Johnson, P. (2021) 'Australia labelled untrustworthy, a climate change "pariah" after stoush with French president, COP26', *ABC News*, [online]

5 November, Available from: https://www.abc.net.au/news/2021-11-05/australia-morrison-criticised-cop26-coal-macron-stoush-qa/100596086.

71 Cited in Tamer, R. (2021) 'Australia wins climate "colossal fossil" award at COP26', *SBS News*, [online] 13 November, Available from: https://www.sbs.com.au/news/article/australia-wins-climate-colossal-fossil-award-at-cop26/vm90jb60v.

72 Eckersley, R. (2021) '"The Australian way": how Morrison trashed brand Australia at COP26', *The Conversation*, [online] 12 November, Available from: https://theconversation.com/the-australian-way-how-morrison-trashed-brand-australia-at-cop26-171670.

73 Lord Deben cited in LoPresti, L., Chalmers, M. and Carabine, A. (2021) 'Scott Morrison accused of failing to understand the "urgency" of climate change', *ABC News*, [online] 8 November, Available from: https://www.abc.net.au/news/2021-11-08/scott-morrison-cop26-doesnt-understand-urgency-climate-change/100602228.

74 Morrison, C. cited in Anon (2021) '"Can-do capitalism" to drive climate innovation, PM tells Victorian Chamber', *Victorian Chamber of Commerce and Industry* website, [online] 10 November, Available from: https://www.victorianchamber.com.au/news/can-do-capitalism-to-drive-climate-innovation-pm-tells-victorian-chamber.

75 Keynes, J.M. (1936/2018) *The General Theory of Employment, Interest, and Money*, Cambridge: Palgrave.

76 Keynes, *The General Theory*, p 142.

77 Danner, M. and Young, G. (2003) 'Free markets and state control: a feminist challenge to Davos man and Big Brother', *Gender & Development*, 11(1): 82–90.

78 Danner and Young, 'Free markets', p 86.

79 Goodman, P.S. (2022) *Davos Man: How the Billionaires Devoured the World*, New York, NY: HarperCollins.

80 Goodman, *Davos Man*, p 8.

81 McQuaig, L. and Brooks, N. (2013) *The Trouble with Billionaires: How the Super-Rich Hijacked the World (and How We Can Take It Back)*, London: Oneworld.

82 Goodman, *Davos Man*, p 5.

83 Njehu, N. (2020) 'In Davos, my only message was to abolish billionaires', *Open Democracy* website, [online] 31 January, Available from: https://www.opendemocracy.net/en/oureconomy/davos-my-only-message-was-abolish-billionaires/.

84 Njehu, 'In Davos'.

Chapter 7

1 Berlin, I. (1991) 'Pursuit of the ideal', in H. Hardy (ed.), *The Crooked Timber of Humanity*, New York, NY: Alfred A. Knopf, pp 1–19.

2 Berlin, 'Pursuit of the ideal', p 14.

3 Harris, M. (2016) 'Isaiah Berlin, negative liberty, and neoliberalism', *SSRN*, [online] 12 November, Available from: https://ssrn.com/abstract=3248569 or http://dx.doi.org/10.2139/ssrn.3248569.

4   Statista (2023) 'The 20 countries with the most billionaires in 2023', *Statista* website, [online], Available from: https://www.statista.com/statistics/299513/billionaires-top-countries/ [Accessed 13 October 2023].

5   Berlin, 'Pursuit of the ideal', p 11.

6   Qureshi, Z. (2023) 'Rising inequality: a major issue of our time', *Brookings* website, [online] 16 May, Available from: https://www.brookings.edu/articles/rising-inequality-a-major-issue-of-our-time/.

7   Williams, Z. (2023) 'The problem with tech bro philanthropy', *The Guardian*, [online] 7 November, Available from: https://amp-theguardian-com.cdn.ampproject.org/c/s/amp.theguardian.com/commentisfree/2023/nov/07/the-problem-with-tech-bro-philanthropy.

8   History.com. (2023) 'Occupy Wall Street begins', *History* website, [online], Available from: https://www.history.com/this-day-in-history/occupy-wall-street-begins-zuccotti-park [Accessed 1 September 2023].

9   Obama, B. cited in Greene, B. (2011) 'How "Occupy Wall Street" started and spread', *US News* and *World Report*, [online] 17 October, Available from: https://www.usnews.com/news/washington-whispers/articles/2011/10/17/how-occupy-wall-street-started-and-spread.

10 White, M. (2016) *The End of Protest: A New Playbook for Revolution*, Toronto: Knopf.

11 Stewart, E. (2019) 'We are (still) the 99 percent', *Vox*, [online] 30 April, Available from: https://www.vox.com/the-highlight/2019/4/23/18284303/occupy-wall-street-bernie-sanders-dsa-socialism.

12 Kelsey-Fry, J. quoted in Geraghty, L. (2021) 'It's been 10 years since the Occupy protests. What did they achieve?', *The Big Issue*, [online] 14 October, Available from https://www.bigissue.com/news/activism/its-been-10-years-since-the-occupy-protests-what-did-they-achieve/.

13 Milkman, R., Luce, S. and Lewis, P. (2021) 'Did Occupy Wall Street make a difference?', *The Nation*, [online] 17 September, Available from: https://www.thenation.com/article/society/ows-occupy-zuccotti-protest/.

14 Stiglitz, J. in Anderson, J.A. (2021) 'Some say Occupy Wall Street did nothing. It changed us more than we think', *Time*, [online] 15 November, Available from: https://time.com/6117696/occupy-wall-street-10-years-later/.

15 Fight for $15 (2023) *Fight for $15* website, [online], Available from: https://fightfor15.org/ [Accessed 23 October 2023].

16 Cited in Greenhouse, S. (2022) '"The success is inspirational": the Fight for $15 movement 10 years on', *The Guardian*, [online] 23 November, Available from: https://www.theguardian.com/us-news/2022/nov/23/fight-for-15-movement-10-years-old.

17 Levitin, M. (2021) *Generation Occupy: Reawakening American Democracy*, Berkeley, CA: Counterpoint, p 4.

18 Anderson, 'Some say'.

19 Kealy, C. (2021) 'A decade on, Occupy Wall Street's legacy on income inequality', *Aljazeera*, [online] 17 September, Available from: https://www.

aljazeera.com/economy/2021/9/17/a-decade-on-occupy-wall-streets-legacy-on-income-inequality.

[20] Emmenegger, P. and Lierse, H. (2022) 'The politics of taxing the rich: declining tax rates in times of rising inequality', *Journal of European Public Policy*, 29(5): 647–651.

[21] Piketty, T. (2013) *Le Capital au XXIe siècle*, Paris: Seuil.

[22] Piketty, T. (2013) *Capital in the Twenty-First Century*, Cambridge, MA: Harvard University Press.

[23] Piketty, T. quoted in Sherter, A. (2014) 'Economist says U.S. inequality reaching "spectacular" heights', *CBS News*, [online] 5 June, Available from: https://www.cbsnews.com/news/economist-says-u-s-inequality-reaching-spectacular-heights/.

[24] See also Piketty, T., Saez, E. and Zucman, G. (2023) 'Rethinking capital and wealth taxation', *Oxford Review of Economic Policy*, 39(3): 575–591.

[25] Tanenhaus, S. (2015) 'Hey, big thinker', *The New York Times*, [online] 25 April, Available from: https://www.nytimes.com/2014/04/27/fashion/Thomas-Piketty-the-Economist-Behind-Capital-in-the-Twenty-First-Century-sensation.html.

[26] Cowburn, A. (2016) 'Thomas Piketty, leading left-wing economist, resigns from Labour Party role', *The Independent*, [online] 29 June, Available from: https://www.independent.co.uk/news/uk/politics/thomas-piketty-resigns-from-labour-party-role-a7108891.html.

[27] Yglesias, M. (2019) 'Elizabeth Warren's proposed tax on enormous fortunes, explained', *Vox*, [online] 24 January, Available from: https://www.vox.com/policy-and-politics/2019/1/24/18196275/elizabeth-warren-wealth-tax.

[28] Weil, D. (2023) 'How economic inequality is fueling authoritarianism: Nobel laureate', *The Street*, [online] 8 September, Available from: https://www.thestreet.com/economy/economic-inequality-fueling-authoritarianism-nobel.

[29] Stiglitz, J. (2023) 'Salvaging global democratic politics requires far-reaching economic reforms', *The Guardian*, [online] 2 September, Available from: https://www.theguardian.com/business/2023/sep/01/global-democratic-politics-economic-reforms.

[30] United Nations (2023) 'The Sustainable Development Agenda', *United Nations* website, [online], Available from: https://www.un.org/sustainabledevelopment/development-agenda/ [Accessed 4 October 2023].

[31] United Nations (2015) *Resolution Adopted by the General Assembly on 25 September 2015, Transforming Our World: The 2030 Agenda for Sustainable Development*, 21 October. New York, NY: United Nations.

[32] Wintour, P. (2023) 'Western leaders defend slow progress to end global inequality as UN summit starts', *The Guardian*, [online] 19 September, Available from: https://www.theguardian.com/world/2023/sep/18/un-summit-sees-western-leaders-defend-slow-progress-to-end-global-inequality.

[33] Lederer, E.M. and The Associated Press (2023) 'UN chief sees a world "becoming unhinged" and a completely absent leadership: "we seem

incapable of coming together to respond"', *Fortune*, [online] 20 September, Available from: https://fortune.com/asia/2023/09/19/un-general-assembly-guterres-world-unhinged-incapable-coming-together/.

34 G20 (2023) 'About G20', *G20* website, [online], Available from: https://www.g20.in/en/about-g20/about-g20.html [Accessed 23 November 2023].

35 Tax Extreme Wealth (2023) 'G20 leaders must tax extreme wealth', *Tax Extreme Wealth* website, [online], Available from: https://taxextremewealth.com/ [Accessed 4 October 2023].

36 Amladi, D. (2024) 'How are billionaire and corporate power intensifying global inequality?', *Oxfam* website, [online] 14 January, Available from: https://www.oxfamamerica.org/explore/stories/how-are-billionaire-and-corporate-power-intensifying-global-inequality/.

37 OECD (2021) *Does Inequality Matter? How People Perceive Economic Disparities and Social Mobility*, Paris: OECD.

38 Qureshi, Z. (2023) 'Rising inequality: a major issue of our time', *Brookings* website, [online] 16 May, Available from: https://www.brookings.edu/articles/rising-inequality-a-major-issue-of-our-time/.

Index